D0450257

# DARK POOLS

# DARK POOLS

HIGH-SPEED TRADERS,
AI BANDITS, AND THE
THREAT TO THE GLOBAL
FINANCIAL SYSTEM

## SCOTT PATTERSON

CROWN
BUSINESS
NEW YORK

Published in the United States by Crown Business,
an imprint of the Crown Publishing Group,
a division of Random House, Inc., New York.
www.crownpublishing.com

CROWN BUSINESS is a trademark and CROWN and the Rising Sun
colophon are registered trademarks of Random House, Inc.

Crown Business books are available at special discounts for bulk
purchases for sales promotions or corporate use. Special editions,
including personalized covers, excerpts of existing books, or books
with corporate logos, can be created in large quantities for special
needs. For more information, contact Premium Sales at (212) 572-2232
or e-mail specialmarkets@randomhouse.com.

Library of Congress Cataloging-in-Publication Data
Patterson, Scott, 1969– .
    Dark pools : high-speed traders, AI bandits, and the threat to the
    global financial system / by Scott Patterson. — 1st ed.
        p. cm.
    1. Electronic trading of securities. 2. Online stockbrokers. I. Title.
    HG4515.95.P284   2012
    332.640973—dc23             2012003096

ISBN 978-0-307-88717-7
eISBN 978-0-307-88719-1

Printed in the United States of America

Book design by Barbara Sturman
Jacket design by Laura Duffy
Jacket photography: (swirl) Design Pics/Ryan Briscall;
(numbers) Mark Segal

10 9 8 7 6 5 4 3 2 1

First Edition

*For Eleanor*

Had there been full disclosure of what was being done in furtherance of these schemes, they could not long have survived the fierce light of publicity and criticism. Legal chicanery and pitch darkness were the banker's stoutest allies.

—FERDINAND PECORA

# CONTENTS

# DARK POOLS

# LIGHT POOL

Loudspeakers boomed Eminem's hit single "Without Me" as Dan Mathisson stepped onto a low-slung dais in the Glitter Room of Miami Beach's exclusive Fontainebleau Hotel. Greeting Mathisson: the applause of hundreds of hedge fund managers, electronic traders, and computer programmers, the driving force behind a digital revolution that had radically transformed the United States stock market. They had descended on the Fontainebleau for the annual Credit Suisse Equity Trading Forum to rub elbows, play golf, swap rumors, and bask in the faded glory of the hotel where stars such as Frank Sinatra, Elvis Presley, and Marlene Dietrich had once sipped cocktails and lounged in private poolside cabanas.

Smartly clad in a light blue cotton shirt and charcoal-gray suit, sans tie, a soft pink Credit Suisse logo illuminated on the wall behind him, Mathisson was pumped. He loved the Miami Beach conference. Over the years, it had become the Woodstock of electronic trading. Closed to the press, the March 10, 2011, gathering was a private congress of wealthy market wonks who'd created a fantastic *Blade Runner* trading world few outsiders could imagine, a worldwide matrix of dazzlingly complex algorithms, interlinked computer hubs the size of football fields, and high-octane trading robots guided by the latest advances in artificial intelligence.

Mathisson was an alpha male of the electronic pack. In another life, the bespectacled five-seven onetime trader would have been teaching students quantum physics or working for Mission Control at NASA. Instead, starting in 2001, he'd devoted himself to building a space-age trading platform for Credit Suisse called Advanced Electronic Systems. He was an elite market Plumber, an architect not of trading strategies or moneymaking schemes but of the pipes connecting the various pieces of the market and forming a massive computerized trading grid.

Plumbers such as Mathisson had become incredibly powerful in recent years. Knowledge of the blueprints behind the market's plumbing had become extremely valuable, worth hundreds of millions of dollars to those in the know. The reason: A new breed of trader had emerged who focused on gaming the plumbing itself, exploiting complex loopholes and quirks inside the blueprints like card counters ferreting out weaknesses in a blackjack dealer's hand.

Mathisson was keenly aware of this. Since launching AES, he'd been a firsthand witness of the powerful computer-driven forces that had irrevocably altered the face of the stock market. He'd created AES's original matching engine—the computer system that matched buy and sell orders—which by early 2011 accounted for a whopping 14 percent of U.S. stock-trading volume, nearly one billion shares a day. He was the brains behind Guerilla, the first mass-marketed robot-trading algorithm that could deftly buy and sell stocks in ways that evaded the detection of other algos, a lethal weapon in the outbreak of what became known as the Algo Wars.

Operating in forty countries across six continents, AES was a moneymaking machine. In 2008, a year when most of Wall Street was single-mindedly engaged in the act of self-destructing, AES had pulled in about $800 million, making it the most profitable arm of Credit Suisse. That number—that $800 million—was just one reason among many why Mathisson's words on that Miami Beach stage meant serious business.

But while the Miami confabs had always been about business, they were also about celebrating, and they typically involved a conga line of cocktail parties, pool parties, and dance clubs. In years past, after the day's long string of speeches and presentations, Mathisson's right-hand man, a charismatic, larger-than-life sales machine named Manny Santayana, would troll the local clubs, pick out the best-looking local girls, and tell them about the *real* party packed with millionaire traders looking for a good time.

Santayana always joked that he never threw *parties*. He threw *networking events at a socially accelerated pace*. Santayana was king of the socially accelerated pace. He ran poker tournaments for traders in the exclusive Grand Havana Room in Manhattan, dinners for bankers at the Versace Mansion in Miami Beach. All year long, there were networking events at a socially accelerated pace around the world—in Tokyo, Singapore, Zurich, London, Oslo, Paris, Hong Kong.

But an iron rule on Wall Street is that every party leads to the inevitable hangover. As Mathisson looked out over the audience, he knew Santayana wouldn't be trolling clubs for bleach-blond babes this year. A freakish stock market crash on May 6, 2010—the so-called Flash Crash—had revealed that the computer-driven market was far more dangerous than anyone had realized. Regulators were angry, fund managers furious. Something had gone dramatically wrong. Senators were banging down Mathisson's door wanting to know what the hell was going on. A harsh light was shining on an industry that had grown in the shadows.

Mathisson was ready to confront the attack. He hit a button on the remote for his PowerPoint presentation. A graph appeared. A jagged line took a cliff-like plunge followed by a sharp vertical leap. It looked like a tilted V, the far right-hand side just lower than the left.

"There's the Flash Crash," he said. "We all remember that day, of course."

The chart showed the Dow Jones Industrial Average, which took an eight-hundred-point swan dive in a matter of minutes on May 6 due to glitches deep in the plumbing of the nation's computer-trading systems—the very systems built and run by many of the people sitting in the Glitter Room.

The audience stirred. The Flash Crash was a downer, and they were restless. It was going to be a long day full of presentations. Later that night, they'd be treated to a speech by the Right Honorable Gordon Brown, former prime minister of the United Kingdom. Ex–Clinton aide James Carville would address the group the following morning. (It was nothing unusual. Past keynote speakers at the conference had included luminaries such as former Federal Reserve chairman Alan Greenspan, former secretary of state Colin Powell, and the onetime junk-bond king Michael Milken.)

Mathisson hit the button, calling up a chart showing that cash had flowed out of mutual funds every single month through 2010, following the Flash Crash. Legions of regular investors had become fed up, convinced the market had become either far too dangerous to entrust with their retirement savings, or just outright rigged to the benefit of an elite technorati.

"This is pretty damning," Mathisson said soberly, noting that the outflows continued even as the market surged higher later in the year. "Even with a historic rally, mutual fund outflows continued through December. This is cause for concern in the U.S."

Mathisson hit the button.

A grainy photo of President Barack Obama appeared, along with his notorious quote from a December 2009 episode of *60 Minutes*: "I did not run for office to be helping out a bunch of fat cat bankers on Wall Street."

Mathisson's point was clear: The feds are going to come down on this industry like a sledgehammer if we don't fix the system from within, fast. "We have to do something," he said.

The heart of the problem, Mathisson explained, was that fast-moving robot trading machines were front-running long-term investors on exchanges such as the New York Stock Exchange and the

Nasdaq Stock Market. For instance, if Fidelity wanted to buy a million shares of IBM, the Bots could detect the order and start buying IBM themselves, in the process driving up the price and making IBM more expensive. If Fidelity wanted to sell a million shares of IBM, the Bots would also sell, pushing the price down and causing Fidelity to sell on the cheap.

To escape, the victims of the front running were turning to dark pools.

"Why are people choosing to send orders to dark pools instead of the displayed markets?" Mathisson asked his audience. "They're choosing dark pools because of *a problem in the lit markets*."

A controversial force in the market in the 2000s, dark pools were private markets hidden from investors who traded on the "lit" pools such as the NYSE and Nasdaq (in the industry, any venue where trading takes place, including an exchange, is known as a *pool*). Large traders used dark pools like a cloaking device in their efforts to hide from robo algos programmed to ruthlessly hunt down their intentions like single-minded Terminators on exchanges. But unlike exchanges, dark pools were virtually unregulated. And the blueprints for how they worked were a closely guarded secret. As such, there were highly paid people on Wall Street, often sporting Ph.D.s in fields such as quantum physics and electrical engineering, who did nothing all day long but try to divine those secrets and ruthlessly exploit them.

The new wave of dark pools epitomized a driving force in finance as old as time: secrecy. In part a solution to a problem, they were also the symptom of a disease. The lit market had become a playground for highly sophisticated traders—many of the very traders sitting in Mathisson's audience—who'd designed and deployed the robo algos that hacked the market's plumbing.

Sadly, the exchanges had helped make all of this possible. They provided to the high-speed trading firms expensive, data-rich feeds that broadcast terabytes of information about specific buy and sell orders from giant mutual funds to the Bot algos. So much information that it could be used to engage in the hit-and-run tactics regulators, fund managers, and senators were screaming about. This was all playing out every day, every *nanosecond*, in the lit markets—a frenzied dance of predator and prey, with Mathisson's peers playing the part of the swarming piranha. Every single investor in the United States was involved—and at risk.

Mathisson was all too aware of this dynamic. Indeed, in 2004, he'd created a dark pool of his own called Crossfinder. It was so successful that it had gone on to become the largest dark pool in the world. By 2011, roughly 10 to 15 percent of all trading took place in dark pools, and Crossfinder accounted for a significant chunk of that volume.

Why? The exchanges had gotten in bed with the Bots. Now investors were fed up, Mathisson argued.

"The policies of today's exchanges cater to the needs of high-volume, short-term opportunistic traders," he said. "The pick-off artists."

The audience visibly tensed.

To an outsider, Mathisson's statement would have seemed relatively innocuous. To the insiders—those sitting in the room—it was a shocker. It was an *outrage*. It wasn't what Mathisson said. Others had been attacking the speed Bots. What was shocking was that *Dan Mathisson was saying it*. Mathisson, one of the architects of the electronic system itself, one of the elite Plumbers—*he was trashing it.*

Pick-off artists!

Mathisson knew what he was talking about. Because the dirty little secret of most dark pools was that they relied on those very same pick-off traders he was trashing. Indeed, they'd been AES's bread and butter for years. In Wall Street parlance, the Bots helped provide the *liquidity* behind the massive AES pool, the rivers of buy and sell orders the turtle-slow average traders—the mutual funds, the pension funds—relied on when they wanted to buy or sell a stock.

While Credit Suisse monitored Crossfinder for manipulative Bot behavior, it still depended on the Bots' steady flow. Mathisson's promise to clients running away from the Bots in the lit pools was that over-the-top hit-and-run gaming activity would be kept to a minimum. Egregious violators were kicked out of the pool. But there was little he could do to entirely stop it.

In short, the dark pools themselves were swarming with predator algos. The dynamic spoke to how powerful the Bots had become.

And there was no place to hide.

Mathisson's kind of straight talk was not heard on Wall Street unless something very troubling was going on behind the scenes. He knew that regulators were zeroing in on the industry. He wanted to be ready.

Mathisson laid out his case. Before electronic trading came along in the 1990s, most markets operated on a floor. Market makers—the people who buy and sell all day long on behalf of investors, collecting a small slice of the deal for their troubles—were able to sense which way the market was going simply by looking around them, staring into the nervous eyes of another trader, watching a competitor frantically rush into a pit and start selling—or buying. *General Electric is in trouble. IBM is about to surge.*

With electronic trading, a placeless, faceless, postmodern cyber-market in which computers communicated at warpspeeds, that physical sense of the market's flow had vanished. The market gained new eyes— *electronic eyes.* Computer programmers designed hunter-seeker algo-rithms that could *detect*, like radar, which way the market was going.

The big game in this hunt became known as a *whale*—an order from a leviathan fund company such as Fidelity, Vanguard, or Legg Mason. If the algos could detect the whales, they could then have a very good sense for whether a stock was going to rise or fall in the next few minutes or even seconds. They could either trade ahead of it or get out of its way. The bottom line: Mom and Pop's retirement accounts were full of mutual funds handing over billions of dollars a year to the Bots.

Dark pools like Crossfinder had (for a while at least) evened the game in the Algo Wars, giving traditional investors a place to hide.

But the evidence was now all too clear: The Bots in their relentless quest for the whales had thoroughly infiltrated the dark pools. And it was all cloaked in the darkness of a market mired in complexity and electronic smoke screens.

Mathisson, for his part, had decided to fight back. To beat the speed traders at their own game, in 2009 he'd launched a turbocharged trading algorithm called *Blast*. Blast pounded its fleet-footed high-speed opponents with simultaneous buy and sell orders like a machine gun. The firepower of Blast was so overwhelming that it forced high-speed traders—who controlled upwards of *70 percent or more* of all stock-market volume by the late 2000s—to cut bait and run for cover.

Blast was effective. But Mathisson needed more. Now Mathisson had a new weapon in his arsenal. He wasn't attacking the very firms that had been AES's meal ticket for nothing. He had an angle: yet another extraordinary machine.

He called it Light Pool.

Light Pool would weed out the "opportunistic" traders, he told the audience. Using metrics that could detect the pick-off artists, Light Pool would provide a clean market where natural traders—investors who actually wanted to buy a stock and hold it for longer than two seconds—could meet and do business. The information about buy and sell orders inside Light Pool wouldn't be distributed through a private feed. It would go directly to the consolidated tape that *all* investors could see, not just the turbo traders who paid for the high-bandwidth feeds from the exchanges.

"All those sleazy hidden order types won't be there," Mathisson said. "We'll create criteria like 'Are you a pick-off artist?' This is effectively going to eliminate the pick-off flow. We're going to be transparent."

Mathisson looked meaningfully at the audience—packed with the very pick-off artists he was attacking—and said something he knew would get their attention.

"There will be no black box."

■ ■ ■

MATHISSON knew, of course, that he was fighting against time, and he secretly worried that there was nothing he could do to close the Pandora's box that had been opened in the past decade. The Plumbers had always believed that a problem with the machine could be fixed with a better machine.

But what if the problem wasn't inside the machine? What if it was the all-too-human arms race itself, a race that had gripped the market and launched it on an unstoppable and completely unpredictable path? Because with inscrutable algos blasting away across high-speed electronic networks around the world, with trading venues splintering into dozens of pieces, with secretive trading firms spreading their tentacles across the globe, the entire market had descended into one vast pool of darkness. It wasn't only the everyday investors who were in the dark—even the architects of the system itself, the Plumbers, were losing the ability to keep track of the manic activity.

And as trading grew more frenetic and managed by mindless robots, a new risk had emerged. Insiders were slowly realizing that the push-button turbo-trading market in which algos battled algos inside massive data centers and dark pools at speeds measured in billionths of a second had a fatal flaw. The hunter-seeker Bots that controlled trading came equipped with sensors designed to detect rapid, volatile swings in prices. When the swings passed a certain threshold—say, a downturn of 5 percent in five minutes—the algorithms would instantly sell, shut down, and wait for the market to stabilize. The trouble was that when a large number of algorithms sold and shut down, the market became *more* volatile, triggering *more* selling.

In other words, a vicious self-reinforcing feedback loop.

The Flash Crash had proven this wasn't merely a fanciful nightmare scenario bandied about by apocalyptic market Luddites. The question tormenting experts was how far the loop would go next time. Progress Software, a firm that tracks algorithmic trading, predicted that a financial institution would lose one *billion* dollars or more in 2012 when a rogue algorithm went "into an infinite loop . . . which cannot be shut down."

And since the computer programs were now linked across markets — stock trades were synced to currencies and commodities and futures and bonds — and since many of the programs were very similar and were massively leveraged, the fear haunting the minds of the Plumbers was that the *entire system* could snap like a brittle twig in a matter of minutes. A chaotic butterfly effect could erase everyone's hard-earned savings in an eyeblink and, for kicks, throw the global economy into yet another Wall Street–spawned tailspin.

The pieces were already in place. Exchanges from Singapore to China to Europe to the United States were linking up through a vast web of algo traders dabbling in every tradable security in the world. The threat had grown so tangible that it even had a name: the Splash Crash.

Worse, because the speed traders had pushed aside the more traditional long-term market makers, a rapid unwind could create a "double liquidity void" — a lack of short- and long-term buying, in the words of the Bank of England economist Andrew Haldane. With artificial intelligence algos thrown in the mix, the behavior of which was entirely unpredictable and unstable, algos that could trigger their own form of self-reinforcing mayhem, the odds of a market calamity were even higher.

The Plumbers would never admit that the system they'd built was deeply flawed, of course. They'd instead talk about shock absorbers and circuit breakers and risk metrics that would stop the madness before it spun out of control. But deep inside, they knew that it was more than possible. They knew that, as the high-octane global trading grid became faster, more and more driven by computers souped-up on light-speed AI systems, *it was inevitable.*

Unless, that is, something was done to stop it.

# PART I

DAISY, DAISY, GIVE ME
YOUR ANSWER DO.
I'M HALF CRAZY, ALL FOR
THE LOVE OF YOU.

—HAL, 2001

# MACHINE v. MACHINE

CHAPTER ONE

# TRADING MACHINES

A rising winter sun cast pale golden light into the otherwise dark and quiet office in downtown Stamford, Connecticut. Haim Bodek, the founder of Trading Machines LLC, squinted at the light through bloodshot eyes and returned his gaze to a stack of five flat-screens on his desk. The only sound in the room was the low hum of dozens of Dell computer towers and several Alienware Area-51 gaming computers.

The sound of the Machine.

It was December 2009. Bodek hadn't been up all night swilling fine wines and schmoozing with deep-pocketed clients at four-star restaurants in Manhattan. He didn't need to. His firm traded for its own account, and Bodek answered only to himself and to a few wealthy partners who'd bankrolled the firm.

He wouldn't have it any other way. No twitchy investors pulling cash every time the market dipped. And no prying questions about the state-of-the-art Machine he'd created.

No one knew how the Machine worked but Bodek.

But now the Machine wasn't working. Even worse, Bodek wasn't sure why. That's why he'd been up all night. If he didn't solve the problem, it could destroy Trading Machines—and his career.

What made the Machine tick was a series of complex algorithms that collectively reflected a two decades' tradition of elite trading strategies. Bodek had personally designed the algos using a branch of artificial intelligence called *expert systems*. The approach boiled down the knowledge gained by experts in market analysis and crunched incoming market data in order to make incredibly accurate predictions. It combined various models that financial engineers had used over the years to price options—contracts that give the holder the "option" to buy or sell a stock at a particular price within a certain time frame— with new twists on strategies that savvy traders had once used to haggle over prices in the pits.

But many of those old-school strategies, geared with cutting-edge AI upgrades that permitted them to compete head-to-head in the electronic crowd, were nearly unrecognizable now. The market had entered a phase of such rapid mind-throttling change that even the most advanced traders were in a fog.

The problem that threatened Trading Machines, Bodek believed, was a bug hidden in the data driving his ranks of algos, hundreds of thousands of lines of code used by the computer-driven trading outfit that he'd launched with sky's-the-limit dreams in late 2007. The code told the Machine when to trade, what to trade, and how to trade it, all with split-second timing.

Bodek, whose seriously pale skin, high forehead, and piercing olive green eyes gave him the appearance of a Russian chess master, was a wizard of data. It was the air he breathed, the currency of his profession. An expert in artificial intelligence, he'd made a career of crunching masses of numbers, finding form inside chaos. To discover order in the ocean of information that made up the market required incredible computer power and ingenious trading systems.

Bodek had both. He was so skilled at discovering patterns in the market's daily ebb and flow that he'd risen to the top of the trading world, working first at an elite Chicago firm, packed with math and physics Ph.D.s, called Hull Trading, then inside a top secret quantitative derivatives operation at Goldman Sachs, before taking over a powerful global desk at UBS, the giant Swiss bank. In 2007, he broke out on his own and convinced twenty-five top-notch traders, programmers, and quants (an industry term for mathematicians who use quantitative techniques to predict markets) from across Wall Street to join him. He set up shop in Stamford and launched Trading Machines just as signs emerged of an impending global financial crisis. It had amounted to one of the most ambitious trading projects outside a large investment bank in years.

Despite the bad timing, Trading Machines had fared well in its debut, posting a tidy profit during a time when most of Wall Street was imploding.

Then something went wrong with the Machine. Bodek was on a mission to fix it. Whatever *it* was.

As the morning progressed, Bodek's team of traders and programmers filed into Trading Machines' third-floor office space. They stepped gingerly around Bodek as if he were a hair-trigger land mine.

The slightest pressure could set off an explosion. Not of anger— Bodek was as levelheaded as a fighter pilot—but of talk. Bodek was a legendary talker, a deep well of stories and analogies and long digressions and digressions on digressions. His was a mind trained to focus on minutiae, and it could be exhausting for listeners exposed to its relentless probing, like a powerful searchlight that never stopped sweeping the ground for new information. He could rarely get far into a conversation before he would say with extreme urgency something along the lines of "What I'm trying to say is there are five points I need to make before we can address the first of those ten points I mentioned earlier." Inside the firm, this was known as "getting Haimed."

Bodek wasn't in the mood to talk that morning. His eyes darkly circled, he sat frozen in his chair, staring at his stacked monitors, mumbling to himself in fits and starts, his hands rising on occasion from his keyboard to pincer his blade-shaved head above the ears as if he were trying to squeeze more juice from his sleep-deprived brain. All the stress had taken a toll. While he was just thirty-eight years old, he appeared a good decade older.

Bodek's entire Wall Street career, from Hull to Goldman Sachs to his own trading desk at UBS, had been one long march from victory to victory. Whenever faced with an obstacle no one thought he could overcome, he'd pull off a miracle. Failure had never seemed possible.

And yet here it was. He could see it, there, on his five screens, in the data that tallied up the firm's dwindling profits. As Bodek sat there, mystified by the behavior of an electronic trading ecosystem *he'd helped invent*, he focused his formidable brain power on figuring out what the hell was going on.

The answer that would solve his problems was also there, he thought, on those screens, hiding amid all the data.

*But where?*

Bodek had little idea that the answer would reveal one of the most explosive controversies of the modern-day stock market.

SHORTLY before 9 A.M., Bodek's partner, Thong-Wei Koh, a six-foot-two crack mathematician from Singapore, took his seat a few desks from Bodek. The two founders didn't exchange a word. They'd been fighting tooth and nail for the past few months. A partnership that had started with visions of glory had descended into a bitter daily feud.

TW was obsessed with mastering risk. At UBS, he'd designed a trading system so ingenious that it could *never* lose a large amount of money—at least according to the math. But now, at Trading Machines, risk was everywhere. He was drowning in it. He'd become so stressed out by the firm's problems that he'd come down with chronic stomach cramps.

Bodek, for his part, was wracked by headaches and insomnia. He began to stir out of his morning torpor as the start of the trading day neared. It was 9:15 A.M.

Time for the War Song.

Bodek plugged his iPod into a dock and pressed the play button. Pounding electric guitar chords screeched from the dock's speakers: the manic Viking heavy metal he loved—and everyone else in the room loathed. As a teenager, Bodek had played drums in a thrash band. Ever since, his taste in music had gone one way: loud, angry, violent.

He was trying to teach his team a lesson with the music. It was how he viewed trading: It *was* war. Us against them. The market was the field of battle. The weapons: brains aided by powerful computers and lightning-fast algos.

Head nodding to the earth-shaking metal, Bodek stood wearily from his chair, his tie hanging loosely around his wrinkled white shirt. While Bodek always dressed the part of a white-shoe banker—gold cuff links, silk tie, patent-leather shoes—he relished the contradictions his outfit implied as the Viking metal pounded away. Once, on a dare at a metal show in 2007, he'd leapt into a raging mosh pit dressed in his suit and tie . . . and lived to tell about it.

Clearing his throat, he rapped for good luck the Spartan helmet perched atop one of his monitors and clapped his hands.

"All right, guys," he said, machine-gun drums and psycho guitar riffs pulsating off the walls of the office. "Yesterday was bad. We got killed again. But we can't give up. We've got to fight this motherfucker! We've got to keep focused! *Stay with me!*"

There was a reason for urgency. That summer, word had gotten out on the grapevine that Trading Machines was foundering. Now Bodek's top guns were getting poached by competitors who sensed blood in the water.

To keep the ship afloat, Bodek was doing the work of three employees, staying at the office all night writing code, testing new strategies, digging deep into the guts of the Machine to figure out what had gone wrong. But he couldn't do much more, and he needed everyone to pitch in if the firm was going to right itself.

"I know it looks bad, but we can turn it around, I know it," Bodek said. "We can do it! Today we're going to fucking *kill it*, OK! Now, let's go!"

Everyone turned to his set of screens and started working. Right as the market opened, Trading Machines got whacked. For months it had been the same. Death by a thousand cuts. Sheer torture. As the nicks and cuts mounted, TW watched in frustration, obsessively clicking a pen, sighing, letting out brief bursts of anger, muttering curses under his breath.

Suddenly, the Machine froze. Trading stopped. TW pounded his fist on the desk. "What the fuck is going on, Haim!" he shouted, glaring sharply at Bodek.

This had happened before.

Bodek started to scramble, calling up the code he'd worked on overnight. "Must be a bug," he muttered, frantically typing.

"Goddammit!"

Groans echoed around the trading room.

Bodek combed through the code and quickly found the problem. A half hour later, Trading Machines was up and running again — only to keep taking losses, again and again, like clockwork.

TRADING Machines' nightmare started in the spring of 2009. Bodek had been on a trip to Hawaii for a relative's wedding. For a brief moment, he'd had time to relax and reflect on all he'd accomplished in the past decade, since joining Hull. He had it all. Money. A beautiful wife, a classically trained musician with the mental chops to match Bodek himself. A beautiful house on the beach in Stamford. Three beautiful children. Most important: He had his freedom.

When he returned to Trading Machines' office in early June, he instantly grew worried. The firm's profits were dropping sharply. Bodek started combing through the nuts and bolts of the Machine, hunting for the problem. He couldn't find it. Since then, Trading Machines had been getting hammered, day after day, bleeding away its gains. It was still making money, but its profits had been reduced by $15,000 *a day* — sometimes more — all through the summer and into the fall. Now, its gains weren't enough to keep up with the firm's costs, especially the nosebleed salaries Bodek had promised to get all that top-gun talent and the expensive technology his strategy demanded.

It was a terminal path. Eventually, the firm would run out of cash. The clock was ticking on Trading Machines.

THROUGH that December morning and into the afternoon, Bodek sat immobile in his chair, mesmerized by his stack of screens. He barely moved, aside from his fingers flying at the keyboard, his bloodshot eyes darting from screen to screen.

This wasn't unusual. Bodek almost never left his chair during the trading day. He didn't eat or even drink water until the market closed at 4 P.M. He rarely spoke. As he sat there, watching the numbers stream by, he was peering into the depths of the market, reading it like an Egyptologist scanning faded hieroglyphics.

*There's Goldman coming in. That's UBS. Hell, I designed that trade myself in 2005. They're screwing it up.*

Bodek's Machine was screwing up, too. He saw it happen all day long. He knew its signs.

Like now.

His eyes widened as he saw another wave coming in. He was tracking the SPDR S&P 500 exchange-traded fund widely known as the Spyder. The Spyder was one of the most heavily traded securities in the world—and one of Bodek's favorites. It was hovering a few pennies above $112.

Like mutual funds, ETFs represent a basket of stocks, bonds, or other assets such as gold. They're traded as a unit and mimic the value of the underlying assets. Unlike mutual funds, they can be traded continuously on exchanges—like a stock. The first ETF, the Spyder, was created in 1993. It tracked the S&P 500, an index of five hundred of the largest public companies in the United States. Other ETFs tracked the Dow Jones Industrial Average—the Diamonds—and the Nasdaq 100—called the Qs due to its QQQ ticker symbol.

The funds were like thermometers tracking the health of the market. As such, computer-driven funds, as well as everyday traders, watched them like hawks for any blip in performance.

One of those blips was about to happen. All was quiet in the room. Perhaps too quiet. Everyone was waiting for the Machine to act. Bodek caught his breath. Now . . .

*Not again.*

"Oh fuck," Bodek muttered.

The Machine's strategy involved rapidly buying and selling stock options. The trouble: Options tend to be extremely volatile and risky. Because of that, options traders normally offset their positions using stock—or an ETF. If the Machine bought an option giving it the right to buy Apple at a higher price within two weeks, it would turn around and sell short Apple stock to protect the position. If the value of the option to buy Apple declined, Trading Machines would make up some of the losses with the short bet on the stock. It was like an insurance policy against a drop in the value of the option.

Crunching the data spit out by the options market was an enormous task. In the U.S. options market alone, hundreds of thousands of messages were produced *every second*. To sort through the data in real time required computer power of the highest order, and intelligent systems to make sense of it.

Any kink in the strategy could cause it to bleed pennies and nickels. And that's exactly what was happening to Trading Machines' stock trades.

Bodek flinched. Over the years, he'd developed a second sense for when the market was about to make a move. He could feel a shift coming.

In a flash, the Spyder ticked down a few cents to $112. The move was so fast the human eye couldn't see it. A person looking at a screen would see a blur, a wiggle at the edge of motion, but it would seem as if nothing had happened.

*But the Machine saw. . . .*

What had happened? An aggressive seller had moved in and dumped the Spyder at $112—a round number typically used by humans, not computers. That triggered sensitive alerts in algorithms that tracked the market, pulling some into the market and causing them to sell, or to buy.

Algo triggered algo. Bids flew into the market at lightning speeds.

Before he could blink, Bodek's Machine made a calculation: The market would keep falling. To profit from the dip, it shot an order to powerful computers that ran a Nasdaq-owned exchange that specialized in options. It was an order to buy options tied to the Spyder that would benefit from a further decline.

The Machine was now holding an option position on the Spyder that was the equivalent to being short $1.4 million worth of the ETF.

But there was risk involved. The Machine needed to protect itself in case the option suddenly rebounded. Anything could cause it. Breaking news. A wave of big buyers. Other machines piling on. In order to insure itself, it had to turn around and *buy* the Spyder—the ETF itself—enough to guarantee against a big loss. The Machine would make money around the edges of the trade, on the marginal difference between the price of the options and the ETF. Such trades didn't make huge profits, but conducted thousands of times a day, they added up.

Bodek's fists clenched and his stomach churned as the digits detailing the trade flew across his screen. He'd seen it happen over and over again. The moment that was killing Trading Machines, when the Machine traded stock or ETFs to hedge its risks.

The Machine was ready to move. Through its high-speed connections its "auto-hedger" started spitting into the market orders to buy Spyders. The orders flew into a connected grid of massive server farms that linked electronic trading pools based in obscure townships across the New Jersey countryside. These pools made up the cyber-trading floor of the twenty-first century, a faceless, placeless cloud of data flying through fiber-optic cables at lightning speeds.

First, the Machine sent orders to a server it owned inside a state-of-the art data center in Cataret, New Jersey. The data center held giant computers that ran one of the four public exchanges in the United

States, Nasdaq. Trading Machines' server was connected directly to the exchange's computers inside the data center.

Not finding enough trades available at the right price, the Machine shot out buy orders to a data center in Weehawken, New Jersey, hitting the BATS Exchange. Orders had also been sent to a data center run by the New York Stock Exchange in Weehawken.

But the algos the Machine created and unleashed into the pools weren't surviving. They were being devoured. The algos seemed frozen, and the trades weren't getting executed.

Meanwhile, the Machine was exposed with its big option bet.

It was naked. And everyone in the room knew it.

TW snapped. "Shit!" he shouted, chucking his pencil at his keyboard, throwing his hands in the air.

Traders started cursing, watching Bodek's Machine flounder. The market was rebounding, generating an instant loss on the $1.4 million option short. It wouldn't be so bad if the Machine had bought enough Spyders—but the bug in the algos, or whatever was plaguing them, was putting the brakes on the execution. It was almost as if the auto-hedger had pushed the market back up with its orders.

It was spooky. Bodek racked his brain.

*Why wouldn't the auto-hedger buy into a declining market?*

It made no sense.

The firm's small group of human traders swung into action, scrambling to send in buy orders manually, bypassing the Machine. In seconds, the Spyder had bounced sharply, hitting $112.05.

Suddenly, a wave of orders from the Machine's auto-hedger flowed in—at the worst moment, *after* the bounce. The Machine bought thousands of shares, moving aggressively, at the same time paying high fees charged by the exchanges. Bodek had designed his Machine to avoid the fees—to in fact *get paid* for providing trades to the market—but time and again he was slammed with fees. That was part of the bug, he thought.

It was a disaster. Combined with the manual orders filled by the traders, the firm was suddenly far too overexposed—it would lose money if the market fell. But the Machine had been trying to *benefit* from a drop. It had been flipped upside down.

Traders across the floor tried to adjust, but it was too late.

In a rapid avalanche, the market tumbled, the Spyder shooting below $112, just as the Machine had predicted. But because it was overexposed, the firm lost money.

Bodek's head sunk.

The entire trade had taken thirty seconds.

Soon after the closing bell rang at 4 P.M., Bodek stood from his chair, eyes bleary from staring at the screen day and night, head pounding from sleep deprivation. His traders and programmers, slumped in their seats, looked up at him with dejection. Bodek was supposed to be their meal ticket, the genius who was going to build a powerhouse and make everyone rich. Bodek knew they were beginning to lose faith in him.

"So we got screwed again," Bodek said, rubbing a hand worriedly along the back of his head. "But we learned something today. And that's all we can do, keep learning, keep trying. It isn't supposed to be easy. That's why we get paid. See you guys tomorrow."

Bodek was starving. He hadn't eaten all day. He darted outside, grabbed a burger from the seedy-looking McDonald's across the street, and returned to his desk. During the next few hours, most of Trading Machines' team filed out. By 6 P.M., the office was empty—except for Bodek, who started, once again, combing over the day's trades, amounting to more than fifty thousand transactions, on his five screens.

# CHAPTER TWO

# THE SIZE GAME

As a child, Haim Bodek had been as comfortable in a physics lab as most children felt on a jungle gym. His father, Arie Bodek, was a world-renowned particle physicist at the University of Rochester in upstate New York, and he expected nothing less from his son. As a graduate student at the Massachusetts Institute of Technology, Arie had made discoveries described in his doctoral thesis that proved critical to groundbreaking findings in particle physics. His work helped establish the existence of the quark, a fundamental element underlying all matter.

But over the years Arie Bodek's role in the discovery had been obscured and largely forgotten. When the 1990 Nobel Prize for Physics was awarded for discoveries tied to the development of the quark model, he was little more than a footnote. Despite several Alfred P. Sloan Fellowships, seven hundred publications, a Panofsky Prize — the top prize in particle physics — and a host of other professional titles and awards, the elder Bodek never got over missing the Nobel.

Haim was expected to make sure such a travesty wasn't repeated in the Bodek family. While his father, constantly absent doing lab work around the world, never helped Haim with his studies, he still held his son to the highest standards. The only way to win attention was through outstanding academic achievements, even in grade school. Young Bodek proved to be a prodigy—quick to understand difficult concepts and capable of remarkable original insight. He was, to all appearances, a savant. A young genius.

But he rebelled. As a teenager, Haim started to resist his father's pressure to fill his shoes. He dyed his hair black and became a drummer in a thrash band. He hung out with a rough crowd and often didn't come home for weeks. When Haim was seventeen years old, in 1988, his father made a prediction. At a family gathering, he openly lamented his son's lack of discipline.

"He will never win the Nobel Prize!" he pronounced.

Haim didn't need to remind his father that he'd never won the prize, either. Despite the emotional pain the prediction caused him, it also touched a deeper, intellectual chord. In order to achieve the future that he (rather than his father) desired, he needed to be able to *predict* the future.

But how can you predict the future?

Is it possible to gather and analyze enough data to increase the chances of correctly predicting future events? With the growth of computer power in the 1980s, it was a tantalizing question. But *massive* computer power was needed to mine the terabytes of data related to a particular question about the future, such as "What is the likelihood that Haim Bodek will win the Nobel Prize?" The machine would have to analyze the lives of all past Nobel Prize winners, how they fared in grade school, their eye color, their ancestors, *their DNA* . . . and on and on, before checking the data against Haim Bodek's own extensive history to find matching patterns.

In the late 1980s and early 1990s, such computing power simply wasn't available to anyone outside corporate giants such as IBM and the military-industrial complex. The supercomputer of that time performed on the level of today's iPad. The Internet, a trove of data today, was in its infancy. There was no Google, no Wikipedia, no Twitter. Theories about predicting the future using computers were fantasies at best.

But the question stayed with Bodek—even after he graduated from high school (despite skipping all of his senior-year finals), even after he used his sky-high SAT scores (making up for lackluster grades) to get into the University of Rochester, where he started pursuing his dream of predicting the future by immersing himself in study of the emerging science of artificial intelligence.

He also started dating his future wife, a striking brunette music scholar named Elizabeth Bonheim. She was beguiled by Bodek's reckless, bad-boy attitude, as well as his dazzling mind. While Bodek wasn't the most diligent student, he consistently scored at the top of the class on tests. Elizabeth would watch with dismay as Bodek skipped nearly every one of his classes, then crammed in a semester's worth of high-level math in a single night before acing the exam and screwing up the grade curve for everyone.

After graduating in 1995 with degrees in mathematics and cognitive science—the latter is the study of the mind as a machine that processes information—Bodek found work at Magnify, an Oak Park, Illinois, high-tech outfit run by Robert Grossman, a pioneer in techniques to mine giant databases for information. Bodek quickly proved his mettle at Magnify. With Grossman and several other researchers he helped write a seminal paper on predicting credit card fraud based on massive data sets. Using "machine learning," a branch of artificial intelligence that deployed algorithms to crunch large blocks of data, the system could detect patterns of fraudulent transactions. One red flag might be a $1 credit card purchase at a gas station followed by a $10,000 splurge at a jewelry store (signaling that the thieves were testing the card before trying to make a big score).

Visa vetted the system, found that it complemented their own methods, and quickly implemented it to stop the $10,000 jewelry purchases. In essence, it was predicting the theft and thereby preventing it, scanning three hundred thousand transactions an hour. It was a computerized crystal ball, forecasting the future with a combination of math and semiconductors.

During his downtime, Bodek started reading about a new trend: applying artificial intelligence methods to the stock market. *Neural nets* had become a hot topic on Wall Street, at least according to a number of books Bodek had come across. Firms were reportedly dabbling in *fuzzy logic* and *genetic algorithms*, *machine learning*, and *expert systems*, all branches of AI. Bodek, an expert in all of the above, became convinced that he could use his vast skills to predict stock moves and make a fortune in the process. He'd also become engaged to Elizabeth and was looking for a way to pad his bank account.

In the summer of 1997, he visited a Chicago-based recruiter for banks and hedge funds—private investment firms that make big wagers on behalf of wealthy investors—named Ilya Talman. He said he wanted to forecast the direction of the market using AI.

Talman looked at Bodek as if he were a madman. "How do you think a guy who's twenty-six and has no experience is going to do that?" he said. "And who the hell is going to hire you? No one, that's who."

Besides, no legitimate firm was using neural nets or fuzzy logic to predict the market, he explained. All the books Bodek had been reading were full of hype. "You have to get a normal job and work your way up the ranks," Talman said.

Bodek scoffed. "I'm not going to do some normal shitty programming job," he said. Days later, he was leafing through the *Chicago Tribune* employment section and came across an ad mixed in among jobs for real estate brokers and construction workers. "Data mining neural net worker to forecast market," the ad read. No company name was given, just a phone number.

Bodek brought the ad to Talman. "You said there were no jobs for me," he said. "Look, they're advertising market forecasting jobs in the *Chicago Tribune*!"

Talman looked into the ad. It had been placed by an obscure firm called Hull Trading. Talman knew about Hull. It was the elite of the elite, a printing press for money.

"There's no way you're getting into Hull," he told Bodek. "All they have is Ph.D.s."

"Just get me the interview," Bodek said.

AFTER a grueling interview process, Bodek landed a job at Hull in September 1997. Among the most sophisticated finance outfits in the world, Hull Trading specialized in stocks and stock options. Founded in 1985 by mathematician, trader, and blackjack whiz Blair Hull, the firm was a hive of physicists and computer scientists. Many had worked at Fermilab in Batavia, Illinois, a high-energy physics research facility just outside of Chicago. It was a place Bodek's father knew well. It had played a key role in the discovery of the quark and he had worked there on and off many times over the years. While Bodek wasn't on a path to win a Nobel Prize, his father was proud that he'd landed among a group of his old Fermilab colleagues.

Bodek's first assignment at Hull was to use machine learning— the same branch of AI he'd used at Magnify—to create algorithms to predict the direction of the stock-option market.

It was the beginning of a dramatic trading evolution on Wall Street and among the first salvos in the coming Algo Wars.

At the time, the algos that most firms used to trade were mindless drones, like single-cell organisms acting according to a basic set of rules designed by programmers. They would scan the market for signals, like primitive animals programmed to eat everything in sight. Has the average price of Microsoft risen 1 percent in the past half-hour? Yes. Buy Microsoft. *Chomp.*

But the stock market had proven too clunky for the sophisticated, dynamic AI algos that could adjust to changing market conditions on the fly—algos that could *learn*, *predict*, and *adapt* like a human trader. This was mostly due to the annoying presence of *humans* in the system.

When Hull hired Bodek in 1997, the stock market was largely divided into two parts: the New York Stock Exchange, where traders swapped big, blue-chip stocks such as IBM and General Electric through registered brokers and "specialists" on the iconic floor of the exchange; and the Nasdaq Stock Market, where roughly five hundred market makers competed to buy and sell stocks, often hotdog tech names such as Intel, Cisco, and Apple, on behalf of clients. NYSE trading was conducted on the floor of the Big Board at 11 Wall Street, where participants swapped information through wild hand signals and shouted orders; Nasdaq market makers largely operated over the phone. Nasdaq stock orders were sometimes input electronically, but few trades took place without a human getting in the middle.

While the humans had developed their own complex ecosystem, they didn't interact well with computers. The behavior of the specialists and market makers was unpredictable. Responses to buy and sell orders could vary. Mistakes were made, upsetting the rigid computer-driven systems, which depended on precise order.

A change was needed: a new pool for the algos to face off in. A *computer-driven* pool where they could evolve and grow in their natural environment, developing their own ecosystem. Like fish in water, computer trading programs worked far better when operating on other computers (rather than the testosterone-fueled floor of the NYSE or the trading desks of Nasdaq market makers). And it was even worse in the options markets, Bodek's chosen field of battle. That's why three months into the job, Bodek shifted gears and quickly moved on to prove himself in other parts of the firm, focusing mostly on European options markets, which were more electronic. In short order, he became one of Hull's top electronic-trading strategists.

Then, in 1999, Goldman Sachs shelled out half a billion dollars to buy Hull. It marked a massive shift inside Goldman—the quintessential old-guard white-shoe Wall Street firm—toward electronic trading. The shift would pave the way for Goldman's rise to power in the 2000s, when it emerged as one of the most aggressive and sophisticated trading goliaths in the world.

Bodek was conflicted by the move. A giant Wall Street bank had suddenly swallowed up his life. He'd always thought of himself as an outsider who played by his own rules, a maverick who happened to have the mind of a world-class scientist. Hull, a hothouse of eccentric Ph.D.s and boy wonders like Bodek, encouraged his outsider self-image. Goldman, on the other hand, was the epitome of the establishment, of faceless Wall Street power.

He decided to stick it out, to discover what Goldman was like from the inside. He felt in ways like a spy who'd penetrated the enemy's inner sanctum. He'd see what it was all about and decide for himself whether it was good, evil, or neither.

At Goldman, Bodek became a cog in the market's rapidly evolving machinery. The system was becoming increasingly electronic, driven by powerful computers that could execute trades in less than a second. Human dealers—the NYSE specialists and Nasdaq market makers—were getting pushed aside by the computer networks, electronic pools designed by experts such as Dan Mathisson at Credit Suisse where the trading algos designed by experts such as Bodek could face off and do battle. When Bodek had first joined Hull in 1997, the pools had only existed in embryonic form and weren't yet large enough for his AI trading system to work.

By the early 2000s, the entire system was in flux. The new pools evoked a water-filled world of frictionless trading: Island, Archipelago, Liquidnet. Some were fully transparent or "lit," such as Island, where all orders were out in the open, reported by electronic data feeds that anyone could access. Others, such as Liquidnet, were dark. Trading took place in secret beyond the prying tentacles of the hunter-seeker algorithms. With electronic innovations such as Island and Liquidnet and the rise of algorithms that swam in their pools, the market was evolving like a living organism, shape-shifting into something entirely new. And the algorithms were changing, too. They were no longer the dumb single-cell virus-like creatures operating on simple orders. (Has Microsoft's average price risen 1 percent? Buy.) They were learning how to adapt in the new pools, morphing into more advanced predators. Many were geared up with advanced AI systems that could quickly detect hidden market signals using the high-bandwidth data feeds and react in a flash, learning and changing their behavior along the way.

Known as "order-awareness algos," they harvested data during the execution of a trade and shifted gears in milliseconds. Beneath the technical bells and whistles, however, something more sinister was going on. "Order awareness" seemed to be another phrase for "statistical front-running"—using streams of data to trade ahead of those massive whales.

With the new electronic pools, the machine-learning algorithms Bodek had once toyed with at Hull became viable.

As the Algo Wars heated up, Ph.D.s devised new algos to defend against the hunter-seeker algos. The algos started feeding on one another. They weren't only programmed to gobble up passive food in the market—fat whale orders to buy a million shares of Intel, sent down by a fund manager. They were dynamic, aware, capable of watching *other algos*, anticipating their moves—and eating them, too. A mutual fund's algo order to buy Intel would follow strict instructions designed to fake out the hunter-seekers: *Only buy when many other traders are buying (hiding in the crowd). If the price moves up too quickly, such as ½ percent in two minutes, stop buying. If the broader market falls quickly, stop buying.*

Some algos were encoded with a randomizer, causing them to shift erratically between strategies, in order to hide the patterns of their moves. They were like hunted prey attempting to cover up their tracks through feints and dodges. With no order for the hunter-seeker radars to detect, it was easier to operate in stealth mode.

But the hunter-seekers adapted to the new stealth techniques and watched for them, anticipating every move—even the seemingly random ones. Every trade left a signal, a trail of bread crumbs. The hunter-seekers were experts at sniffing them out.

The mindless algos had evolved into dangerous beasts of prey. They were getting *smart*. They had names such as Shark, Guerilla, Stealth, Thor, Sniper. It was digital warfare taking place inside massive computers. Billions were at stake.

BODEK didn't stay long at Goldman. Most of Hull's top people had already left, and the creative magic that had driven Hull's machine for years had been suffocated by Goldman's embrace, he felt. In 2003, Bodek landed at UBS and set up shop at the bank's massive Stamford headquarters. *The Guinness Book of World Records* had dubbed UBS's Stamford trading floor the largest in the world. The size of two football fields at one hundred thousand square feet, it sported fourteen hundred seats and five thousand monitors. It was a computerized trading machine of vast proportions, juggling more than a trillion in assets a day.

Bodek's mandate was to build an options-trading desk that could go head-to-head with the likes of Hull—and he succeeded in spades. His first signal achievement was an entirely new options trading strategy called *dynamic sizing*. In September 2003, soon after he'd arrived at UBS, he developed a monster algorithm to dominate all others. Using the bank's capital, the algorithm would play an electronic game of chicken by spamming options exchanges with massive orders designed to push aside smaller competitors. By doing so, it got more favorable trades. The idea behind it was simple: Because certain exchanges gave priority to firms that placed large orders, a fat trade could leap ahead of everyone else.

Based on a formula, Bodek's algo would dynamically shift the size of its orders to get the best response. Only a small part of the trade would ever get executed, because the trader on the other side wasn't remotely as large. An order to buy one thousand contracts of Intel options might purchase only one hundred contracts, since that's the most that were offered. It was high-stakes electronic poker, and for a time Bodek was winning every hand.

Bodek called it the Size Game.

His desk quickly racked up big profits playing the Size Game. In short order, other trading firms copied the strategy, triggering a new algo arms race. The game reached absurd levels as firms posted orders as much as fifty times the amount they wanted to trade in order to leap ahead of the competition. As the algos interacted, dialing sizes up and down in order to game one another, the traffic of information shooting through the trading network spiked. It was a classic example of algorithmic evolution. Firms rigged algos to game other algos, dynamically shifting the size of their orders to win the race.

It didn't always work perfectly. Bodek's system was coded with a bad-trade-detection alarm that would blast a loud Homer Simpson–esque "DOH!" whenever a trade was moving against it. One day, after a trader turned on a new feature across the entire portfolio, the bad-trade-detection system went manic, screaming out more than five hundred "DOH!"s in four seconds, like a high-frequency mix tape gone berserk. Bodek's traders soon couldn't bear to watch *The Simpsons*, since the sound triggered a gut-level panic mode, a twisted traders' version of post-traumatic stress disorder.

Volumes surged to insane levels. In 2005, the Size Game nearly crashed the OPRA feed—run by the Options Price Reporting Authority—the data pipeline feeding the option trading pools.

On Wall Street, of course, such events are hailed as career-making victories. By 2006, Bodek was jointly in charge of UBS's elite electronic volatility trading desk, with hundreds of millions of the bank's capital at his fingertips. He worked alongside Thong-Wei Koh, or TW, his future partner at Trading Machines. Bodek and TW were fish out of water at UBS, two confirmed math nerds in a sea of testosterone-fueled traders. They used to say that they were dolphins in a pool of sharks (dolphins are known for cooperating in order to defeat predators).

Their skills neatly balanced out. Obsessed with risk, TW carefully managed the desk's operation to make sure it didn't blow up. Bodek was more of a gunslinger, pushing the edge of the envelope to maximize returns.

But he still wasn't satisfied. He often thought back to his rebellious days as a drummer in a thrash band, and the idealism he and his hacker pals had adopted in the early nineties, when a new vision about using technology to break apart the power structures of society had become a rallying cry. The mantra became *information wants to be free*—and brilliant programmers would do everything they could to make it happen. Then the Internet came along, and information on many levels *was* free. It was a victory for the technorati.

But Bodek was still working for a bank; *he* wanted to be free, to pursue his own dreams. In 2007, he and TW started to discuss launching their own operation, one that would run its own money using Bodek's brilliant strategies and deep knowledge of the market, backed up by TW's obsessive risk-management skills.

Besides his desire to break out on his own, Bodek also saw that a number of technical changes in the options market were coming, such as a shift from pricing of options in fractions to decimals. Typically, an option trader could buy an option for, say, $1 and resell it for $1.05. Decimal pricing would change that—an option trader might buy the option for $1 and be able to resell it for only $1.01. The shift would make it cheaper for regular investors to get in on the game, but it would make it more difficult for the big boys to make the fat profits they'd grown accustomed to. The difference between buy and sell prices would shrink. Profits of five or ten cents per contract could shrink to a penny. The Size Game would be crushed—any firm that put in massive orders would be risking too much for too little reward.

To make money, a firm had to be streamlined, able to trade at prices that its competitors thought weren't profitable enough—at least according to the rules of the Size Game. Rather than hit home runs, Bodek wanted to play Small Ball: consistently hit lots of singles and doubles and drive up the score. By creating a new game while the old outfits were still trying to play the one he'd invented, Bodek would

once again have the jump on everyone. And it would be so much easier to do this when he was running his own show. Or so he thought.

In the fall of 2007, the two heads of UBS's electronic volatility
trading desk handed in their resignations and launched Trading Machines a mile away, in a small office in downtown Stamford. On a clear
day, Bodek could see UBS's hulking headquarters from a window in
his new digs.

Times were good for Bodek. To celebrate his and Elizabeth's tenth
wedding anniversary, on October 26, 2007, they tossed a lavish party
at the luxurious Waveny House in New Canaan, Connecticut, the former estate of Texaco founder Lewis Lapham. Thrown at the height of
the Wall Street bubble, the party was a midnight masquerade ball and
cost $60,000. Soon after, Bodek purchased a black BMW Z4M coupe
with red leather seats. He called it the Batmobile.

Bodek quickly began scouring Wall Street for top talent, and he
found eager takers among the trading desks of the most elite banks
and hedge funds in the country. Word got around that Bodek and TW
were building the Next Next Thing in Stamford, a cutting-edge trading operation that reputations would be built on. They turned down
dozens of résumés from programmers and traders that most startups
would have killed for.

They moved fast. In November 2007, Trading Machines launched
with $20 million. While small by some standards, it was deemed sub-
stantial for a high-speed trading outfit—and spoke to the economics
of the business. Fast traders make money by picking up pennies and
nickels on thousands of trades a day. Because they move in and out of
positions so rapidly, they can recycle a small amount of cash over and
over again. Imagine lowering a water-powered generator into a stream
of water. The faster the stream, the more energy it generates. The ability to scale up to massive volumes with seemingly little risk—in effect
causing the stream to flow more rapidly—was a major reason why
high-speed trading had become one of the industry's hottest strategies
by the late 2000s.

Trading Machines was among the elite at this approach. Deploying roughly $5 million in capital—the rest was set aside for expenses—Trading Machines in a single day typically executed 17,000 stock trades and 6,500 options trades. Bodek's trades were all managed by the Machine. At the guts of the Machine was a computer program he called *Pi*, a reference to the number as well as the 1998 movie by Darren Aronofsky that depicts a paranoid mathematician's quest to unearth universal patterns in nature in stock market data. Pi was designed to make a small amount of money for each option or stock traded. Make enough trades, and those pennies and nickels could add up to a significant chunk of change—as long as the strategy worked as designed.

Powered by more than one hundred IBM Blade servers, the Machine was plugged into seven options markets, four stock exchanges, and several dark pools. It was fully automated (though traders could jump in and manually trade under certain circumstances) and extremely aggressive. Calculating that most firms wouldn't have the ability to make a profit by rapidly trading options in the decimal era, Bodek believed he'd have a golden opportunity to become a major player by taking the risk and, with TW's help, deploying models sophisticated enough to manage the risk.

Trading began in August 2008. The strategy Bodek designed was the culmination of a complex algorithmic trading tradition that had started at Hull and that he'd carried on at Goldman and UBS. He'd started with the premise that he could model the theoretical value of all options as implied by the price of the underlying stock. Throughout the trading day, there were small swings in the prices of the options that signaled to the Machine that they had swung away from their true theoretical value. That meant an opportunity. If the price swung too high, the Machine would sell the option, expecting to profit when it declined. If the price fell too much, the Machine would buy it. The key was to have a model that was both accurate and fast, because other machines were trying to beat it to the punch. The Machine had to have massive power so it could calculate these values over and over again and enter the orders into the market thousands of times a minute.

It was fierce combat. Trading Machines was locked in competition against thousands of players sporting Ph.D.s in everything from quantum physics to electrical engineering to biochemistry. If most of the computer models they deployed judged that Intel was about to rise sharply from $20 a share, the machines would pound the market with buy orders. Sellers, at the same time—often using similar models—rammed up their prices rapidly.

Imagine it: hundreds of thousands of orders flying into the market each second through high-speed connections, fighting to be in front of all the others. Just as quickly, as stocks bobbed and weaved, those orders were canceled and resubmitted at different price points—at different exchanges and dozens of other trading venues, such as dark pools (incredibly, a staggering *90 percent* or more of all orders placed into the stock market were canceled).

Every second, all day long, every day, this happened again and again and again, trades fizzing through fiber-optic cables laced around the world. The action was so rapid and heavy that no human could do it. It had to be run by machines—high-frequency traders, the speed-freak robot traders of Wall Street. These firms traded both at very high speeds (speeds measured in the millionth or even billionth of a second) and at very high frequencies, meaning the orders they pumped into the market were incredibly *frequent*, often to the tune of thousands a second. The frenetic frequency of the orders, combined with the insane speeds at which they flew into the market, had created an entirely new market ecosystem that seemed more like something from *The Matrix* than a place for investors to stash their hard-won earnings.

Bodek knew all about the speed traders. Hell, *he was one of them.* Trading Machines was as tooled-up as could be, state-of-the-art as a space shot. Its computer layout alone cost more than $3 million a year.

But there were several important differences between Trading

Machines and most other high-speed outfits. Bodek's firm specialized in options, whereas most speedsters focused on stocks and ETFs. They were apples and oranges. Options markets were relatively slow compared with stocks. To Bodek, the speed traders of the stock market were insanely fast, turning over positions in a matter of a few seconds. His firm typically held a portfolio of options contracts that rotated at a much slower pace. The high-frequency dimension of the options business centered on managing its risk and inventory as the market shifted. While high-speed to most investors, Trading Machines was a lumbering turtle compared with the rising new breed of speed Bots in the stock market.

Bodek had also become concerned about the widespread use of artificial intelligence in the market. The options market, with its massive volatility, seemed particularly resistant to AI, which tended to rely on markets behaving in a relatively orderly fashion.

He thought of AI like a weather-monitoring system for the market—it could detect when the weather was changing and *learn from new patterns* as it evolved. If the market was like a vast, ever-changing weather system, the AI Bots were like satellites that could sense when a cold front was moving in, or a patch of sunny skies. What's more, they could predict patterns by looking for new clues— 60 percent of the time a sudden drop in temperature means a thunderstorm is moving in. *Run for cover. . . .*

The trouble, Bodek believed, was that the market could be far more volatile than the weather. It could go from a hundred degrees to subzero in a matter of minutes. No AI system could ever sense such wild swings. And if it did, it would likely overreact and make the swings *worse*.

That's why Bodek preferred to trust his own brain. While he used AI methods such as expert systems to build his algos, he preferred to maintain control throughout the trading day. That's why he never left his seat, not even for a bathroom break.

And *it was working*. Unlimited riches seemed at Bodek's fingertips. Trading Machines was his best shot at the big time—running his own fund, building a trading empire to span the globe. He'd planned to use his windfall to fund research efforts to combat genocide, a long-held dream that went back to his grandparents' narrow escape from Poland after the Nazi invasion of 1939. Bodek had already helped fund one of the earliest Darfur information projects in 2003 and had spent more than $100,000 on projects to intervene in atrocities around the world. But he wanted to do much more.

Then the Machine stopped working, and Bodek channeled every bit of his brain power toward fixing it. Like the obsessive mathematician in the movie *Pi*, he shut out all distractions, including his own family, and dove into the data. He even stopped driving the Batmobile, promising himself he'd use it again when he'd solved the mystery. For months, it sat in his front yard, gathering rust.

But nothing was working. He'd started wondering if the problem plaguing Trading Machines wasn't an internal bug. Perhaps, he thought, darting in and out of his screens were the footprints of an entirely different breed of high-frequency trader, one that made moves he'd never seen before.

Maybe, he thought, *the game itself* had changed. It was as if weather patterns that had existed for years had disappeared entirely. This was not the same stock market he'd encountered at UBS, when he helped run one of the world's largest derivatives trading desks. The very ecosystem of the market itself, driven by the latest advances in the Algo Wars, seemed to have shifted and morphed into something new and, to Bodek, profoundly disturbing.

# CHAPTER THREE

# ALGO WARS

The Algo Wars had broken out in the late 1990s with the appearance of a small band of computer-savvy trading operations—later dubbed high-frequency traders—with obscure names such as Automated Trading Desk, Getco, Tradebot, and Quantlab. They arose in isolated pockets around the country. Chicago; Mount Pleasant, South Carolina; North Kansas City; Houston; New York. Tiny at first, by the late 2000s they zipped in and out of stocks at speeds measured in one-millionth of a second and accounted for more than two-thirds of all trading of U.S. stocks.

They were so skilled, so efficient, and so fast that they made money nearly every single day. Trading their own cash, they were only interested in short-term profits and rarely held positions overnight. In many ways, they acted like market makers, the ever-present middlemen who bought stocks when others wanted to sell, sold when others wanted to buy. But they were almost entirely unregulated and operated in the shadows of the financial industry.

Many of the high-speed firms deployed massive amounts of leverage, or borrowed money, as much as fifty to one by the late 2000s (for every dollar they owned, they borrowed another *fifty dollars* from banks and brokers in the hope of amplifying their profits). As the financial meltdown of 2008 showed, massive leverage can quickly un-ravel and trigger devastating, out-of-control meltdowns.

Over the years, the speed traders worked hand in hand with the architects of the electronic pools, the exchange Plumbers who catered to their needs like fashion designers wooing movie stars. To the pools, high-frequency trading (commonly called HFT) was like a magical elixir. It brought massive volume, resulting in massive profits. Since the pools made money by executing trades, the more volume they received, the more money they raked in.

To lure the traders, the pools offered a smorgasbord of special services. At the top of the list was *information*: hard data about the state of the market as well as the activities of *other traders*. They provided expensive data feeds that channeled a fire hose of information to the Bots, which parsed it in microseconds—and reacted in microseconds. The firms that could crunch the data, detect patterns, and react first won the race.

The exchanges also offered beneficial status to the firms that poured the most liquidity into their pools. On Nasdaq, a firm that sent twenty-five million shares *a day* into its market could qualify for one of its top "tiers," which allowed the firm to pocket higher trading fees. On Direct Edge, the top tier once went to firms that sent *forty million shares a day* into its pool.

The Algo Wars evolved with AI. If an algo could dynamically adapt to new patterns in the data in the heat of battle—in the midst of the trading day—it could operate more efficiently. In the morning, stocks might trade according to one trend, carried higher by momentum; then in the afternoon they might operate according to a new dynamic as investors cashed in their gains. Such trends rippled through the electronic pools in waves throughout the day. The algos tried to surf the waves without getting swamped.

As they plunged into the pools, the AI Bots started generating entirely new patterns—waves of their own—creating a new trading ecosystem: a market that changed and morphed minute by minute, reacting dynamically to its own twists and turns as in a digitized hall of mirrors. A market that almost seemed *alive.*

As Bodek dug further into the never-ending complexities of high-frequency trading in the stock market, he felt as if he'd finally come out the other end of his father's dream and was once again back in the realm of particle physics. The complexity of the interactions of all the orders was mind-bending.

Part of the complexity derived from one of the primary goals in this nanosecond race: to literally get *paid to trade.* Beginning in the late 1990s, a small group of electronic trading venues—upstart rivals to the NYSE and Nasdaq—launched a payment system that gave trading firms an incentive to send buy and sell orders to their computerized matching engines. Firms that "made" a trade happen got paid a fraction of a cent per share, while firms that "took" the trade paid a fraction of a cent per share (the *take* fee was typically slightly higher than the *make* fee, and the exchanges pocketed the difference). Eventually, this "maker-taker" system became the de facto method of trading for the vast majority of the U.S. stock market.

Imagine a grocery store in which you can haggle over prices. The grocer is willing to sell you an apple for $1. You, however, are offering to pay 95 cents for the apple. If the grocer agrees and takes your lower offer, *he pays the take fee* while *you get the make fee.* If, however, you decide to give in and pay $1 for the apple, *you* pay the take fee and the grocer gets the make fee. Whoever gives in and crosses the spread between the bid and the offer pays.

The system rewards patience and puts a price on speed. Maker-taker provides an incentive for firms to put up lots of price points. Patient "market makers" can perpetually put up quotes and wait, pocketing the fees. More aggressive and motivated traders who simply must have that apple right now (or must sell that apple—or that Apple stock—right now) are more willing to pay the fee.

Maker-taker amounted to a frenetic game of musical chairs, with computer-driven firms popping in and out of stocks with the singular goal of snatching the fees.

The exchanges loved it, since it boosted their revenues. That, in turn, made the high-frequency firms that specialized in winning the maker-taker game *very* important to the exchanges. "The maker-taker pricing model makes high-frequency traders the exchanges' most valuable customers both through an increase in trading fees and an increase in market data that gets generated," the trade journal *Advanced Trading* noted in a June 2011 article.

Vast sums were at stake. Once a month, firms that "made" a lot of trades, typically high-frequency trading outfits, received checks from the exchanges paying them for their service. At the same time, firms that *took* the trades, typically slow-moving large mutual funds but also outfits such as Trading Machines that specialized in options but had to trade large sums of stocks, got stuck with a bill. In 2008, for instance, the NYSE and Nasdaq alone paid out $2 billion in "make" fees (while collecting even more in "take" fees). And since high-speed traders gravitated to the more speed-friendly exchanges BATS and Direct Edge, the total amount was surely much higher.

It was a game within a game, and it inspired all sorts of perverse behavior. Heavily traded stocks such as Citigroup and Intel became beloved by fee-seeking high-speed firms, since the more trades that occurred, the more fees they could collect. Some firms reportedly ramped up trades at the end of the month—even if the trades were losses—simply to surpass specific volume-level targets at the exchanges in order to boost their fees (firms that averaged, say, fifty million shares a day would get better deals).

Regular investors, of course, had little idea about the massive transfer of wealth that was taking place—or that the exchanges, in thrall to the speed-traders' oceans of volume, were in on the game and getting paid right alongside the high-frequency traders.

In some ways, the market had come full circle. The outfits that could afford the best bandwidth and reach the highest tiers and knew exactly how the Plumbing worked had an advantage over everyone else. It was exactly like the specialist system of old, in which insiders lined their pockets at the expense of everyone else. In ways, however, it was worse, because these new computer-driven masters of the universe were almost entirely unregulated. No one was keeping their eyes on the Bots' activities. No one could, since no computer on earth could capture all of the manic nanosecond action.

It was a new version of the old stock market—and highly toxic.

Bodek began to think it had become broken at its core. *If I'm swinging at market phantoms, buying too high, selling too low, what chance do ordinary investors have?*

It was so complex. The number of destinations for trading stocks was maddening. There were four public exchanges: the NYSE, Nasdaq, Direct Edge, and BATS (the latter two, which specialized in high-speed trading, appeared on the scene in 2005 and 2006, respectively). Inside each of those exchanges were various other destinations. The NYSE had NYSE Arca, NYSE Amex, NYSE Euronext, and NYSE Alternext. Nasdaq had three markets. BATS had two. Direct Edge had EDGA, which had no "maker-taker" system, and EDGX, which did.

Then there were the dark pools. Giant banks ran most of them. Credit Suisse owned the largest, Dan Mathisson's Crossfinder. Goldman Sachs's Sigma X was a close second. There was Liquidnet and Posit and Pipeline. Nasdaq's European dark pool was called NEURO Dark. Chicago's Getco (short for Global Electronic Trading Company), the largest and most powerful high-frequency trading firm—it was likely the most active trading operation the world had ever seen—also ran a pool called GETMatched. In all, there were more than fifty dark pools in the United States.

While dark pools had been originally designed for large investors as a haven from the hunter-seeker algos, by the late 2000s most had been thoroughly penetrated by Bots. Indeed, they couldn't operate without them. This led to new problems: *toxic dark pools* swarming with predator algos designed to front-run large trader orders and game the lit market—the very problem Dan Mathisson was trying to fix with Light Pool.

Then there were the *internalizers*. Hedge funds such as Citadel Investment Group, based in Chicago, a giant New Jersey shop called Knight Trading, and banks such as Citigroup or Bodek's old haunt UBS *bought orders* from retail brokers such as TD Ameritrade, Charles Schwab, and E*Trade and executed the trades inside their own computer pools. They matched buy and sell orders "internally," rather than route them to an exchange. A day trader snapping up a hundred shares of Apple from her home office account had little chance of ever actually trading on the NYSE; instead, she was interacting with a sophisticated program crafted by a team of Ph.D. quants working for a giant Chicago hedge fund or a secretive desk within a Swiss bank. The effect was to remove from the rest of the market the mom-and-pop retail flow and segregate it within isolated pools. And while the internalizers bragged about the quality of their execution, investors using those systems would have been wise to wonder just *why* a Chicago hedge fund or Swiss bank wanted to pay millions of dollars a year for their orders.

The market was pools within pools, all connected electronically, forming a single sloshing pool of dark electronic liquidity. By 2012, the amount of stock trading that took place in dark pools and internalizers was a whopping *40 percent* of all trading volume—and it was growing every month.

Even the lit markets were unfathomably complex, run by giant computers that processed secret trading strategies designed by physicists, chemists, Ph.D. mathematicians, AI computer programmers. The strategies were dueling and dodging, processing orders at mind-boggling rates. In late 2011, for instance, Nasdaq rolled out a platform called Burstream that gave clients the ability to get data in six hundred nanoseconds—six-hundred-*billionths* of a second—with its "Nano-Speed Market Data Mesh" system. In the options market, nearly nine million orders flowed through the system each second, overwhelming computer programs and making a hash of trading information.

All of that turnover was having a real-world impact on stocks. At the end of World War II, the average holding period for a stock was four years. By 2000, it was eight months. By 2008, it was two months. And by 2011 it was *twenty-two seconds*, at least according to one professor's estimates. One founder of a prominent high-frequency trading outfit once claimed his firm's average holding period was a mere *eleven seconds*.

No one—*no one*—truly knew what was taking place inside the guts of this Frankenstein's monster of a market.

# CHAPTER FOUR

# 0+

In early December 2009, Haim Bodek finally solved the riddle of the stock-trading problem that was killing Trading Machines. He was attending a party in New York City sponsored by a U.S. exchange. He'd been complaining for months to the exchange about all the bad trades—the runaway prices, the fees—that were bleeding his firm dry. But he'd gotten little help, and he'd finally stopped using the exchange altogether.

At the bar, he cornered an exchange representative and pushed for answers. The rep asked Bodek what order types he'd been using to buy and sell stocks. Order types were how trading firms "talked" to exchanges, the language they used to communicate their intentions. They determined how a buy or sell order interacted with other orders. A "market order" essentially told the exchange to "buy the stock now no matter what!" They were for urgent traders who didn't care if the market moved in the next few seconds. "Limit orders," used by many professional traders, specified that an investor wanted to buy or sell a stock within a "limit." A limit order might tell the exchange to buy Intel for up to $20.50—but no higher. They protected investors from sudden swings.

They were the kind of orders Bodek used at Trading Machines. That's what he told the exchange rep.

The rep smirked and took a sip of his drink.

"You can't use those," he told Bodek.

"Why not?"

"You have to use other orders. Those limit orders are going to get run over."

"But that's what everyone uses," Bodek said, incredulous. "That's what Schwab uses."

"I know. You shouldn't."

As the rep started to explain undocumented features about how limit orders were treated inside the exchange, Bodek started to scribble an order on a napkin, detailing how it went into the exchange. "You're fucked in that case?" he said, shoving the napkin at the guy.

"Yeah."

He scribbled another. "You're fucked in that case?"

"Yeah."

"Are you telling me you're fucked in *every* case?"

"Yeah."

"Why are you telling me this?"

"We want you to turn us back on again," the rep replied. "You see, you don't have a bug."

Bodek's jaw dropped. He'd suspected something was going on inside the market that was killing his trades, that it wasn't a bug, but it had been only a vague suspicion with little proof.

"I'll show you how it works."

The rep told Bodek about the kind of orders he *should* use — orders that wouldn't get abused like the plain vanilla limit orders; orders that seemed to Bodek specifically designed to *abuse* the limit orders by exploiting complex loopholes in the market's plumbing. The orders Bodek had been using were child's play, simple declarative sentences sent to exchanges such as "Buy up to $20." These new order types were compound sentences, with multiple clauses, virtually Faulknerian in their rambling complexity.

The end result, however, was simple: Everyday investors and even sophisticated firms like Trading Machines were buying stocks for a slightly higher price than they should, and selling for a slightly lower price and paying billions in "take" fees along the way.

In part, it had to do with a massive market-structure change instituted by the Securities and Exchange Commission in 2007. Known as Reg NMS, short for Regulation National Market System, it had been an attempt to bind together the fragmented electronic marketplace into a single interlinked web of trading—a true national market system. The only way to do this, a team of technocrats at the SEC decided, was to mandate that any order to buy or sell a stock had to go to the venue that had the best price. If an investor placed an order to buy Intel at the NYSE, where it was selling for $20.01, and there was a better price at Nasdaq, say $20, the order would instantly be routed to Nasdaq. The prices were shared among exchanges and dark pools on an electronic ticker tape called the Securities Information Processor, widely known as the SIP feed.

While Reg NMS made some intuitive sense, it also spawned a vast tangle of complications. Now all trading venues had to constantly monitor the price of a stock (or hundreds or *thousands* of stocks) on every trading venue, all the time, a feat that required industrial strength computer power. Because of this linkage, the national market system regulated when the best bid or offer for a stock was permitted to change within each exchange or dark pool.

If prices changed, one result could be that an order placed into an exchange's trading queue was either rejected, routed to another exchange, or kicked to the back of the queue—the lineup of buy or sell orders ranked according to priority (whoever was first in line got the trade).

This made life very complex for obsessively detail-oriented firms that wished to microscopically control every aspect of how their orders were treated by an exchange—and evidently some complained about it. The exchanges, eager to please their most-favored clients, rolled out new order types that would solve the problem (while these order types were free, many firms without the proper Plumber expertise and exchange guidance couldn't use them).

The special order types that gave Bodek the most trouble—the kind the exchange rep told him about—allowed high-frequency traders to post orders that remained hidden at a specific price point at the front of the trading queue when the market was moving, while at the same time pushing other traders back. Even as the market ticked up and down, the order wouldn't move. It was locked *and hidden*. It was dark. This got around the problem of reshuffling and rerouting. The sitting-duck limit orders, meanwhile, lost their priority in the queue when the market shifted, even as the special orders maintained their priority.

Why would the high-speed firms wish to do this? Recall those maker-taker fees that generate billions in revenue for the speed Bots every year. By staying at the front of the queue and hidden as the market shifted, the firm could place orders that, time and again, were paid the fee. Other traders had *no way of knowing* that the orders were there. Over and over again, their orders stepped on the hidden trades, which acted effectively as an invisible trap that made other firms pay the "take" fee.

While that seemed intuitively unfair, it was even *worse*. Bodek learned that when his limit orders were re-posted in the queue as the market ticked due to the complex Reg NMS quirks—when the market went higher or lower, trade orders were frequently reshuffled—they were often dropped *right on top* of the hidden orders, forcing Trading Machines to pay the fee.

It was fiendishly complex. The order types were pinned to a specific price, such as $20.05, and were hidden from the rest of the market until the stock hit that price. As the orders shifted around in the queue, the trap was set and the orders pounced. In ways, the exchange had created a dark pool *inside* the lit pool.

"You're totally screwed unless you do that," the rep at the bar said.

Bodek was astonished—and outraged. He'd been complaining

to the exchange for months about the bad executions he'd been getting, and had been told nothing about the hidden properties of the order types until he'd punished the exchange by cutting it off. He was certain they'd known the answer all along. But they couldn't tell everyone—because if everyone started using the abusive order types, no one would use limit orders, the food the new order types fed on.

Bodek felt sick to his stomach. "How can you do that?" he said. "Isn't that illegal?"

The rep laughed. "It probably should be illegal, but if we changed things, the high-frequency traders wouldn't send us their orders," he said.

They'd go to other pools that had similarly abusive order types.

As he drove home that night, Bodek processed what he'd been told. Nearly every trading firm in the United States—mutual funds, bank desks, pension funds—used limit orders to buy and sell stocks. They were the meat and potatoes of the professional trading world. The market had been *designed* for limit orders. An insiders' term for the market itself was a "central *limit order* book"—a CLOB in the industry jargon. No less than *USA Today* told investors that "the best, easiest and free way for investors to protect themselves in this era of electronic trading is to use so-called limit orders" that safeguard against "short-term disruptions that might be caused by computerized trading." But a representative for a U.S. exchange had just told Bodek *not* to use limit orders, which were getting picked off by high-speed traders like ducks in a pond.

BODEK thought practically nonstop for days about what the exchange representative had told him that night at the New York party. The way that the abusive order types worked made him think back to a document he'd been given by a colleague that summer as he researched what was going wrong at Trading Machines. The document was a detailed blueprint of a high-frequency method that was said to be popular in Chicago's trading circles.

It was called the "0+ Scalping Strategy."

Bodek suspected that there might be a link between the order types and the strategy.

Riffling through his files, he quickly found it. While the document didn't say which firm used the strategy, he'd been told by the colleague who'd given it to him that one of the most successful high-speed firms employed it, or something closely akin to it. Due to the sophistication of the strategy, he'd guessed from the start that it was probably written by a Plumber.

There was another giveaway that it had originated in Chicago, where Bodek had worked for several years at Hull Trading: "scalping." To a trader, scalping didn't mean the same thing it meant to most people—a suspicious-looking guy peddling tickets for a sporting event or rock concert outside a stadium. In trading, scalping was an age-old strategy of buying low and selling high—very quickly. It was a common practice on the floors of futures exchanges that populated the Midwest—the Kansas City Board of Trade or the Chicago Mercantile Exchange. The 0+ Scalping Strategy was apparently a futures-trading technique that had been transformed into a computer program.

Bodek started reading. Page two of the document laid out the purpose of the 0+ strategy. "Simple Goal: use market depth and our order's priority in the Q to create scalping opportunities where the loss on any one trade is limited to '0' (exclusive of commissions)."

Bodek paused at that. Essentially, the author of the strategy was saying that its primary goal was to *never lose money*—the loss on any trade was "0." In theory, this could be done through a scalping strategy. By being first in the "Q"—shorthand for the queue in which orders are stacked up, like theatergoers waiting in line for their tickets—the firm could always get the best trade at the best time.

But what happened when the firm *didn't* want to buy or sell? Bodek kept reading.

"**GOAL RESTATEMENT**: use the market depth and our order's priority in the Q to create scalping opportunities where the probability of a +1 tic gain on any given trade is substantially greater than the probability of a –1 tic loss on any given trade."

*Aha*, Bodek thought, *market depth*. That was a reference to the orders *behind* this firm's orders, the other theatergoers waiting in line. The 0+ trader is assuming that his firm is so fast and so skilled that it can almost always get priority in the trading queue — be the first to buy and the first to sell. The depth behind it, the other orders, is the rest of the market.

*The author is saying I always want to win (or rather, I never want to lose). His probability of winning — a +1 tick — is "substantially greater" than a –1 tick loss.*

*But how?*

The rest of the market — suckers like Trading Machines or everyday mutual funds — was *insurance*. Under the next heading, called **SIMPLE PREMISES**, the exact meaning of what insurance meant was spelled out.

"If we have sufficient depth behind our order at a given price level, then we are effectively self-insured against losing money. Why? If we get elected on our order, we could immediately exit our risk for a scratch by trading against one of the orders behind us."

In other words, if the 0+ trader buys a stock (gets "elected"), and his algos suddenly detect that the price is likely to fall — they can see a large number of sell orders stacking up in the trading queue — he can flip and sell to the sucker standing behind him, resulting in a "scratch" (no gain and no loss). He can do this because his computer systems can "react fast enough to changing market conditions . . . to 'always' achieve, in the worst-case, a scratch or a cancel of our orders."

Bodek was floored as he realized what this meant. It was the Holy Grail of trading. The 0+ trader was describing a strategy that effectively *never lost*. The rest of the market protected it whenever the firm's algorithms detected the slightest chance that the market was moving against it.

*It's brilliant — and diabolical.*

Bodek thought carefully about what this meant. A firm that has found a strategy that is virtually *guaranteed to win* on every trade has discovered a hole in the market. Trading is all about taking risk, but this author was describing a virtually *riskless trade.*

The situation confronting Bodek and other investors not using the 0+ strategy was challenging, to say the least. It was like driving a car down the freeway, and every time you tried to speed up, another, faster car was in front of you. No matter how many tricks you pulled, this car (a 0+ symbol stamped on its hood, of course) was always leading the pack. The only time you could get around it—when it would suddenly hit the brakes and vanish in the crowd behind you—was when a Mack truck was speeding right at you. Worse, the 0+ trader *was the Mack truck*!

Say your mutual fund manager wanted to buy fifty thousand shares of ExxonMobil. Of course, he wouldn't simply put in an order to buy fifty thousand shares at once. The Bots would eat him alive. He'd carve it up into slices of one thousand shares a piece, or even less. He hits the button. The first one-thousand-share buy order flies into an exchange. Exxon just happens to be trading for $75.20.

But the order isn't executed. It sits there, floundering as sellers suddenly start running away. The Bots—some using the 0+ scalping strategy or a variant of it—have jumped in front of the fund manager's order, angling to buy ahead of him. The buy orders seemingly materialize out of nowhere. They were *hidden.*

The Bots get the trade because they're armed with the special order types that allow them to jump in front of the fund manager. The trades activated because their radar-detector algos sensed that the market was ticking higher.

Why?

They sensed the fund manager's presence.

Suddenly, two hundred shares of the fund manager's order are filled for $75.22. But the rest of the order, eight hundred shares, is still in limbo. The fund manager pounds his desk. What's going on!

Exxon ticks up to $75.22, then $75.24, where he gets another two hundred shares, leaving six hundred unfilled. Exxon hits $75.25, then $75.26.

Adding to the confusion, the fund manager has lost track of where his order has gone. It's not clear where it's posted—the NYSE, Nasdaq, Direct Edge, BATS. Perhaps, he thinks, it's floating between the obscure connections linking all the pools together.

Exxon ticks up to $75.30, then sails clear through to $75.35—and the buy order is hit again. The fund manager gets all of his remaining six hundred shares. He buys some more as the price ticks higher, even sending some orders into dark pools. He buys as the price moves all the way up to $75.50, where the market stabilizes with a dense concentration of sellers, and shares start executing like water. He buys a total of ten thousand shares for an average price of $75.40. He still has forty thousand shares to go.

He decides to wait and sits there watching in disgust as the price crawls back to $75.25. The price is falling now because the Bots sense that the fund manager is sitting on the sidelines. But once he starts buying again, the whole game starts over.

That's how it works. Regular investors, the suckers using those stupid limit orders, buy high and sell low—*all the time.*

Bodek deduced that the 0+ document was in effect describing a subspecies of a vast high-frequency trading *class*—a shared approach that had spread across the industry over the years. It had its own lingo, phrases like "self-insurance," "sweep risk" (the odds of getting blasted by a giant order), and "scratch." That kind of evolution takes time to develop. What's more, it was a lingo Bodek had never heard before, not at Hull, not at Goldman, not at UBS. It was its own world, one very few people knew about.

Bodek inferred that the 0+ strategy had originally been designed sometime in the mid-2000s. But the market had changed since then, dramatically. There was much more competition. The rules were different. That made it harder for this firm or any other using a similar strategy to always win, to always know where it stood in the queue and to cut and run when things got hot.

The pieces started to fall in place. He thought back to what the exchange rep had told him about the exotic order types. The 0+ strategy needed *new order types* to give it more control over the queue against competitors. Orders that didn't pop up and down a tick—that didn't slip and slide around the order book. An unpredictable plus-one tick or negative-one tick (plus or minus one penny, in other words) could be enough to destroy the strategy, which relied on absolute certainty on a millisecond time scale. It required orders that wouldn't be kicked out of the queue. If the orders were invisible to the rest of the market, even better.

Of course, Bodek couldn't be sure that his theory was correct. But it sure seemed to make sense to him—and helped explain why Trading Machines was getting screwed over and over again in the stock market.

Who else knew about this? Surely, not the mutual funds. Surely, not the poor schlubs trading through their E*Trade and Charles Schwab accounts. Who else had access to this kind of information, the 0+ specs, the details about the order types that abused Reg NMS, a set of regulations designed to protect ordinary investors and give them the best prices?

And who would tell? The exchanges needed the dumb limit orders to feed the sharks, at the same time booking fees from all the trades they triggered. The speed traders who used it were getting filthy rich. Mutual funds were feeding billions to high-frequency traders every year, cash coming straight out of the pockets of everyday investors. It was almost invisible, pennies per trade. Those endless plus-one ticks, the tail-chasing ups-and-downs plaguing fund managers trying to buy their fifty thousand shares of Exxon or IBM or whatever.

The total sum, however, was staggering. Sure, the high-frequency traders provided "liquidity," giving investors the ability to buy and sell. But what was the cost? For mutual fund investors, the cost could be dramatic. Because investments compound over time, small slivers shaved out of each investment amount to a massive loss. One thousand shares of Exxon purchased for $75.50 instead of $75.25 represents a loss of $250. Say that purchase was made when you were thirty years old—that's $250 that you can't reinvest in the stock market, a huge opportunity cost.

These dollars add up. Assuming a relatively modest annual return of 6 percent on the other stocks you *could have* invested that money in (excluding the effects of inflation), that $250 would have turned into more than $2,500 forty years later, when you planned to retire. Multiply that by all trades in all funds over decades, and the cost to ordinary investors over time is virtually incalculable.

This, of course, was the long-term impact. The short-term costs, however, were painfully evident to pros such as Bodek, whose firm was getting nickel-and-dimed right out of existence.

The game had changed. Bodek became increasingly convinced that the stock market—*the United States stock market*—was rigged. Exchanges appeared to be providing mechanisms to favored clients that allowed them to circumvent Reg NMS rules in ways that abused regular investors. It was complicated, a fact that helped hide the abuses, just as giant banks used complex mortgage trades to bilk clients out of billions, in the process triggering a global financial panic in 2008. Bodek wasn't sure if it was an outright conspiracy or simply an ecosystem that had evolved to protect a single type of organism that had become critical to the survival of the pools themselves.

Whatever it was, he thought, it was wrong.

He remembered the exchange rep's words from the party: *totally screwed*.

Ever the scientist at heart, Bodek decided to test the order types to validate the information he'd been given. Back at Trading Machines, he followed the advice he'd been given—he stopped using the sitting-duck limit orders and started using the insider orders. Immediately, his losses abated. His orders weren't getting abused time and again. Bodek felt as if he'd taken a gun that had been pointed at his head and aimed it at someone else. *Someone* was getting screwed.

Just not Trading Machines.

THE options market, meanwhile, began to suffer a breakdown in 2010. Decimal pricing and other changes were instituted, shaking up the Size Game and other strategies the industry had thrived upon. While Bodek had created Trading Machines to benefit from those changes, the other problems hitting his system had gummed up the works. He'd solved one problem by using the new order types, but he now faced a new set of obstacles. The loss of important talent and squabbles over strategies and money were a constant distraction. What's more, the firm had lost a big chunk of the capital it was able to use to trade, reducing its ability to turn a profit. A comeback seemed more and more unlikely.

Bodek wasn't ready to give up, though. He'd been pulling off miracles his whole career. He was sure he'd do so again.

But the rest of the firm was losing faith. The tension mounted in the summer of 2010. Scuffles had been breaking out in the trading room.

One day in July, several traders and programmers checked out for lunch shortly after noon, when the market was in its typical early afternoon doldrums. Others shut down their systems and kicked back to watch the World Cup.

Bryan Wiener, a trader who'd been with Trading Machines since the beginning, sat at his computer hunting for ways to make money. A throwback in a roomful of eggheads, he was a pit trader from Chicago who'd once snorted a line of cayenne pepper on a $200 bet. Wiener wasn't about to sit back and do nothing while the firm bled to death. Busy with one trade on his terminal, he told the trader next to him to make a bet that took advantage of the difference between two exchange-traded funds. It was a small bet, one that might make two grand at best. But money was money. Trading Machines needed it.

The trader, an ex–Navy Seal named John who'd come from the

Chicago hedge fund king Citadel, refused to do it. "What's the point?" he said.

"There's nothing else going on," Wiener said. "Let's do this fucking trade."

John burst red-faced from his seat. "Don't tell me fucking what to do!" he screamed at Wiener.

"Dude, I don't want to fight over a fucking trade," Wiener said defensively. The guy was acting like the insane army recruit Private Pyle in the movie *Full Metal Jacket*, he thought. Totally nuts.

John stormed out. Later in the day, he returned to the office and quit. Other employees were also bailing. The damage seemed irreversible. Bodek, desperate for money, scrambled to find a lifeline. He eventually landed a $10 million infusion from a specialty finance outfit. But the investment came with strict conditions. If Trading Machines' capital shrank to a certain level, the financier could seize the entire company.

By December, it looked certain that the firm was doomed. TW had left months before. With just a few weeks until Trading Machines was seized unless a dramatic turnaround occurred, Bodek decided to roll the dice by scaling up volumes. With TW and his obsessive risk controls out of the way, Bodek could push the Machine to its limits. Perhaps if he let it rip, the system would work more efficiently.

And parts of the Machine performed wonders. Unleashed, it was able to juggle huge volumes. For a few days, it traded more than 5 percent of Spyder options, a phenomenal achievement by a firm starved for cash.

But it was too late. Bodek had picked a bad time for his Hail Mary pass. In late 2010, the U.S. options market was coming under massive pressure as all the structural issues that had hit Trading Machines metastasized and hit everyone else, too. There was the problem of hedging in the stock market, which had become a devil's game of tag with high-speed traders. Then, two of the largest options exchanges converted to a maker-taker model in imitation of the stock market. The

entire options industry reeled. The trading unit for one of the largest
options firms in the world, Interactive Brokers, posted a $24 million
loss for the fourth quarter of 2010, one of its worst quarters ever. Interactive was run by Thomas Peterffy, a legend in the options trading
industry and one of Bodek's idols. If Interactive was taking losses, the
entire industry was in trouble.

In February 2011, Chicago high-speed giant Sun Trading laid off
forty employees and shut down its high-frequency options desk. Even
Getco, the elite high-speed operator, was struggling in options. The
entire options business, one of the most important markets in the
U.S. financial system, appeared to be seizing up. Few knew what was
going on.

Bodek believed he did, but there was nothing he could do about
it. The dream was over. In March 2011, Trading Machines was wound
down. The wealthy investors who'd bankrolled the operation told
Bodek he wasn't needed anymore.

EVERYTHING was shifting, evolving at high speeds, all in the dark.
The evolution of algorithms pumped up on massive high-frequency
engines and cutting-edge AI had reached a tipping point. The algorithms were changing so rapidly, devouring one another so viciously
in the daily microsecond skirmishes of the Algo Wars, that the market seemed poised on the edge of either a mind-blowing evolutionary
leap—or a cataclysmic implosion. Its own architects, ace Plumbers
such as Dan Mathisson at Credit Suisse, could barely keep pace with
the changes. It was a lab experiment in real time, with no turning
back. Mathematicians, computer programmers, and physicists were
conducting a grand experiment on the global financial system—one
of the most chaotic, unpredictable forces on the planet, prey to the
whims of people with their all-too-human fear and greed. They were
building the rocket ship even as it blasted off into space.

The consequences reached deep. David Weild, a former Nasdaq
executive, made the case that because speed-obsessed computer trad-

ers gravitated to stocks that were heavily traded—which meant they could easily buy and sell them in split seconds—they commonly ignored small stocks, which didn't trade as often.

Look no further than the 0+ strategy for the reasoning behind this approach.

"The simplest implementation of this strategy will be more effective in relatively . . . deep and liquid markets that tend to trade both sides of TOB [the order book] before moving to a new price level," it read, "and less effective in thin, relatively illiquid, and volatile markets. For the purposes of this writing, we will assume that this strategy will only be implemented in slow, deep, and liquid markets."

The result: Trading in shares of small companies was drying up, and fewer companies were issuing stock in initial public offerings. From 1991 to 2000, an average of 530 companies went public every year in the United States. By the end of the 2000s, the average had dwindled to 126 companies a year, according to Weild. This had helped lead to a broad drop-off in the number of public companies. In 1997, there were about 8,200 public companies. By 2010, there were roughly 4,000. For the broader economy, this was disastrous, cutting off access to public markets for companies that needed cash to grow their businesses and hire more employees. With everyday investors losing faith in the market itself, frightened away by the manic volatility, the brain-twisting complexity, and the rising risk of flash crashes, a crucial cog in the nation's economic engine was coming unglued.

The complexity had become so deeply ingrained, so self-reinforcing, that even aces such as Bodek were befuddled and outraged. With mass computerization, the entire market had become cloaked in a stealthy electronic order flow that shifted digitized money across continents and oceans at speeds that defied logic. The most elite high-speed trading gurus were often at a loss to explain how the market actually worked.

Because the market was so dark, conspiracy theories became rampant. Rumors spread that some firms were sending waves of orders to jam up exchange matching engines—the core computers that paired up buy and sell orders—hoping to profit on discrepancies in prices across multiple pools. Microsoft might trade for $25 on one exchange, and $25.02 on another, presenting an opportunity. Sophisticated tricks known as "layering," "spoofing," and "quote stuffing," in which computers gamed the electronic pools with phantom orders, were said to be unbridled. Insiders talked of trading outfits based in countries such as China, India, and Russia that manipulated prices around the world through sophisticated computer games.

Warnings of an attack on the financial system from outside the United States were mounting. One of the most vocal critics was John Bates, a computer scientist who in the early 2000s launched a firm that built trading algorithms using an AI technique called complex event processing. A decade later, Bates worried that the explosion of computer trading threatened the stability of the financial system on a global scale. "Fears of algorithmic terrorism, where a well-funded criminal or terrorist organization could find a way to cause a major market crisis, are not unfounded," Bates wrote in a February 2011 article. "This type of scenario could cause chaos for civilization."

Neil Johnson, a University of Miami physicist who studies complex market patterns, warned in a February 2012 interview of a "global war between competing computer algorithms" that could cause a "big systemwide collapse" in which the stock market shatters like broken glass. The market, he said, had evolved into a "lake full of different types of piranhas" devouring one another in a high-speed frenzy. In a working paper he co-authored—"Financial Black Swans Driven by Ultrafast Machine Ecology"—Johnson showed that the market in the past few years had undergone "an abrupt systemwide transition from a mixed human-machine phase to a new all-machine phase character-ized by frequent black swan events with ultrafast durations."

It was a brave new world that few people outside Wall Street knew existed. And it was growing at an exponential rate. In the market rout of August 2011, when stocks fell 20 percent in a matter of days because of escalating concerns about the European credit crisis, message traffic—the beehive humming of all those orders—exploded. Nanex, a high-tech firm that tracks speed trading, processed a staggering one *trillion* bytes of data in all U.S. stocks, options, futures, and indexes on a single day. That was quadruple the peak spikes of information the market had seen just two years earlier.

Nanex had detected within the noise a curious pattern—a high-frequency algorithm it called *the Disruptor*. The Disruptor whacked the market with so many orders that it effectively *disrupted the market itself.* That caused traders—like Bodek at Trading Machines—to become so frustrated by the bad results that they effectively pulled out and shut down (or replied in kind with their own computerized weapons, such as Credit Suisse's Blast).

The Algo Wars were leaving a path of destruction in their wake. "HFT algos reduce the value of resting orders and increase the value of how fast orders can be placed and cancelled," wrote Nanex researcher Eric Hunsader. "This results in the illusion of liquidity. We can't understand why this is allowed to continue, because at the core, it is pure manipulation."

And what about the Securities and Exchange Commission? The nation's top stock-market cops were clearly outgunned. In May 2011, SEC chairman Mary Schapiro told Congress that "the Commission's tools for collecting data and surveilling our markets are wholly inadequate to the task of overseeing the largest equity markets in the world."

It was as if the FBI were admitting that it couldn't track organized crime. Everyone, it seemed, was in the dark.

WHERE had it all come from? Bodek believed it all went back to the architects of the market itself: *the Plumbers*. The Plumbers had designed the pipes of the system, the digital computer networks linking traders to exchanges, exchanges to exchanges, dark pools to dark pools, including the fiendishly clever order types that Bodek believed had tripped up Trading Machines. Many of them had first worked at the exchanges and moved on to join trading outfits, where they helped create programs to interact with and exploit the very systems they'd built.

Bodek, while still trying to make a go of Trading Machines, had realized he needed Plumber expertise himself. So he hired a stock market programming expert he'd heard about at UBS, a Russian-born computer whiz named Mike Lazarev. Lazarev had been working on Wall Street since the late 1990s. He'd dropped out of college to work at Island, the state-of-the-art electronic pool that had been the launching pad for high-speed trading and AI Bots. He was an insiders' insider, one of the behind-the-scenes architects who knew in extreme detail how the plumbing of the market's vast electronic system had been pieced together.

Even though Lazarev could only do so much for Trading Machines, he was amazed by Bodek's never-say-die attitude. He'd known a virtual army of virtuosos and blinding geniuses during his programming career on Wall Street, and there was little question that Bodek stood out as one of the most intelligent and hardworking people he'd ever met.

But there was one person Lazarev had come across, years ago, who was more intelligent than Bodek or anyone else he'd known. Like Bodek, this person was obsessed with inner details of how markets worked—and in fact had been the prime mover in the creation of the high-speed market that was now coming apart at the seams. He was a high-school dropout who'd taken on Wall Street's most formidable power brokers—and destroyed them—a shy, idealistic outsider who'd been fined for his alleged ties to one of the biggest frauds in stock market history, a computer programming wizard, a reclusive genius who'd never been photographed in public and who had for years avidly fought to avoid the public eye.

He was the King of the Plumbers: Joshua Levine, the creator of Island.

# PART II

WE DETERMINED THE BEST
THING FOR US TO DO
WAS BASICALLY TAKE THE
HUMAN BEING OUT OF
THE EQUATION.

—BERNARD MADOFF

# BIRTH OF THE MACHINE

# CHAPTER FIVE

# BANDITS

Joshua Levine darted up Wall Street among throngs of bankers, traders, and specialists in their bespoke suits, patent-leather shoes, and slicked-back hair. An impish figure of five-six with a wide-open boyish face and bullet-shaped head, the eighteen-year-old computer programmer looked nothing like them. His severe buzz cut, worn tennis shoes, and ragged jeans gave him the appearance of an army recruit gone AWOL. He shouldered a backpack full of scribble-filled notepads, wrinkled printer paper, textbooks about complex computer languages, schematics for newfangled computer chips, technical manuals for stock market trading systems.

While Levine at first glance may have seemed the epitome of a teenage slacker, he was, in fact, supremely focused. Acquaintances quickly discovered this when they met the intense gaze of his copper brown eyes.

It was 1986. The bull had come roaring back in the financial capital of the world after the punishing doldrums of the 1970s. Peter Lynch was in the midst of his historic run at the helm of Fidelity Investments' Magellan Fund. Warren Buffett, the Oracle of Omaha, was becoming a household name. It was the Wall Street of Michael Lewis and Gordon Gekko, of hostile takeovers and the Reagan Revolution.

Times were good and getting better. Denizens of the Street were more than ready to celebrate.

Levine couldn't have cared less about the bull market. The programmer had little interest in trading or making money. His mind was focused on a single subject: changing the world through computers.

Heading west toward Trinity Church on the western terminus of the famed street, yellow cabs darting by along the deep and narrow canyon of skyscrapers, worried-looking men storming out of subway stations, Levine glanced up at the sculpted Georgia marble façade and Corinthian columns of the New York Stock Exchange, imperious as a Roman temple. Central exchanges such as the NYSE had first cropped up around the coffeehouses of Amsterdam, London, and Paris in the seventeenth century. Founded in 1792 by twenty-four men under a buttonwood tree, the NYSE had maintained a virtual monopoly on stock trading in the United States for nearly two hundred years. As such, it represented everything Levine hated about Wall Street. The inside information, the special deals, the secrecy of the connected.

The *money*. The *power*. The *Big Board*.

Trading at the NYSE took place on the floor of the exchange, beyond the ken of everyday investors, amid the haggling of a select group of insiders. Only after the trades occurred did the NYSE report prices to the consolidated tape, giving Joe Schmoes a clue about where the market was going—or, rather, where it had been. The NYSE was in many ways a massive dark pool.

Levine felt there had to be a better way. A geek among computer geeks, Levine, like Haim Bodek, was a child of the 1980s, a time when PCs were just beginning to creep into middle-class households. It was also a time when a revolutionary idea had emerged among a subculture of scientists and computer hackers who understood that the rising force of digital communication presented a remarkable opportunity: *Information wants to be free*. These activist programmers saw themselves as an enlightened high-tech guerilla army who could use technology to hack the System and liberate information in all its permutations, making it available to the masses. In the process, they would crush the privileged elite. And there were few institutions that represented power and privilege more brazenly than the NYSE, a monopoly that had a stranglehold on the trading of the largest companies in the world—blue-chip giants like General Electric, Walt Disney, and IBM.

While other venues such as Nasdaq could technically trade NYSE-listed stocks (or vice versa), it rarely happened because the NYSE specialists controlled the market for their stocks. That dominant position allowed them to provide the best prices, and investors had little reason to go elsewhere. Still, the specialists charged hefty fees for their service. There were also widespread rumors that the specialists used their inside information to front-run customer orders (Fidelity wants to buy one million shares of IBM? I think I'll buy a little myself . . . *first.*)

Levine intuitively didn't trust it. He walked past the building and through a mob of tourists gawking, posing, snapping Kodak Instamatics. The NYSE as it then existed was doomed, and he knew it. It was only a matter of time.

Joshua Levine had always been drawn to the city lights. Born in a Manhattan hospital on December 31, 1967, the son of a Park Avenue psychopharmacologist, he was raised in the middle-class suburbs of New Rochelle, a half hour's drive north of Manhattan. Growing up, he would often make his way down to the city to visit his father's Upper East Side office on 76th Street, just a short walk away from Central Park and the sprawling Metropolitan Museum of Art.

No good at sports, shy with girls, Levine at a young age became obsessed with computers. He quickly saw that computers would transform how the world worked in ways few people could understand. By the time he was seventeen, he was the programming equivalent of a chess grand master. He decided to drop out of high school and try to make his way as a freelance programmer. There were few places that needed programmers at the time more than Wall Street.

Walking down Broad Street, Levine cut in front of the fortress-like former headquarters of J.P. Morgan, known as the Corner. Its massive limestone-block entryway still bore pockmarks from a terror-ist bombing in 1920. A stone's throw down the street sat the headquar-ters of Goldman Sachs, the most powerful private bank in the world.

Finally, Levine reached his destination: a broker dealer called Russo Securities. Levine was quickly learning the ins and outs of Wall Street at Russo. For instance, basics such as the fact that "brokers" trade on behalf of clients, like mutual funds—the broker part of the designation—and for their own account, which is the "dealer" side of the business. He'd recently taken a job as a runner for Russo, owned by a tight-knit family that lived on Staten Island and specialized in trading penny stocks. The job included mundane tasks such as bird-dogging paperwork and stock certificates between brokerages and the floor of the NYSE. Levine often found himself darting along the floor of the Big Board, mounds of discarded trade tickets and crumpled tickertape underfoot, trying to find the assistant of a broker or spe-cialist who had a stack of stock certificates he needed to retrieve for Russo.

It was a maddening scene. Traders screamed out orders in huge packs to besieged specialists, everyone frantically scribbling numbers on scraps of paper to keep track of it all. The traders used weird hand signals to indicate how many shares they wanted to buy or sell, other signals to indicate price. Whoever could signal the fastest won the trade. It was chaos. And so unnecessary, Levine thought. The enor-mous paperwork—and waste—astounded him. Why not wire the trades through a computer?

As Levine wound his way through Russo's tightly packed office, he looked around. He saw a few computer terminals, but for the most part everyone was working over the phone.

Suddenly, a gruff voice from the trading desk called out to him.

"Hey, kid, come here," hollered Shelly Maschler from a cluttered desk littered with piles of stock certificates and cigar ash. Maschler was wearing a tight-fitting dark blue polyester jacket and wide lemon-yellow tie.

"Hi, Shelly," Levine said, slightly out of breath. "What's up?"

"Can you come out to my house this weekend?" Maschler said. "I need some more work on my satellite dish."

"No problem," Levine said. "Look, I gotta run."

"Sure, kid," Maschler replied. "I'll tell my wife to fix you some roast beef."

As Levine scurried off, Maschler leaned back in his chair and lit up a half-smoked Macanudo cigar, smiling and thinking, *I like that fucking kid.*

SHELDON Maschler was a bull of a man, stocky as an NFL lineman—and as intimidating. Known to his friends as Shelly, Maschler was a hard drinker—his favorite elixir was Dewar's scotch whiskey on the rocks—and chain smoker of fine Macanudo cigars. His head was massive, cinder block–shaped, and seemed welded onto his powerful body without the refinement of a neck. He was known to never back down from a fight and was more than willing to play dirty if he thought the situation called for it. His black hair thickly greased and combed straight back from a fierce widow's peak like an oil-tipped spear, Maschler looked like a cross between the Count on *Sesame Street* and the Chicago Bears' Dick Butkus.

The teenage Levine wasn't intimidated by the burly trader. Levine reveled in Maschler's fearlessness, his *I-don't-give-a-flying-fuck* attitude toward the Street's fat cats. Both from Jewish families, they saw up close how much of the U.S. banking system was run by a club of white Protestant power brokers with Ivy League degrees. Happy to stick it to the big boys whenever he got a chance, Maschler would help teach Levine that the powers that be on Wall Street were often straw men who could be knocked down with brains, balls, and—if necessary—brute force.

Maschler had recently left a nationwide brokerage based in Newark, New Jersey, called First Jersey Securities. A notorious penny-stock pump-and-dump outfit, First Jersey was run by an evil-genius scam artist named Robert Brennan. Brennan had gained fame in the 1980s for a string of ads in which he zipped around in a Sikorsky helicopter, passing American landmarks such as the Grand Coulee Dam while espousing the virtues of First Jersey's ability to fund small start-ups. The ads, which invited viewers to "Come Grow With Us," appeared during nightly news shows and even the Super Bowl. Maschler quickly rose within the ranks at First Jersey and by the mid-1980s was running its Jersey City office.

When allegations of ties to organized crime and stock scams threatened to bring First Jersey down in 1986, however, Maschler quickly jumped ship. He was pulling in some cash from a sports-betting outfit he ran on the side, and the last thing he wanted was extra scrutiny from the law. To keep his hooks in Wall Street, he landed a job at a firm run by a few Staten Island acquaintances: Russo.

Word about a tech-savvy whiz kid willing to work for peanuts quickly reached Maschler's ears. Ham-fisted with electronics, Maschler hired Levine for odd jobs at his home in the Staten Island development of Heartland Village. In exchange for roast beef sandwiches or a new color TV set, Levine helped repair the satellite dishes and computer modems Maschler used for his home office.

Maschler soon realized that Levine was far more than your typical Wall Street runner. The sprightly programmer had been gobbling up every computer manual and technical book on market structure he could lay his hands on. He worked like an animal, running for Russo during the day and poring over ponderous technology manuals at night.

On Wall Street, of course, youthful ambition is as common as pinstripes and golden parachutes. Maschler had little idea that Levine's aspirations went far beyond the commonplace dream of endless riches nurtured by the legions of bright-eyed strivers who flocked to lower Manhattan every year. Because as Levine sponged up the technical details of the market's plumbing, he had begun to cobble together a revolutionary vision: a vision of how the market could work—and *should* work—if run by computers. Scribbling digits on a ticket, watching traders scramble to get prices on the phone, seeing all the bad data, the old data—it wasn't even *data*, it was useless noise—Levine foresaw a market in which all information streamed seamlessly through microprocessors. Computer programs could match buyers and sellers, who could easily look up on a screen the price for any stock they wanted to trade. They could see how many shares were available and how much they cost. Best of all, with all data available at the press of a button, investors wouldn't get fleeced by the unscrupulous insiders who hoarded all the information.

At the time, nearly all stock transactions in the United States went through human middlemen. In theory, investors could simply meet on the street and exchange stock certificates for cold hard cash. Centuries ago, that often occurred—on Broad Street itself (or its curb, which came to be known as the Curb Market). In practice, it was more efficient to create a central place where professionals could act on behalf of investors, taking a slice of the action for their troubles, of course.

On the Nasdaq Stock Market, these people were known as market makers or dealers. On the NYSE, they were called specialists, the descendants of those twenty-four men who'd founded the Big Board in 1792. They were the grease that made the market's wheels spin—and the doorkeepers to the temple's riches. Everyone from Warren Buffett and Peter Lynch to Aunt Millie and Uncle Joe relied on these middlemen to buy and sell stocks on their behalf (Buffett and Lynch, of course, got much better treatment than Millie and Joe). In exchange for their services, the middlemen tacked on a fee called the "spread," the difference between what they paid for a stock and the amount they charged to sell it back to investors. Think of a specialist like a car dealer named Big John who buys a Mustang from Ford Motor for $30,000 and sells it to his customers for $35,000—Big John's $5,000 profit on the deal is the spread.

Levine hated this system. Like toll collectors on a bridge, specialists and market makers put themselves at the heart of the money flow,
picking off dimes and quarters that added up to billions a year. It was
nothing less than a transfer of wealth from ordinary Americans trying
to save for retirement into the pockets of the financial elite.

So Levine had an idea: Why not let investors *bypass the middlemen* and trade directly with one another? Why not create a computer
program that would automatically bring together buy and sell orders
when prices matched?

The plan amounted to nothing less than taking the Wall Street
out of Wall Street. It was simple. It was the future. And the bigwigs
Levine would go on to pitch the idea to told him repeatedly it was utterly impossible, if not insane.

Levine didn't believe them.

ALL of Levine's hard work—the late hours devouring computer textbooks and trading manuals—quickly paid off. Soon after his eighteenth birthday, he passed the National Association of Securities
Dealers' (NASD) Series 7 exam. The credential gave him the license
to become a professional trader and operate as a broker dealer, one of
the very middlemen he despised. (To beat the system, he had to learn
its rules.) Then, in 1987, Levine left Russo and formed a consulting
outfit called Joshua Group Limited. He was nineteen years old.

Bare bones in the extreme, Levine's office was nothing more than
a PO box at Wall Street Station in downtown Manhattan. Clad in
T-shirts, tennis shoes, and blue jeans, he pitched his vision for automated computer trading to dozens of dubious Wall Street executives.
He told them that a computer could efficiently track their orders, eliminate mounds of paperwork, and save millions. More often than not,
they laughed him out of their oak-paneled offices—if he even made it
past their front doors.

But a few bit, and eventually he established a reputation as a brilliant programmer with dirt-cheap fees. By his early twenties, Levine

had deals with an A-list of top Wall Street clients: Shearson Lehman Hutton, the predecessor of Lehman Brothers; Steinhardt Partners, one of the biggest hedge funds in the United States; and Herzog Heine Geduld, one of the largest dealers in over-the-counter stocks (those not traded on a major exchange such as the NYSE). For Wang Financial, a firm that used private telephone lines to supply market data to money managers, he designed Shark Marketlink, a computer interface that downloaded and displayed real-time market information. By the late 1980s, the software had been deployed in hundreds of offices around the country.

Levine's ability to land such clients spoke to his jaw-dropping skills as a programmer—and to the fact that he had virtually no competition. Few people at the time believed computers could play more than a marginal role on Wall Street. Beyond record keeping or putting a quote up on a screen, it seemed to many that computers were little more than a tool to help the experts ply their trade on the phone or face-to-face. It was a people's business built on three-martini lunches.

Levine thought otherwise.

He briefly enrolled in the elite electrical engineering program at Carnegie Mellon University in Pittsburgh. But his freelance career proved too successful, and he quickly dropped out. Levine's aversion to school had nothing to do with a lack of ambition or ability. He was simply so far ahead of his classmates—and often his teachers—that he had no need for a degree. It would be a waste of time when he could be doing *real* work, making *real* money. Levine's formal education came to an end in February 1988, when he earned a high school equivalency diploma from the State of New York.

His top priority was peddling software for the Joshua Group. A major coup was a consulting job writing code for Tiger Management, a giant hedge fund firm run by legendary trader Julian Robertson. Known inside Tiger as JoshQuote, the program, through a computer, printed stock quotes on trading desks and facilitated trades. Levine also designed JoshDOT, a program that trading firms could use to quickly enter orders into the NYSE's Designated Order Turnaround system, or DOT, which electronically routed orders to specialists on the exchange floor (ironically, the orders were given to typists, who hammered out the trades on specially designed typewriters, a system that would remain in place until the mid-2000s).

As he honed his knowledge of how the NYSE floor operated, Levine grew even more certain that he was dealing with an institution trapped in the Stone Age. It couldn't last. The face-to-face haggling over prices on trading floors was doomed. He didn't know if its end would come in ten years, or thirty. But it *would* come. It was simple math. Because in the future, there would be *too much trading* of NYSE stocks for human beings to handle the load. Volume had been ramping up in the 1980s as the economy took off, and the odds were high that it would keep rising. Humans would be outgunned.

Computers manned by multiple traders, however, could juggle limitless numbers of stocks, far faster than a guy named Vinnie frantically scribbling orders on a ticket and wildly flashing hand signals to the pit. The future was automation. It was obvious.

Levine saw another problem: spreads. He couldn't understand why stock prices were quoted in spreads of one-eighth of a dollar (or, more often, one-quarter of a dollar). Why not price stocks like everything else in America—*in pennies*? People could buy a box of cereal for $2.45, but they couldn't buy a stock for the same price.

It all went back to the eighteenth century, when the Spanish dollar, buoyed by conquests in the Americas, served as the world's currency. Spanish merchants often sliced up doubloons into eight pieces as forms of payment—so-called pieces of eight. Hence, U.S. stock prices traded in eighth-of-a-dollar slices because conquistadors such as Hernando Cortés and Francisco Pizarro hacked their way across North and South America centuries before.

Levine thought the convention was not only antiquated, it was outright theft. It made spreads artificially wide, handing outsize profits to market makers and specialists. It was as if a car dealer who bought a Mustang from Ford for $30,000 could *only* resell it for $35,000. A competitor who wanted to sell the same model Mustang for $32,500 couldn't, according to the Street's centuries-old rules. The fat profit was the equivalent of a rustproof body undercoat, and the buyer had to pony up for it whether he wanted it or not.

Market makers had their excuses, of course. It would be impossible to price all the stocks they traded in penny increments, they said. Fractions were so much easier. Levine countered that computers could easily price stocks in pennies.

Why not switch?

In a word: greed. The dealers and specialists who controlled the NYSE and Nasdaq were the very people who would be smashed by penny pricing. The chance that they or the exchanges would *ever* consider switching to pennies was zero.

Levine knew that change would have to be forced on the powers that be from the outside. There was far too much money at stake. It might take years, but the change was inevitable. And when it did come, the dealers and specialists would be out of a job.

And if somehow Levine could make it come quicker . . . all the better.

In 1987, Shelly Maschler left Russo to take over the trading arm for a small Brooklyn brokerage called Datek Securities. Like Russo, Datek specialized in penny stocks, which large banks tended to overlook. But its founder, Aaron Elbogen, a friend of Maschler's from his Brooklyn youth, wanted to expand the business into more heavily traded Nasdaq stocks. He asked Maschler if he'd be interested in running a Datek office in downtown Manhattan, and Maschler agreed. In July 1987, he set up shop at 50 Broad Street, a twenty-story, horseshoe-shaped building constructed in 1915. Infested with rats, the building was falling apart after years of neglect. But the location was prime, steps away from big players such as the NYSE, Goldman Sachs, and J.P. Morgan.

Founded in 1971, Datek was a quiet shop that processed about a hundred transactions a day for its small-fry clientele—far less than the heavy flow Maschler had juggled at First Jersey and Russo. To beef up the operation, Maschler brought along a small team of seasoned traders he'd worked with over the years. Soon after they arrived, Datek's trading volume started to take off. Maschler and his band of no-holds-barred traders forcibly ground out markets for the small stocks and started sending through hundreds, then thousands of orders a day.

Everything was running smoothly. Maschler's aggressive tactics worked well as the market rocketed higher in the late summer and fall of 1987.

Then, disaster struck. Black Monday: October 19, 1987, the worst one-day collapse in the history of the U.S. stock market. Firms such as Datek were left flapping in the wind as the stocks they traded plunged in value. As the market imploded, Maschler and his traders tried to salvage their positions, repeatedly picking up the phone to call Nasdaq dealers and unload their stocks. But the phones kept ringing unanswered as the dealers stuck their heads in the sand. The market crashed, resulting in astonishing losses. By the end of the day, the Dow Jones Industrial Average was down a monstrous 23 percent.

Like nearly every other trader, Maschler got clobbered, though he didn't lose everything. The same couldn't be said for a business associate of Maschler's, a small-time New Jersey broker named Harvey Houtkin.

Houtkin's firm, Rushmore Securities, imploded on Black Monday, losing $2.5 million. Left with a ravaged portfolio, Houtkin asked Maschler if Datek would liquidate the rest of his holdings, a thankless and not particularly profitable job. Maschler, who needed all the business he could get, said yes.

Months later and somewhat back on his feet, Houtkin told Maschler he'd discovered curious loopholes in a Nasdaq system that processed small trades from everyday mom-and-pop investors. Called the Small Order Execution System, or SOES, it allowed the brokers for small investors to place orders directly with market makers through a computer system. No phone calls necessary. Implemented in 1985, SOES was rarely used at first. Most market makers traded over the phone or used a computer system called SelectNet, which displayed bids and offers on a screen and allowed traders to place orders through a window on their terminals, much like a primitive instant message system. While run on a computer network, SelectNet didn't actually implement the trade. It merely transmitted information about bids and offers to human market makers, who executed the trades by hand.

Black Monday's slew of unanswered phone calls by Nasdaq dealers sparked a media backlash. Ordinary investors had been hung out to dry as the insiders saved their own skins. In a bid to stave off the heat, Nasdaq made SOES mandatory. All market makers were required to automatically buy or sell at their current quotes up to one thousand shares of most widely traded Nasdaq stocks. On SOES, they couldn't choose to ignore a thousand-share trade in favor of a better trade coming from a pal at Goldman Sachs or Morgan Stanley. To ensure that market makers didn't ignore SOES, the system was automated. Executions were instantaneous.

The new-and-improved SOES went live on June 30, 1988. Houtkin, who'd studied the computer plumbing of Nasdaq in the 1970s as a student at Baruch College, instantly saw that he could game SOES for a quick buck. By automating SOES, Nasdaq had unwittingly unlocked a back door into its private club. Desperate to rebound from his Black Monday meltdown, Houtkin leapt at the chance.

Maschler, of course, wanted a piece of the action, and Houtkin gave him the scoop. First, he told Maschler, he needed a computer equipped with Nasdaq Level II Workstation software — *Level II* simply meant it had access to market makers' best quotes — that provided a direct link to SOES. The computer would monitor the activity in a stock, such as Microsoft. It posted all the bids and offers by the various market makers in Microsoft and tracked them as they changed throughout the day.

Nasdaq stocks typically had a dozen or more market makers competing to buy and sell. They entered their orders by hand through their Level II Workstations. Some moved faster than others. On SOES, a small fortune could be made in the fleeting delay between moves, Houtkin told Maschler.

When the market for a stock started to shift—say, offers to sell Microsoft jumped from $50 to $50¾, while the buy offers rose from $49¾ to $50¼—some market makers might be caught napping, still offering to sell at $50.

That meant that for a brief moment, free money was on the table. A market maker was offering to sell Microsoft for $50 even as another was offering to buy for $50¼. With a few keystrokes, Houtkin could rapidly snap up a thousand shares of Microsoft for $50 a piece from the slowpoke market maker. Seconds later, he could turn around and unload it for $50¼, an instant profit of twenty-five cents a share. For a thousand-share order, that added up to a quick hit of $250.

Rinse, repeat. Dozens of such trades a day added up to real money. Since the trades were typically a thousand shares, the numbers weren't insignificant: at $50 a piece, a thousand shares of Microsoft cost $50,000.

Houtkin didn't realize it, but he was mimicking a trading strategy, perfected on the floors of Chicago's futures trading pits, called *scalping*. It was in many ways the same spread-capturing strategy that Nasdaq market makers used. The difference was that market makers made money from buying and selling to regular investors. Scalpers like Houtkin made money *off the market makers.*

Houtkin knew he'd discovered a gold mine. Such free-money scenarios rarely occur in real life on Wall Street, but one existed on SOES—one that happened over and over again *all day long, every day.* Maschler, of course, loved it.

Nasdaq market makers hated it. The $250 profit for Houtkin

amounted to a $250 loss on their end, since they could have sold the stock for the higher price or bought for a lower price. SOES forced market makers to become more diligent about the stocks they juggled. It wasn't easy. They often handled twenty or thirty stocks at a time. Without a sophisticated computer system, it was nearly impossible for them to keep track of all their stocks at once. Houtkin and Maschler could focus on just a few stocks and whack them time and again. Outraged, pockets picked, the market makers starting calling Houtkin and Maschler the "SOES bandits."

At first, the practice was dubbed Tube Watching—a play on old-fashioned tickertape watching—due to the unusual sight of a trader staring bug-eyed at a computer screen all day. "Compared to this, the New York ticker tape is like yesterday's newspaper," Houtkin told *Barron's* reporter Thomas Donlan in late 1988.

Donlan foresaw that SOES trading was far more than a new kind of trading—it was an evolutionary shift "in which technology is gradually replacing exchanges, specialists and dealers with a mechanical marketplace. Trades need no longer be based on mutual trust and a history of good relations; they can now take place with impersonal avarice between cutthroat traders who never meet."

Nasdaq's bigwigs were stunned when they saw what the bandits were up to. Nasdaq had stipulated that licensed broker dealers couldn't use the system to trade on their own behalf—they could only use it to execute orders for clients, ordinary investors who wouldn't dream of buying a thousand shares of Microsoft one minute and selling them a few minutes (or seconds) later.

But Houtkin had unearthed another loophole. Since he no longer ran a brokerage after his firm imploded on Black Monday, he could trade independently as an individual investor—the very kind SOES was designed to help. And since he had the skills of a master trader, he could make SOES sing like a concert violinist playing a Stradivarius.

Maschler, for his part, began trading on SOES himself, only far more aggressively than Houtkin. He didn't worry about the niceties of masquerading as a mom-and-pop retail investor. He simply let it rip, rules be damned—and he quickly taught his team at Datek how to play the SOES game as well.

As he did so, Maschler began racking up more and more enemies across Wall Street—including Houtkin. The two partners were soon slugging it out for dominance in the SOES battlefield. Houtkin, the eventual, embittered loser, once told a *New York Times* reporter that "rules weren't rules" for Maschler, who "had a street mentality, and under him Datek operated in the bowels of the industry."

An epic fight lay ahead. Nasdaq, controlled by its nationwide confederation of market makers, began gearing up for a battle that would last more than a decade. The SOES bandits would take crippling blows, and no wonder: They were going up against some of the most entrenched powers on Wall Street, where they were seen as insidious worms slowly devouring the lunch of the market makers—the lifeblood of Nasdaq.

The first wave of attacks came almost immediately. In a letter to the SEC in 1988, the NASD—the regulatory arm of Nasdaq—wrote that "order entry firms and their customers have been engaging in practices which could seriously impact the viability of SOES. . . . The NASD believes that these trading practices are undermining the integrity of the system."

The gloves were coming off.

WHILE Maschler's Datek traders were good at SOES, they had little edge over skilled competitors such as Houtkin. That quickly changed after Josh Levine began tinkering with Datek's SOES trading system.

Levine was still working at Russo and freelancing, but he started to poke around Datek's operation at 50 Broad Street soon after he'd heard they'd been using an automated trading system. While he didn't know the ins and outs of SOES at first, he quickly caught on—and liked what he saw. The greedy fat-cat insiders were getting their lunches eaten by Datek's hit-and-run traders. It was a thing of beauty, a pristine example of how technology could shift the ground beneath the entrenched elite and transfer the power to their smarter, faster rivals.

Datek's grizzled traders at first didn't know what to make of the slight, baby-faced programmer named Josh. The most they knew about computers was that their kids spent too much time playing Pac-Man and Asteroids at the arcade. Soon enough, they were in awe of Levine. He could fix a computer bug in minutes or make a few tweaks that would turbocharge their systems. He struck everyone he met as a self-taught genius, always three steps ahead of them in conversations and producing simple solutions to the thorniest problems.

Oddly, Levine fit right in among the renegade outsiders at Datek. Like them, he had little respect for the pin-striped bankers who ruled the Street. He'd found a home, literally. Early on in their partnership, Maschler let Levine use an empty apartment in Brooklyn in exchange for his technology skills.

It was a potent mix. Maschler's aggressive anything-goes band of desperado traders and Levine's home-spun computer genius quickly turned Datek into a deadly guerilla trading machine aimed squarely at the heart of Wall Street. Together, they would take on some of the most powerful forces of finance, the giant banks, such as Goldman Sachs and Morgan Stanley, that controlled a vast amount of the market. Levine's vision of a computer-driven market would devastate the human dealers and open up the market to everyone.

But years later, the consequences of this approach, in a supreme twist, were to result in a market far more dark and secretive than anything Levine ever could have imagined. A market of secret algorithms, black boxes, dark pools, and mammoth computer centers where programmers measured trades by the billionth of a second. A market so chaotic, complex, and treacherous that it could cause a brilliant trader such as Haim Bodek to conclude that the entire system was rigged.

# CHAPTER SIX

# THE WATCHER

S oon after learning about SOES trading, Levine started working full-time out of Datek's office at 50 Broad Street. It was the late 1980s. His freelance consulting company, Joshua Group, was juggling several projects at once, writing programs for NYSE firms, banks such as Lehman Brothers, and hedge funds such as Tiger Management. His obsession with trading had turned into a boon for Maschler, who'd become embroiled in all-out warfare against Nasdaq. The burly cigar-chomping trader could see that the vast, nationwide army of Nasdaq market makers would never back down. It was going to be a brutal fight lasting years.

Maschler had started recruiting a fresh batch of young, ambitious traders with a single purpose: to work SOES all the day long like machines. He wanted fresh blood, traders with the stamina and desire to sit in front of a terminal every minute of the day, wide-eyed, hungry, picking off lazy market makers like dead-eyed snipers scoping out a kill.

One of his first hires was Jeff Citron, a recent high-school graduate who possessed everything Maschler was looking for in a trader: street smarts, intelligence, and a boiling desire to get rich quick. A cocky, sandy-haired teenager from Staten Island, Citron had started working full-time as a clerk in Datek's office on July 5, 1988. He was just eighteen years old and making $25,000 a year. Initially, his duties involved making coffee, opening mail, and running errands, but he kept pestering Maschler to let him try his hand at trading.

Most of Maschler's other traders were good—seasoned pros who'd cut their teeth on Wall Street in the dead market of the 1970s and lived to tell about it. But they were befuddled by the Street's hottest new trading tool: the desktop computer.

Citron, a tall, gangly teenager who liked to let his hair grow to his shoulders, was the face of a new generation of trader—the video game player. And Maschler taught him well: how to watch for a slow market maker, how to move fast and take advantage of the opening when stocks took off on overnight news. Maschler had become so good at watching market maker quotes that he liked to say he could tell when a guy on the other side of the screen was taking a whiz, because his quote didn't move.

But eventually even Maschler couldn't compete with Citron.

ONE morning, Citron was sitting before his terminal smirking and rubbing his hands like a ravenous gourmand eyeing a rack of lamb. The other Datek traders in the room looked on with envy. They knew he'd found a kill.

It was just before the opening bell. Citron was flexing his neck muscles like an athlete, preparing for action. It was one of his favorite tricks, one Maschler had taught him. Before trading started, he'd search for a stock that was going to move sharply right out of the gate. Anything could cause it: big news in *The Wall Street Journal*, a rumor on the grapevine. Citron didn't care about the details. He just wanted to know if the stock would move—and who *didn't* know it.

Citron had found a live one, a stock that would be up about $2 a share in early trading. His next move was to hunt for a dealer who was asleep at the switch—or caught in traffic on the way to the office—and hadn't updated his quote from the previous day's session.

Right at the open, Citron made his move. Using SOES, he bought one thousand shares of stock from a market maker whose quote was stale. He then turned around and sold the shares seconds later at the new price, $2 higher, an instant $2,000 gain per trade, minus commissions.

Citron executed the trade roughly *ninety times* that morning before the market maker changed the quote, amounting to a gain of more than $150,000 after fees. The market maker, of course, had just sold a huge chunk of the stock at an extremely low price, amounting to a paper loss of more than $150,000.

Citron didn't give a shit about the market maker. He should have been in the office, glued to his terminal, if he was going to put quotes out.

*A quote was a quote.*

Done with his trade, Citron switched off his terminal, stood, and left the office, beaming. Later that day he was back, his brand-new Mercedes-Benz 500SL convertible parked out front.

DRIVEN by the frantic action of traders such as Citron, Datek quickly became one of the largest users of SOES on Wall Street, far outpacing Houtkin's operation. As Shelly Maschler and his team of traders at Datek kept pushing the envelope on SOES, they became enemy number one among Nasdaq's market makers.

The hatred market makers felt for Datek went well beyond the everyday sparring matches that fueled Wall Street's Darwinian live-and-let-die routine. It was visceral. And, at times, violent.

Take Jerry Rosen. A market maker for Vanderbilt Securities, a broker dealer across the street from Datek, at 43 Broad Street, Rosen knew all about Maschler's old tricks. Maschler would do *anything* to get an order. He had no respect for his fellow market makers, Rosen thought, taking their shitty little thousand-share orders on SOES and ruining the game for everybody. He'd known Maschler since the 1970s when Maschler was an up-and-coming penny-stock dealer in Jersey City. Rosen's boss at Vanderbilt was Morty Kantrowitz, an old-timer who'd helped Maschler get his start on Wall Street.

His boss's connection with Maschler made Rosen paranoid. It seemed as if Datek's traders somehow knew about his positions. It was uncanny. Datek was constantly hitting the stocks he was trading, eating into his profits.

Rosen was convinced Maschler had inside information about his positions and was banging his stocks on purpose. It was personal. Then one morning, Rosen was looking to unload a large position in Airship International, a company that peddled ads on blimps. Out of the blue, Datek offered to sell a measly thousand shares of Airship's stock for 25 cents *less* than what Rosen was offering. That meant Rosen could only sell his own stock for a cheaper price.

He'd been SOES-ed.

Rosen snapped.

"Goddammit!" he screamed as the trade popped up on his Level II Workstation. Bursting out of his office, he darted across Broad Street and bolted up several flights of stairs. The door to Datek's office was open. In a rage, Rosen stepped inside.

"You did it again, I'll fucking *kill* you!" he screamed, racing past Maschler, who was sitting at his desk, and leaping at a Datek trader named Freddy Balbi.

Maschler grabbed a letter opener. As Rosen closed in on Balbi, Maschler lunged, stabbing the letter opener into Rosen's shoulder. Rosen screamed. Blood streamed down his jacket. Despite the wound, he felt lucky, convinced Maschler had been aiming for his heart. "The fat bastard was going to kill me," Rosen would later tell anyone who'd listen.

He called the police, and Maschler was arrested and hauled off to a nearby station. Rosen wanted to press charges. But his boss, Kantrowitz, Maschler's longtime friend, asked him to cool his heels. So Rosen devised a plan. He arranged to meet Maschler at a city diner in Brooklyn.

"If you want to solve this, Shelly, pay me fifty grand," Rosen said across the table. "Or else I'm going to the police."

Rosen had no idea that Maschler was taping the conversation. Soon after the meeting, he told Rosen that if he filed charges he'd sue him for extortion — and he had the tape to prove it.

Rosen never filed.

It was clear to Maschler that he'd shaken up a hornet's nest. Perhaps to escape more attacks from the likes of Rosen, in 1990 he moved Datek's trading operation to his home, 182 Kelly Boulevard in Heartland Village, a ramshackle neighborhood at the very center of Staten Island. He wanted to lay low, but that didn't mean he was slowing down for a second.

He set up shop in his basement, a dank, low-ceilinged space decked out with a few fold-out card tables, a couple of dusty couches, and a large dog. Maschler's right-hand man, Mike McCarty, had an office on the first floor. In charge of Datek's books, McCarty was a terrifying enforcer of Maschler's decrees, with a volcanic temper that could explode in the face of any trader who wasn't pulling his weight. According to office legend, McCarty once ripped a Datek trader from his seat by the hair, dragged him screaming across the trading room, and tossed him out the door. Traders knew to never, *ever* fuck with McCarty.

Levine stayed put at 50 Broad. He occasionally trekked out to the Maschler homestead to tinker with Datek's computers, taking the long ride on the Staten Island Ferry from lower Manhattan. He helped traders get news feeds by hacking into a Standard & Poor's service through satellite dishes on Maschler's roof. His first real business deal with Maschler was a beeper company. While they've been largely consigned to history's dustbin by handheld computers and phones, beepers in the 1980s represented the cutting edge of computer technology, delivering all kinds of information to their owners. Maschler had been an investor in a company that pushed sports scores to beepers, but had a falling out with his partners. He decided to launch his own sports-beeper company and enlisted Levine and Citron to write the computer code in return for co-ownership in the outfit. Levine wrote the backend paging code, while Citron wrote a billing system. Called Sports Box Inc., and based at 50 Broad, it became one of the biggest sports-beeper companies in the country.

But more and more, Levine was working on Datek's trading system. He began logging monumental hours, often working through the night in his apartment or at a cramped office at 50 Broad, dozing off in front of a blinking terminal, struggling to bring what seemed like a fly-by-night day-trading boiler room into the Information Age.

A major advance came in response to the booming volume at Datek as traders such as Citron pushed the limits of SOES. All that volume created a number of logistical nightmares. Every day, after the closing bell, Datek's traders had to tally up all of their moves on paper to figure out how much money they'd pocketed. Each trade was recorded on a printout from the Nasdaq Level II Workstation, so they often had to pore through a stack of hundreds of pages.

Looking for a way to simplify the process, Levine started working on a system that would allow a computer to scrape the relevant information from the trading "blotter"—the record of trades—on the Nasdaq Level II Workstation and input the data in a program. The program could then automatically keep track of each trader's profit and loss. He'd written similar programs for firms such as Tiger and the NYSE. The trouble was finding a way to channel the information off the Level II machine into a desktop computer.

Levine quickly cooked up an idea. Why not route the signal from the printer cable in the Workstation to a PC? Then he'd simply need to create a program to interpret the signal, sift out the relevant information, and track it.

After a few weeks of trial and error, Levine came up with a program to do just that. He called it the Watcher.

WHEN it was first created in 1990, the Watcher was little more than an automated stock-portfolio management system. It would keep track of—or "watch"—a trader's orders and positions and calculate how much the trader had made, a task that in the dark ages of the late 1980s and early '90s was largely consigned to back-office clerks. Levine automated order management for Datek, giving traders the ability to see on their computer screens whether they were winning or losing.

But Levine kept tweaking the program. As he did so, the Watcher evolved from a passive order-tracking system to a state-of-the-art trading machine that could outgun the most sophisticated systems on Wall Street. The PC receiving the order information became the "front end" of the trading platform—the steering wheel driving the trade itself through the market's plumbing. Instead of manually placing orders through the slow, clunky Level II Workstation, traders could buy and sell stocks through the Watcher itself using keyboard shortcuts designed by Levine. They could track multiple stocks at a glance, detecting from the shifts in the bids and offers whether a stock was going to rise or fall in the next minute. Levine's elegant programming enhanced the speed of the system, giving Datek's traders the ability to see shifts in the market before nearly everyone else. It provided flexibility and speed—and was a stepping-stone toward something far more revolutionary.

Turbocharged with Levine's skillful programming, the Watcher dramatically outpaced the Level II Workstations market makers used, giving Datek traders a 360-degree look at the market's order flow, and the ability to place orders far more rapidly than anyone else. And the stock market would never be the same. With the Watcher, as *Forbes* would state two decades later, "a nation of day traders was born."

BUT Levine's goal wasn't simply to bring day trading to the masses. Since working at Datek and learning more about how the market functioned, he'd conceived what amounted to the ultimate heresy on Wall Street: He wanted to make stock trading *free*—for everyone— by leveraging the power of the computer.

It was a jaw-dropping vision. To make it a reality, Levine immersed himself in dense academic studies of market structure, a relatively new field that had sprouted in the 1970s and '80s. Finance professors were contemplating novel approaches to how markets worked, with an eye on making them more efficient. The literature could be wickedly complex, mind-bendingly arcane, long tomes full of obscure terms and difficult equations. Levine lapped it up.

The book that left the most indelible impression was *Reshaping the Equity Markets: A Guide for the 1990s,* by Baruch finance professor Robert Schwartz. Schwartz's sweeping survey of markets in the United States and around the world, from Tokyo to Toronto, was a revelation to Levine. He learned about earlier efforts to create electronic markets, such as CATS, the Computer Assisted Trading System implemented in 1977 by the Toronto Stock Exchange—the world's first fully automated electronic trading system. Markets in Europe and Japan were also dabbling in electronic trading. Of course, none of those markets compared remotely in size or complexity to the United States stock market, Levine's chosen field of battle, which remained dominated by humans.

Schwartz's book was the first place Levine came across an approach to the markets from an abstract, theoretical basis. The only problem: He disagreed with just about everything Schwartz wrote. On computerized trading, Schwartz wrote that while its advantage is "the rapidity with which orders can be electronically transmitted and executed," the drawback is that "speed may also have undesirable consequences if it is not properly controlled." Investors may be better-off at times if "the pace of events is slowed down."

To Levine, that was nonsense. Slowing down trading was the prime tactic of the Nasdaq market maker who didn't want to honor his quote, who wanted to *back away.* One of the primary goals in Levine's ideal trading universe was speed: the faster the trading, the better. Speed forces market makers to be honest. It also encourages more transparency of the minute-by-minute ticks of the market. Instinctively, Levine believed the more visibility, the better. On Main Street, that was the vision of an idealist, a dreamer. On Wall Street, it was the ravings of a lunatic.

But the madness would soon spread from Levine's inner sanctum across the nation—and, in due course, the world. Indeed, the coming flood of free information unleashed by Levine's computer systems would put Datek at the epicenter of the day-trading explosion of the 1990s, which took off as more individual investors gained access to the market through the Internet using software such as the Watcher. The dot-com frenzy that would shake the nation's stock market to its core was gearing up—and Josh Levine was at the center of it.

Maschler, of course, couldn't have cared less about the masses or making trading free. His goal was simple: to get filthy rich as quickly as possible. To capitalize on his new computer weapon, Maschler started hiring more and more young traders, often kids from Staten Island, fresh out of high school, with no trading experience at all. It became a Maschler trademark: find a struggling hungry kid from the streets who could never make it in the big leagues, show him the ropes, make him rich, and win his loyalty.

"Shelly had a whole group that he brought in from Staten Island," recalls Moishe Zelcer, Datek's longtime accountant. "He acted as their father figure. He recognized talent. Even when guys were down and out, when he saw talent, he'd use it. And they were so devoted to him. Loyalty was the absolute rule."

# CHAPTER SEVEN

# MONSTER KEY

One day in Shelly Maschler's basement, the new hub of Datek's operation, a Staten Island trader named Joe Cammarata and another trader agreed to race each other to see who could be the first to buy a thousand shares of Apple for $24 a share. Cammarata, rushing to get the order into the system, screwed up by putting the wrong stock symbol into his Watcher trading program. The other trader beat him to the punch on the first few hundred shares. In frustration, Cammarata put in a new order to buy Apple for $28 a share — and it was filled instantly, *at $24*, beating the other trader.

This was confusing. By rights, the trade should never have been filled, Cammarata thought. He called a contact at Nasdaq and explained what had happened. His contact explained that the $28 order to buy was filled first because of a protocol known as "price-time priority." Orders put into the Nasdaq order book were assigned a time stamp that prioritized orders with the same price. The earlier the order, the higher the priority. Orders with better prices, however, jumped to the front of the line — even if they were made later. And because another market maker was willing to sell for $24, that was the price Cammarata got.

A lightbulb went on. Cammarata realized that he could instantly buy or sell a stock for the best price in the order book. He put in another order to buy Apple for $50 a share—expecting to leap to the front of the queue. But the order was rejected. Calling his Nasdaq contact again, he learned that the system worked only for prices up to *20 percent* higher or lower than the best bid or offer in the system.

Cammarata had unwittingly stumbled on a hidden loophole in SOES—*price beats time*. If he saw a bid or offer he wanted to hit, he simply needed to enter a price 20 percent away from the bid or offer and the trade would be his, *instantly*. If a market maker were bidding to buy Apple for $24 a share and sell it for $24¼, a typical quarter-point spread, and Cammarata wanted to buy, he'd enter a bid for a thousand shares 20 percent higher than $24¼, about $29. If he wanted to sell, he'd make an offer to sell for $19⅛, roughly 20 percent lower than the bid.

The advantage of this was simple: Often on SOES, traders making the same bid and offer for a stock lined the queue. The trade went to the firm that placed the order first. Cammarata had discovered a way to leap over the queue, make a ridiculous offer, and *still get the best price*. He could offer to buy Apple for $29, far higher than the going price, and get it for $24¼.

To automate the process, he created a keyboard shortcut that gave him the ability to jump to the front of the queue at a moment's notice. And for weeks, he outpaced every other trader at Datek. Some even thought he was cheating. But he kept his secret quick-draw gimmick to himself. Eventually, after another trader figured out his trick, Cammarata decided to pass it on to Levine.

The result was one of the most powerful stock-trading tools of the nineties: the Monster Key, a program created by Levine inside the Watcher that gave traders the power to blast orders into SOES like a tommy gun. Whenever they saw a trade they wanted to hit instantly, they simply typed in their order and punched the Monster Key. While Cammarata ballparked the 20 percent difference in his head, the Monster Key program instantly calculated the price using an algorithm.

Armed with the Monster Key, the Watcher now allowed traders to buy and sell stocks at a velocity never before seen. A trader could type a symbol into the Watcher and hit Shift B to buy one thousand shares of a stock—or Shift S to sell one thousand. The algorithm behind the key would instantly calculate a price that was 20 percent up or down.

The Monster Key was one of the original trading algos, among the first of a growing arsenal of digital weapons in a coming cyberwar that would eventually marshal the most sophisticated techniques in computer science. The Key could be dangerous, a sure way for reckless traders to lose massive sums of money. Good traders, however, could rack up huge profits.

More trading algos would come. Levine designed Bombs, then SuperBombs. They were the embryonic algos of the high-tech Guerillas, Stealths, and Snipers of the coming decade of the Algo Wars.

At the time, Levine didn't have to worry about competitors. He was so far ahead of the pack that he was playing a game few even knew existed. While primitive, the Monster Key in its day was deadly. Citron, Cammarata, and other Datek traders began racking up huge gains trading on SOES. Using the Key, "you could be a high-school dropout from the wrong side of the tracks and be a millionaire in a month," says Peter Stern, who in 1996 helped launch Datek Online, Datek's discount brokerage for day traders.

THERE was one major problem with the guerilla trading operation Levine, Citron, and Maschler were building at Datek. Nasdaq had designed SOES for retail investors, not professional traders. To make it *appear* as if Datek's orders were coming from regular investors, Maschler signed up "nominee accounts" for the firm and collected a small investment from the nominees. Datek promised the nominees a fixed rate, say 12 percent of their investment. At the end of each trading day, Datek would assign its SOES orders to the nominee accounts. Any profit above the fixed-rate payments was pocketed by the house: Datek itself.

In short order, everyone at the firm signed up friends and relatives to Datek accounts. It was easy money—*too* easy. One person recalls that Citron told him that Datek could provide him a *guaranteed* 30 percent annual return. Datek effectively became a hedge fund clone with hundreds of small investors (including a number of grandmothers living in Queens, according to an SEC official who later investigated Datek). The trouble was, SOES wasn't designed for hedge funds, and there were strict rules prohibiting such abuses. Maschler didn't care. In his eyes, Nasdaq was the corrupt operation. He was only giving it what it deserved.

There were technical hurdles to overcome for Datek's nominee system to work. Since every trade got a time stamp indicating when it was executed, it was difficult to *retroactively* assign trades to customer accounts. At first, traders would physically wind back the time-stamp clock to the time the trade occurred and punch the ticket with the client's name.

When Datek's trading volume skyrocketed with innovations such as the Watcher and the Monster Key, this process became far too cumbersome. To solve the problem, Levine designed an automated computer system to allocate trades to nominee accounts and time stamp them. All profits above the fixed rate were transferred into Datek's coffers. This system was called the Wire.

There were other issues Maschler & Co. had to deal with, including the growing backlash from Nasdaq market makers—and Nasdaq itself.

"ARE you threatening me?" shouted Peter, a market maker for the Minneapolis investment bank Piper Jaffray.

Peter was on the phone with Maschler, who was complaining about how Peter had handled a trade involving just five shares.

"What do you mean, am I threatening you?" growled Maschler. "I already *have* threatened you, you dumb Minneapolis cocksucker!"

Maschler slammed down the phone in disgust. Another market maker had backed away from his offer to trade a stock.

It was a problem Datek's traders were running into more and more. Since traders could only put in so many SOES orders a day due to NASD restrictions, they were forced to execute some of their trades over SelectNet, the Nasdaq-operated system in which traders placed orders through a window on their Level II Workstations.

Since SelectNet wasn't automated, that gave the market makers an option—they could ignore the trade or *back away* from it (by law they were supposed to execute the trade if it was the best price in the market, but Nasdaq market makers didn't always act as if the law applied to them). Worse, outside of SOES, market makers weren't obligated to trade at their quoted price for more than one hundred shares.

Increasingly, Datek traders would punch in an order to buy a stock on SelectNet and watch in fury as the order sat there, ignored. When they picked up the phone to ask the market maker why he wasn't selling when the offer was right there on the screen for the world to see, more often than not the answer was a terse "A hunnet, sold a hunnet." That meant the dealer had already sold a hundred shares of the stock and the quote was stale—*or so he said.*

The Datek traders knew when they were being lied to, and frequently erupted in profane outbursts, such as Maschler's tirade against Peter.

Maschler knew the NASD enforced its rules when it wanted to. Increasingly, the regulator was training its guns on Datek. In 1991, the NASD fined Datek $10,000 and smacked Maschler himself with a $50,000 fine for violating SOES rules. In May 1993, the NASD fined Maschler $5,000 and suspended him from trading for a day. The charge: "profane and indecorous language," an astonishing charge in an industry that was never known for its decorous language. The NASD complaint didn't include any specific examples of said language, but it did pile adjective upon adjective to communicate how indecorous it actually was: "calculated," "graphic and protracted," "sexually denigrating," "gross, vile, and disgusting."

In his defense, Maschler said the language stemmed from disputes over trades. He asserted his rights to free speech, adding for good measure that everybody did it. "Traders can't say a sentence without cursing," he told *The Wall Street Journal*.

There were other, far more serious charges. In 1993, the NASD found that Datek was splitting up SOES orders into various trading accounts to get around its restrictions. It suspended Maschler and his entire Staten Island office from executing NASD transactions for six months.

During the hearings, Maschler displayed a stunning irreverence toward the regulators. One day, he showed up in bathing trunks and a T-shirt that read NASDAQ SUCKS. The judge, outraged, tossed him out, telling him to come back in a different shirt the following day. Maschler did as ordered—wearing a T-shirt that read NASDAQ SUCKS in different colors.

Regulators were quickly crawling all over Maschler's ragtag office. One day, a typical one in the market for Datek, each trader sat staring at his Watcher in Maschler's basement, all decked out in their standard work uniform—baggy shorts, T-shirt, tennis shoes or flip-flops. Suddenly, they all noticed an odd presence in the room: two men in crisp suits looming in the stairwell door.

Maschler exploded like a grenade.

"Who . . . the FUCK . . . are YOU!" he screamed, jumping from his seat and jabbing his Macanudo in the air.

"We're from the SEC," one of the suits said. "We're looking for Sheldon Maschler."

"Who the FUCK let you in!"

"The door was open."

"If my fly was open, would you suck my dick?"

The Datek traders buckled in their seats, struggling to contain their laughter.

"Now get upstairs and RING THE FUCKING BELL!" Maschler roared.

The two SEC officials sheepishly crept back upstairs—and rang the bell. Maschler pressed the intercom button.

"Hello, who is it?" he said calmly.

There was a pause. Then, "It's the SEC."

"Come on down!"

Maschler greeted them warmly, all smiles, backslapping. "Now, wasn't that easier?" he said, waving around his Macanudo and blowing smoke right into their faces.

BY 1994, as Datek kept growing, Maschler had shut down his basement operation and moved back to 50 Broad. He understood that as the fight over SOES heated up, it was best to be in the center of the action—and as close as possible to Levine. He set up shop in a tenth-floor office, just down the hall from the programmer. In short order, Levine's peaceful research lab was transformed into a raucous frat house. His shoe-box office was tight, cramped, crawling with computer gear. One small, grit-slathered window looked out over Broad Street. Baker's racks lined a wall from floor to ceiling. Two-dozen flickering PC monitors were sardined along the racks, displaying streaming rows of glowing digits. Coils of wires, Ethernet cables, and power cords snaked in all directions, finding egress into weird openings in the floors, walls, and ceiling—or just disappearing into mounds of trash.

Trash was everywhere—on the racks, the tables, perched atop PCs. Mostly, of course, it was on the floor. The floor *was* trash. Chunks of ancient candy bars, apple cores, blackened orange peel, coffee grounds. Stacks of *Popular Electronics* and *Investors Business Daily*. An oscilloscope. Milk cartons. Mostly empty plastic Coke bottles. Computer keyboards, several broken. An eighteen-inch lizard named Greg sat in a giant climate-controlled terrarium. The door often couldn't be closed because of the creeping clutter. With space so tight, Levine usually stood, furiously typing on several keyboards hooked to Dell computer towers.

It was chaos, though to Levine it all seemed perfectly in order; if asked about a missing document or research report, he'd plunge his arm into a seemingly indistinctive mound of junk and with a flourish retrieve the missing item.

Directly outside Levine's den was another kind of barely controlled chaos: the Datek trading room. A constant *clickclickclick* blended with a fugue of profanity. Dozens of Datek day traders sat hunched before long card tables, tense, eyes welded to their computer monitors, watching their Watchers, banging keyboards — *clickclickclick* — shouting, cursing, screaming "LOOK AT MICROSOFT!!!" or "LOOK AT INTEL!!!" or "LOOK AT FUCKING APPLE!!!"

At other times, the room was dead silent as traders seemed hypnotized by their flowing screens, a silence interrupted only by the clicking of keys or the high-pitched squeals of mice stuck in the glue traps scattered about the floor. A haze of cigarette and cigar smoke hovered along the ceiling of the trading room, seeping into Levine's computer-lined cave, to his constant annoyance (he didn't smoke). It was a rough-and-tumble crowd — but they were hungry, young, and hardworking. The seasoned traders put the new recruits through their paces, showing them when to hit the bid, when to wait, when to get out of the way quick because the market was swinging against them. Their Watcher orders armed with the Monster Key hit the market at top speed, gunned from their computers through dedicated T1 lines, high-speed cables that could transmit data at roughly fifty times the rate of a normal telephone hookup.

They were Maschler's bandit army, the rejects of Wall Street, the city college kids from the backwaters of Staten Island, Queens, and the Bronx, the ones who didn't stand a chance at a big bank like Goldman or Morgan. Dumb boiler-room mutts — but they had a secret weapon: Josh Levine. With Levine creations such as the Watcher and the Monster Key at their fingertips, they could out-trade the very best in the business. They could grind Goldman to a pulp. They could make Morgan cry.

A-chomp his cigar, Maschler roamed the office like a wolf hunting fresh meat, constantly urging his traders to push the envelope — to trade faster, more aggressively, to *destroy* the Nasdaq market makers, his mortal enemies. Again and again he bellowed "FUCK 'EM, FUCK DA BASTAHDS."

New recruits learned at the feet of top-dog traders like Citron (still in his mid-twenties) or Maschler's eldest son, Erik. After a few weeks, cub traders were handed $300,000 to $400,000 to play with. Stakes could rise to $1 million or more. The traders kept a slice of their profits, and Datek pocketed the rest (with a fraction handed back to the "nominees").

Most traders focused on the high-volume stocks, like Microsoft and Intel, since they moved up and down a lot and were easy to jump in and out of. They were *flat* when the day began and *flat* when it ended — in other words, no one held positions overnight, since news in the early morning, or after the close, could kill a position.

All that trading, of course, wasn't going unnoticed on Wall Street — or in Washington, D.C.

DATEK was now in the crosshairs of the most powerful securities regulators in the land, the SEC and the NASD. The SOES bandits, in the view of the regulators, were spreading like a virus. A 1992 NASD study found that 80 percent of SOES share volume in the fifty most active Nasdaq stocks came from the bandits.

To protect itself, Nasdaq started to circle the wagons. It made a move to cut the number of shares a trader could buy or sell in a single pop from one thousand to five hundred. It placed a limit on the number of SOES orders market makers had to honor to one every fifteen seconds. Then it tried to scrap the SOES mechanism altogether and replace it with a new system that gave market makers a twenty-second grace period to decide whether to honor a quote, making it harder for bandits to ply their frenetic hit-and-run strategies.

Nasdaq's efforts proved largely fruitless. It had little idea that a lone computer genius was crafting its demise from a ragtag office on the tenth floor of 50 Broad Street. Levine, ever fearless, knew the truth. The old boys were mired in the past. The Watcher, and software like it, was the future.

Then he got help from an unlikely source: academia.

IN 1994, two finance professors, Bill Christie and Paul Schultz, published a groundbreaking study based on the trading data of Nasdaq stocks such as Apple and Intel.

The two professors had noticed something very *odd* in the data: Nasdaq market makers rarely if ever posted an order at an "odd-eighth"—as in $10⅛, $10⅜, $10⅝, or $10⅞. (Recall that this was a time when stocks were quoted in fractions of a dollar, not pennies.) Instead, they found that for heavily traded stocks such as Apple, market makers posted odd-eighth quotes roughly *1 percent of the time.*

When they looked at spreads for stocks on the NYSE or American Stock Exchange, by comparison, they found a consistent use of odd-eighths. That meant Nasdaq market makers must be *deliberately* colluding to keep spreads artificially wide. Instead of the minimum spread of 12.5 cents (one-eighth of a dollar), spreads were usually twenty-five or fifty cents wide. That extra 12.5 cents was coming directly out of the pockets of investors. Add it up, and Nasdaq's market makers were siphoning *billions* out of the pockets of investors.

In early 1994, the two professors put their findings in a paper called "Why Do Nasdaq Market Makers Avoid Odd-Eighth Quotes?" Their findings, they wrote, raised "the question of whether Nasdaq dealers implicitly collude to maintain wide spreads."

The *Los Angeles Times* quickly picked up on the study. On May 26, the paper ran an article stating that the Christie-Schultz study "strongly suggests that the nation's brokerage firms collude with each other to rig over-the-counter trading and ensure themselves artificially high trading profits at the expense of investors."

Inside the SEC, the study erupted like a bomb. The Nasdaq investigation was assigned to a staid, low-key attorney in the enforcement division named Leo Wang. Socially awkward, but aggressive as a pit bull, Wang had gained prestige within the commission for handling a high-profile bond-manipulation case against Salomon Brothers in the early 1990s.

In October 1994, the Justice Department launched an investigation into antitrust law violations by market makers. Wang began his own investigation in November.

He started hammering Nasdaq dealers with subpoenas, demanding transaction records. He hit the jackpot when he forced the firms to hand over truckloads of tape recordings going back years. Traders had been oblivious to the recordings, which were made as a backup in the event of a dispute over the details of a trade. Inside the SEC, the enormity of the task of reviewing the tapes at first seemed daunting— it could take weeks, if not months, to comb through them for evidence of price fixing.

But it proved all too easy: The *very first tape* Wang played revealed two dealers fixing prices.

"What can I do for you?" the first trader on the tape said.

"Can you go one-quarter bid for me?" the second asked, using trader code to boost the price by twenty-five cents.

"Yeah, sure."

"I sold you two hundred at one-quarter. Just go up there, OK?"

"I'm goosing it, cuz," the first trader said, using trader lingo indicating that he was artificially raising the price.

"Thank you."

After the deal was finished, one of the traders, perhaps in enthusiasm over a job well done, struck a different sort of deal over the phone: a drug deal.

The law was about to come down on Nasdaq like a sledgehammer. The investigations by the SEC and the Justice Department would result in a seismic restructuring of the stock market, helping to sideline human market makers and pave the way for the rise of the electronic pools. Indeed, it was that age-old human flaw that in many ways had set the stage for the rise of the machines on Wall Street: greed.

Waiting in the wings to pounce: Josh Levine and Datek.

LEVINE sat ramrod straight in front of his computer screen. "Intel is at one eleven," he said excitedly, watching his Watcher.

Jeff Citron sat back in a large, squashed-looking leather chair, his feet propped on a card table piled high with bits of hardware, yellowing magazines, food wrappers, half-empty Coke cans. He smirked and ran a hand through his long, spindly hair.

He knew exactly what Levine was thinking.

"I have to do this," Levine said.

Citron watched Levine with interest. He never ceased to be amazed by his enterprising companion. It was early 1996. A few years ago, in 1993, the two had officially teamed up, forming their own brokerage. Levine had also started his own broker dealer, Big J Securities. Another company, called Smith Wall Associates, marketed their computer-trading software such as the Watcher. Datek, of course, was their number one customer. The location of all of these firms: 50 Broad.

Despite the new ventures, Levine and Citron remained fiercely loyal to Datek and Maschler. Citron was personally in control of management and policies of Datek Securities. Levine, while never officially employed by Datek Securities, devoted most of his time toward building the software that ran Datek's trading machine.

Levine never stopped tinkering with the Watcher, adding new tricks. He was determined to find more ways to circumvent Nasdaq's market makers—or to at least make them suffer.

That day, all was relatively quiet in the office as Levine started typing. Since the best offer to buy Intel was at $111, he figured some witless market maker wouldn't notice if he dropped in an extra digit.

Taking a breath, he typed in an offer to sell a thousand shares of Intel for $1,111¼.

And a market maker hit him. He broke into a dance.

"I made a million dollars!" Levine shouted, shooting his arms into the air. "I made a million dollars!"

"That was really stupid," Citron said, shaking his head. "You know what's going to happen next."

Levine knew.

Since market makers often focused squarely on the right side of the order—the fraction—they could be tricked into buying far too high or selling far too low. Maschler loved it because it showed the Nasdaq dealers for the subhuman apes he knew they were.

Levine loved it because it forced them to be more honest, more aware. It was *discipline*. That day, he'd found the perfect opportunity.

The phone rang. A Datek trader picked up. "It's about Int-See!" he yelled out, using trader shorthand for Intel's ticker symbol, INTC.

Citron grabbed the phone.

"You the head trader?" he said. "Ah, you like that trade, huh? Not bad, huh?"

He knew the trade was a scratch and negotiated to sell a thousand Intel shares for $111⅞, still a tidy profit—but no million. Levine didn't care. He knew all along that he wasn't *actually* going to pocket a million dollars. Such erroneous trades were routinely canceled. But in another part of his mind, a streaming virtual cyberworld where the numbers on the screen were reality, he had *made a million dollars*.

WITH all its success, Datek started to change. Maschler began poaching recruits straight out of Ivy League schools, trying to burnish the firm's image and, with luck, forge ties with influential power brokers through their blue-blood connections. Many were making hundreds of thousands a year—if not millions. The dream job on Wall Street was no longer a cozy position with a white-shoe investment bank. Now the young blood was gravitating to the quick-draw hedge funds and day-trading outfits like Datek.

Training was fast and focused. Maschler was intent on ripping as much money out of SOES as he could before the candy store was shut down. "We are slick, we are quick, we are smart, and yes, sometimes we take advantage of the system," Maschler told a reporter in 1995. "I look at the gray area and I find loopholes."

Citron, for his part, had become a millionaire many times over. And he found plenty of extravagant ways to spend his newfound riches—fine wines, mansions, jets, helicopters.

What raised eyebrows wasn't that Citron, still in his twenties, was living like a Howard Hughes for the 1990s. It was where he got his new toys: Robert Brennan, the notorious First Jersey penny-stock manipulator who'd employed Maschler in the 1980s. Brennan had declared bankruptcy in 1995 after being fined $75 million for a massive securities fraud, and was selling off the goodies he'd accumulated over the years from his ill-gotten gains.

Maschler tipped off Citron to the fire sale. In 1996, Citron, freshly married, scooped up Brennan's sprawling estate perched on the Manasquan River in Brielle, New Jersey, a popular getaway for Wall Street moguls. He promptly bulldozed Brennan's mansion and built a new one for $3 million, including a copious wine cellar. He also bought Brennan's Gulfstream jet.

While Maschler's connections with Brennan were clear-cut, the links between Citron and Brennan remained murky. Still, the appearance of close ties between the two cast a pall over Datek. The scandal-ridden Brennan had been connected to some of the sleaziest operations on Wall Street. Citron wasn't burnishing Datek's reputation by ostentatiously picking up Brennan's flashy possessions.

Regulators took notice. They had been probing Datek for years, convinced its traders were manipulating the market through SOES. Maschler was constantly under the microscope of the NASD and had even attracted the attention of the Justice Department. The SEC was hesitant to go to Datek for information about Nasdaq market maker abuses—as it had with Harvey Houtkin—because of concerns about its potential ties to organized crime. Whether or not those concerns were justified, they hurt Datek's image in a business where reputation often meant everything. As Datek's visibility in the market grew, the scrutiny shifted toward Maschler's day-trading golden boy, Jeff Citron.

For Levine, however, it was never about the money. Not in the Wall Street sense—where *everything* was about the money. He seemed content to live life on a relatively small scale, renting an apartment in Battery Park in Manhattan, a ten-minute walk to the office. Rather than jetting to the Bahamas, he spent his weekends wandering the streets of Manhattan or Coney Island. His focus wasn't on making millions—it was on changing the market through computers.

He struggled to keep the darker side of Maschler's operation at arm's length. Levine's sole interest in Datek was in using it as a Trojan horse to penetrate Wall Street and attack it from within. And *it was working*. His trick on the market maker with Intel was proof that humans were no good at matching orders between buyers and sellers. Beyond the larcenous spreads they charged, they were prone to bone-headed mistakes.

A computer could do the job far quicker, cheaper, and mistake-free. Humans were in the way. Computers could make information free and let investors trade without the interference of the middlemen.

The pieces were in place. Levine's dream was about to come alive—an electronic pool that brought investors together without middlemen. A pool that was open, seamless, fast, and free.

An island.

# CHAPTER EIGHT

# THE ISLAND

**A** bell rang.

In a blink, Josh Levine hopped to the center of his cluttered office at 50 Broad and shimmied before a camera.

It was one of the stranger manifestations of Levine's ethos of transparency. In 1995, the programmer had installed a video camera in a corner of his office that transmitted live images to his website, josh.com. "Live WebCams," the site read. "Only a few will catch a random nose pick. Will you be one of them? Try your luck, it's free!"

Viewers would typically see Levine's crew-cut bullethead bent over his keyboard, the programmer typing, peering at his monitor, in ragged jeans, T-shirt, and flip-flops, a mound of crumpled trash and stacked computer gear looming behind him. If they looked hard enough, they might even see a large lizard sitting placidly in a giant terrarium.

They may not have realized that Levine could track who watched the videos by the unique Internet Protocol numbers the viewers' computers used. His number one fan was a day trader based in New Jersey. Numbers two and three, in a close tie: the SEC and the NASD.

"If we're so crooked," Levine seemed to be asking regulators, "why would we put ourselves on screen day and night?"

The website also included a button that read "Ring the Bell, Make

Them Dance." If the button was clicked by a viewer, an electronic bell rang in Levine's office, prompting the programmer to jump out of his chair and dance a jig like some crazed digital marionette. "They Have Been Dinged," the site read above the live feed, with a vague reference to "The New Fresh Air Annex."

Anyone watching could reach only one conclusion: This was not your ordinary Wall Street operation. Something very different was going on at 50 Broad. Something revolutionary.

While Levine's antics were a constant source of hilarity at Datek, the traders had a profound respect for the impish programmer. Most thought Levine by far the most intelligent person they'd ever met, or ever would—and they thanked God in heaven that he was on their side.

But there were complications that even Levine couldn't fix. The Nasdaq market makers, and the waves of new rules and obstacles that NASD kept ramming out, were a constant source of anxiety and outrage at Datek. Market makers routinely ignored Datek's SelectNet orders, backing away from their posted quotes, often leading to missed opportunities or, worse, significant losses as traders, struggling to get out of positions in a fast-moving market, were left flapping in the breeze.

One way to get around the problem: find a new pool to play in, a deep market filled with orders that Datek's traders could work with. Aside from the NYSE, which was completely out of touch, there was only one other trading venue that fit the bill: Instinet.

Instinet was the result of the efforts a small number of firms had been making for decades to work around the old boys' club of the New York Stock Exchange. Lots of brokers had NYSE-listed stocks on hand that they would have liked to buy or sell directly to one another, or to investors, in order to avoid the high fees charged by the NYSE middlemen. But it was difficult to get around the fact that the NYSE was the dominant meeting place for NYSE-listed stocks—among the largest public companies in the world. What's more, the NYSE's powerful interests erected all kinds of roadblocks, including lawsuits, to keep brokers from trading its stocks with one another. Still, these firms—including Bernie Madoff's broker dealer, Bernard L. Madoff Investment Securities—kept trying.

As such, Instinet had been founded in 1967 as Institutional Network (it was open only to "institutional" firms such as Fidelity and Merrill Lynch) in order to trade NYSE stocks. It had largely failed at its original goal, but it eventually became the largest electronic trading network for over-the-counter stocks (that is, non-NYSE stocks). It was renamed Instinet in the 1980s, and British media giant Reuters purchased the company for $110 million in 1987.

Instinet was essentially a giant dark pool. Trading through Instinet was completely anonymous and usually took place through a dedicated Instinet computer. To trade through Instinet, a firm needed to "rent" the computer for a modest fee of about $1,000 a month. Firms also needed to pass through a credit committee that allowed access to the Instinet pool only to select members that carried a large amount of capital on their books, essentially locking out anyone without millions of dollars to throw around on fancy technology. In other words, it was yet another insiders' club that Levine despised.

Like Nasdaq's SelectNet, the Instinet computer allowed firms to display their buy and sell orders on a computer screen. These orders weren't available to the general public—Instinet reported transactions to the public only *after* they were completed. As important, the matching process wasn't automated. Living, breathing Instinet traders sitting at desks in Instinet's midtown Manhattan headquarters did the actual grunt work of bringing the buy and sell orders together and settling the deal, usually through a few quick phone calls with the institutions themselves. (Fidelity wants to buy fifty thousand shares of IBM for $100, but Goldman wants to sell a hundred thousand for $100¼. If Fidelity takes seventy-five thousand, Goldman will sell for $100⅛. *Deal.*)

Market makers steadily made inroads into Instinet, which was designed primarily for institutions that made large trades. By the mid-1990s, it had become the largest venue for trading Nasdaq stocks, next to Nasdaq itself, controlling roughly one-fifth of the volume.

That's why Levine became interested in Instinet. If Watcher users could pipe into Instinet's flow, they could bypass Nasdaq completely for many of their trades. No more backing away, no more crappy Nasdaq technology issues, no more Nasdaq bullshit. And while Levine detested Instinet's closed system, he hated Nasdaq even more. Plus, Instinet had better technology.

And so in short order he and Citron arranged a meeting with Instinet executives at their 875 Third Avenue headquarters in midtown Manhattan.

Levine explained that the flow from the Watcher would be a perfect match for the institutional orders that poured through Instinet every day. It would increase Instinet's liquidity, for no cost. And since the Watcher would substantially increase Instinet's volume, Levine and Citron asked for a small reduction in the fees Instinet charged its regular customers.

They were turned down flat.

"Fine," Citron said as they stood to leave. "We'll build our own system and we'll go head to head."

The Instinet response: peals of chin-wagging laughter.

LEVINE wasn't amused. And he knew something the Instinet bigwigs didn't. Trading through the Watcher was *booming*. While Citron's threat to create their own trading pool might have seemed like a joke to Instinet, which counted the largest trading firms in the country as its clients, the reality was that by the mid-1990s, the prime growth market for exchanges was day traders—Watcher's specialty.

As competition ramped up, day trading was increasingly becoming a cutthroat business. SOES rooms were opening up around the country, spread by day-trading prophets such as Harvey Houtkin. The ability to plug directly into the market through a computer and rapidly buy and sell stocks with a mouse click was a revelation for many would-be stock jockeys. This, of course, was well before online trading companies such as E*Trade and Ameritrade had become household names, their cloying commercials daily fare. For most people, the only way to get in on the Wall Street game was through a hometown broker. SOES changed all of that. The fact that the market was in the midst of a raging bull run propelled by high-tech powerhouses Microsoft, Cisco Systems, Apple, and Intel didn't hurt.

At Datek, the armchair SOES traders—and even more seasoned pros like Harvey Houtkin—were gnats on the beast's back. The software they used was pathetically slow compared with the Watcher. That didn't mean it was easy. Other sophisticated trading firms were getting in on the game. And the Nasdaq market makers were learning how to avoid the traps and tricks the SOES bandits had been using to destroy them.

As the game got harder, the pressure on Datek's growing ranks of traders became fierce. Citron and Maschler roamed the floor, packed warrens of cluttered card tables and sweat-drenched traders fueled by fast food and caffeine and whatever other stimulants they could get their hands on. They sat hunched before their streaming tubes, jaws clenched, focused on the flickering data, baseball caps pulled tight over darting bloodshot eyes. The trading room was dripping with testosterone, ultracompetitive young men at close quarters staring all day at a very tangible measurement of success on their screens: the day's profit and loss.

Bad trades resulted in a screamed-out order to hit the floor and do fifty. Fistfights broke out. Computer equipment was tossed about like nursery toys. Look up from your Watcher, and you might see a keyboard or monitor cannonballing across the room into a pocked wall, its former user hunched over his desk fuming at another trade gone sour. Management finally levied a $100 fine for anyone who destroyed a keyboard, $500 for a monitor. The destruction continued unabated.

It was demanding mentally and physically. One particularly focused trader was in his seat every day at 8:30 A.M. and didn't get up or take a drink until 4 P.M., when the market closed, so he wouldn't have to go to the bathroom.

The market was also becoming increasingly volatile. Roller-coastering tech stocks could deliver a trip to day-trader heaven—or hell. Traders talked of *grinding*, the go-nowhere stocks floating directionless all day long; of *head fakes*, the deadly swings made by large traders—the bastard hedge funds, the oh-fuck-me banks like Morgan, Goldman, and Bear Stearns—looking to fool the market before *whipsawing* everyone in the opposite direction and triggering the animal fear of panicked herds bailing out of positions, the bug-eyed gut-rush of *scared money*. Tens of thousands could be lost in minutes, made back the next. No one blinked when a chalk-faced guy doubled over a garbage pail and puked violently, never leaving his seat and trading right through the puke.

All the frantic activity was having an impact on the wider market. As more SOES traders chased the market, *the market itself changed*. Nasdaq market makers started to react defensively when they saw a wave of SOES orders sweep in. They developed tactics to duck and cover—and to fight back.

It was a new kind of market, a market of constant action, of waves and fades, of tricks and ruses. To hide from the bandits, dealers and fund managers starting slicing and dicing their orders, parceling out smaller and smaller chunks of stock in a game of hide and seek. A fifty-thousand-share buy order for IBM could be sliced into "child" orders of a thousand shares—or five hundred or even two hundred shares. Behind the chunks was the "parent" or "iceberg" order, the below-the-surface whale the bandits were licking their chops over.

In years to come, this hunter-seeker, duck-and-dive style of trading would define the very structure of the market, its rules encoded in sophisticated algos with names like Dagger, Sniper, Raider, Thor, Stealth, and Iceberg. They would create electronic pools of dueling programs tricked out with cutting-edge AI backed by supercomputers.

At Datek in the 1990s, it all lived inside the fevered brains of Maschler's bandit army wielding their Watchers. With Watcher, traders could build a hot list of stocks that displayed their activity in a single window. Colors shifted indicating whether a stock was going up or down, who moved, and whether the move changed the spread. Smaller windows tracked a variety of indexes, giving traders a sense of the broader direction of the market.

New traders at Datek started off pocketing 12 percent of their returns. After they earned a Series 7, they made 15 percent; 20 percent for a Series 24 (which earned the holder the ability to manage other traders). Rookies were given little leeway for losses. They were expected to start earning thousands of dollars a day within their first few weeks. After all, they were playing with house money.

There were plenty of examples of big winners like Citron—gifted traders could rake in enormous profits with the Watcher. One ace trader at Datek was said to have made between $25,000 and $35,000 a day, every day, for months on end. George West, a cofounder of Broadway Trading—a SOES firm that also used the Watcher and also was based at 50 Broad—was said to rake in $50,000 to $100,000 *a day*. He could lose as much as well, but more often than not West finished the day in the black. Among his co-bandits, West was known as a *sick* trader.

Few were sicker than Citron. But by the mid-1990s, Citron rarely traded anymore. Still in his mid-twenties, Citron was an *executive*, an empire builder. He wore crisp suits, got expensive haircuts, and bossed people around. Other Datek traders who'd been at the firm as long or longer resented him. But he was Shelly Maschler's golden boy, and *no one* was going to argue with Maschler.

And why complain? The money was phenomenal. Every month, Datek's management threw a party at a rented hall a few blocks from the office. Star traders would be called onto a platform for congratulations in the order of how much money they'd made during the month. Maschler would wrap a beefy arm around the shoulders of his stars and growl, "Great fuckin' month," sloshing Dewar's clasped in one hand, Macanudo in the other.

The festivities continued at the after-parties in local clubs. "Drinks on me tonight," Citron would say, swatting a thousand in bills on the bar.

DESPITE the growing egos—and billfolds—as the millions flowed in, everyone at Datek knew deep down that the key to their success lay in the Watcher. Levine's program let them monitor a hundred or more stocks at once, while Nasdaq market makers typically could track only ten or twenty or thirty. Using the Monster Key, the Datek traders could jump to the top of the queue at a moment's notice and rip the face off anyone in their way.

The volume was enormous. One day in late September 1995, so many orders flowed out of Datek that they crashed Nasdaq's computer system. Orders were delayed for as long as seventeen minutes. The tech-heavy index plunged nearly 3 percent on near-record volume of 523 million shares.

John Wall, head of Nasdaq's market operations, jumped on the phone and called Levine in a rage.

"We're going to pull the plug on you guys if this keeps up!" he screamed.

"That's not fair, John!" Levine shot back. "You're too slow!"

Levine was infuriated that Nasdaq couldn't handle his orders. Roughly thirty-four thousand trades had been sent to Nasdaq from Datek, but only nine thousand were executed. Many orders were completed after the market plunged, resulting in big losses for Datek traders. It was unacceptable.

BY late 1995, a few outside firms, such as Broadway Trading, had started using the Watcher in addition to Datek. As more traders used his system, Levine saw that Watcher traders were often swapping the same stock—*for the same price.* Citron might think Intel was going to go up and start buying, while the trader next to him might think Intel was going to go down and start selling. Whoever was right made money.

This could lead to an odd situation. At times, a trader using the Watcher might offer to sell a stock *for a lower price* than another Watcher user was offering to pay, a perverse situation known as a "crossed market." One trader would offer to sell Intel for, say, $10, while another wanted to buy it for $10½. Rather than trade with each other, they had to go through an intermediary—a Nasdaq market maker who often backed away.

*What if those trades could interact with each other?* Levine thought. He could *cut out the middleman*. Better, the trades could be executed far quicker if they occurred on an electronic network designed for speed.

So starting in 1995, using an amalgamation of computer languages—called Assembly, "C," and FoxPro—Levine built the first iteration of what would become Island. He called them Jump Trades. Using Jump, any two Watcher users could trade directly between themselves without interacting with a market maker. The Watcher automatically booked the trade and reported it to the consolidated tape. Jump Trades were first rolled out on November 13, 1995, when Levine announced the function in an internal e-mail system called Watcher News, used by Datek traders as well as the other clients who used the trading system.

"Auto-Realtime Jump Trades! Now you can do a Jump trade with another trader in realtime and have it AUTOMAICALY [sic] hit your Watcher, his Watcher, the P&L Systems, and the Wire Confirm," he wrote.

But there was a problem. It was hard for one Watcher trader to know when another Watcher trader had a matching order.

Thus were spawned "the Greenies." Levine wrote a program giving Watcher traders the ability to see on their screens open SelectNet orders—trades that hadn't been executed—made by other Watcher traders. The system highlighted the orders in glowing green, setting them apart from non-Watcher orders. When a Watcher trader entered an order to execute against a Greenie quote, Levine's system automatically canceled the order in SelectNet and matched the two orders internally through Jump.

Jump combined with Greenies created a system that was like an internal matching engine for the Watcher.

This was Island in embryo.

On February 9, 1996, Levine sent out a message on Watcher News notifying users that things were about to change.

"One Small Step for Watcher, One Giant Step for Watcher Kind," the message read. "It's called ISLAND."

IN the dark dawn hours of yet another frigid New York morning, Levine dressed quickly and left his apartment in the shadow of the Twin Towers at Battery Park. He trudged through city blocks clogged with treacherous mounds of packed dirt-pocked snow and ice from the year's record-breaking string of storms. It was February 16, 1996. A Friday. Earlier that week, IBM's AI supercomputer Deep Blue defeated world chess champion Garry Kasparov for the first time. Bill Clinton was entering his second term in office. The country was in the midst of a powerful economic boom that would culminate in a massive tech-stock bubble, and Levine and Datek's army of traders would be at the center of it.

The programmer walked east on Wall Street, then turned south on Broad, passing by the marble façade of the New York Stock Exchange. At 50 Broad, he took the elevator to the sixth floor and walked past a few early risers, the wired, sunken-eyed day traders for Datek. Staring at their computer terminals, hugging their steaming coffees, waiting impatiently for the action to start at the opening bell, they nodded to Levine quietly as he passed.

Months earlier, Levine had decamped from the tiny cluttered room on the tenth floor of 50 Broad to a larger room on the sixth.

Despite the uptick in size, the room quickly slouched toward the entropic chaos Levine seemed to thrive in. He brought in an inflatable kiddie pool and populated it with turtles. He grew sea monkeys in a glass jar. An Israeli army bazooka leaned in a corner. The ubiquitous garbage piles, the tech 'zines such as *PC World*, stacks of computer books, pizza boxes, magazines, crunched Coke cans, crumpled computer printout paper, and candy wrappers rose to the ceiling like tropical plants, competing for space with the baker's racks of computers, rows of computer terminals lined up on card tables, electric cords and creeping cables shooting out of the floor and through holes in the ceiling.

Levine shed his jacket, sat down before his monitor, and hit a button. His computer hummed awake. It was time. The pieces were in place. Now he was about to bring to life the heretical idea that he'd been nurturing ever since he was a teenage runner for Russo in the 1980s.

Typing rapidly, he called up the program. Inputting a few instructions and taking a deep breath, he turned it on. Island was alive.

"Island is here!" Levine wrote on Watcher News. "You now have the ability to execute Island orders from the safety and comfort of your own Watcher."

Wall Street would never be the same.

LEVINE was fully aware of Island's game-changing implications. In the lead-up to Island's rollout, he'd sent an internal e-mail on Watcher News boasting, "Island is our new trading system that will change the world."

Proud as a new parent, Levine was also *right*.

In its most basic form, Island was a computer program that simply matched buy and sell orders, bypassing the market makers. After Island matched the trades, it reported them to Nasdaq. The name evoked an "island" of orders where investors could retreat, a digital haven safe from the Nasdaq pickpockets (NYSE stocks at the time were largely off-limits to Island for regulatory reasons).

While simple, the idea was revolutionary. Lightning-fast and cheap to use, Island became the electronic pool that would spawn a whole new breed of trading machines, which would dominate the market in the next decade. Able to meet face-to-face on Island without the meddling influence of slow, unpredictable humans, automated trading algos were able to grow, adapt, mutate, and evolve. The weak algos died away, deprived of their lifeblood: money. The strong algos grew and thrived.

THE Island system was simple, at least on the surface. Traders who subscribed to Island got their data through an electronic feed called IHOST. Later named ITCH, the feed disseminated all information about buy and sell orders in Island—most recent prices, matched orders, the status of a stock, etc. Users might see an "H" pop up next to a stock price on their screen, indicating that trading in a stock had been halted, likely for some market-moving news release. A "W," short for Welcome, told users that they'd entered the Island system. "N" meant Good Night. (In his ITCH user's guide, Levine wrote that "N" meant "It's time to go home. Island is shutting down for the night. See you bright and early tomorrow.")

Another protocol called OUCH provided subscribers a superfast way to plug into Island and enter orders. (ITCH and OUCH didn't actually stand for anything. They were intended to make fun of Nasdaq's proclivity toward using four-letter conventions such as NQDS, Nasdaq Quotation Dissemination Service.)

The system was elegant and fast. What's more, Island published all trades on its website using a program called BookViewer—*for free*. Not only were the best buy and sell orders on the Island system visible, all orders *behind* those orders were visible. If one trader was bidding $50 for two hundred shares of Intel, while another was bidding $50¼ for five hundred shares, and another was at $50½ for one hundred shares, all the orders were there on the screen to see. And the entire book was available in machine-readable form—meaning computers with the right code could instantly track the book and react at lightning speeds.

This was all unheard-of. At the time, it was incredibly expensive for investors to get live stock market data, which was tightly controlled by Nasdaq, the NYSE, and the big trading firms. Websites such as Yahoo Finance or TheStreet.com published prices, but there was a fifteen-minute delay. No self-respecting trader would ever make a bet on fifteen-minute-old information. With Island, anyone could go to BookViewer and see live bids and offers for hundreds of stocks ticking across the screen.

Levine reveled in the taboo transparency—he was cracking open secret information and bringing it to the masses. It was the old hacker mantra: *Information wants to be free.* Levine had practical interests in mind as well, since publishing the data would advertise Island's mind-boggling speed and bring in more users. But his biggest priority was shining a light on the darkness.

Island was the first fully *lit pool.*

The irony of it all: Island was spawned by *bandits*, pick-off artists, professional scalpers exploiting regulatory loopholes, ethically chal-lenged traders like Maschler and Citron searching for the gray areas of the market. The core Datek trading strategy required speed, and Levine had delivered it in spades. Island was *built for bandits*—speed jockeys whose only goal was to jump in and out of a stock in minutes or even seconds. Speed was hardwired into the system, it was the fun-damental principle of Island's existence. This was a system that in the next decade would go on to dominate the U.S. stock market, and even-tually the global stock market.

BEYOND its speed and simplicity, Island's prime selling point was *price.* Trading on Island was dirt cheap. It charged $1 per trade, com-pared with $2.50 on Nasdaq. While trades entered into Island were sometimes executed on Nasdaq because a matching order didn't exist—costing Island $1.50—most were matched on Island itself.

Bottom line: There was nowhere to trade as cheaply or as quickly as on Island. In e-mails on Watcher News, Levine boasted that Island was better than everyone else.

"Island is run by us," he wrote. "We want Island to be good and fair and cheap and fast. We care. We are nice. SelectNet is run by Nasdaq. They don't care. Instinet is run by Reuters. They aren't nice. . . . All you need to get started is a phone line and the will to change your life. You have to take the first step. Won't you join us at Island?"

His world-changing ambitions were clear. On his website, josh.com (Home of the Monster Key), Levine wrote: "Click here to find out more about Island, my newest trading system designed to replace NASDAQ's SelectNet and REUTERS Instinet."

THAT spring, Levine went on a marketing tour to get the word out. He attended a series of trade shows alongside heavyweights such as Bloomberg and Nasdaq and Instinet.

He had a lot to learn about marketing. An important part of putting up a display booth at a trade show involved negotiating with union officials whose employees helped with the heavy lifting—like getting an electricity hookup. Levine was astonished to learn that this typically involved an under-the-table payout of as much as twenty grand. He refused outright, comparing the practice to extortion. There was no way he would compromise his ethics for a trade show.

The result: Island's trade show table generally looked like a grade-school science-fair project. A flimsy grass hula skirt encircled a rickety card table. Sans electricity, Levine sat in shadows—surrounded by brightly lit booths with flashy displays from deep-pocketed competitors like Instinet. Levine tried to hand out dollar bills or Susan B. Anthony coins impressed with an Island stamp, since it cost just a buck to execute a trade on Island.

Most attendees—think Armani-clad traders with Rolex watches

and greasy Gordon Gekko hairdos — didn't want the free dollar. Levine decided to stick to programming. He'd find others to pitch Island.

Better yet, Island would sell itself.

FROM the beginning, Levine's trading pool was humming like a Formula One race car. Using Island, Watcher users could blast trades into the market at speeds never before seen. Market makers were utterly outclassed and outgunned.

While Island had many orders flowing in from Watcher traders and a handful of other SOES firms, it wasn't enough to turn it into a substantial business. Island needed heavy, steady flow from traders that operated with jumbo volumes.

It soon got what it needed.

Not long after Island opened for business in January 1996, an obscure firm called Automated Trading Desk signed up, making it one of the first non-Watcher operations to use Levine's system.

Founded in 1988, ATD was a cutting-edge computer-driven outfit based in Mount Pleasant, South Carolina. It was a pioneer in the field of high-speed automated trading that years later would have a dramatic impact on Wall Street. In the 1980s, a finance professor named David Whitcomb and James Hawkes, a computer engineer who taught at the College of Charleston in South Carolina, had devised algorithms to predict the outcomes of horse races. They eventually applied those same algos to the stock market and launched ATD from Hawkes's Mount Pleasant home.

ATD later designed an artificial intelligence program that could act like a market maker, tracking dozens of market factors, such as trading volumes and the momentum of prices and predicting where prices would go during a period of roughly thirty seconds to two minutes. It called its pricing "engine" BORG, short for Brokered Order Routing Gateway, a nod to the race of evil cyborgs from the popular TV show *Star Trek: The Next Generation*.

In 1996, Whitcomb paid a visit to 50 Broad and met Levine. ATD had been trading on Instinet, but the firm was interested in expanding its scope. The ATD founder was instantly taken with Levine, and in short order his firm started trading on Island. It rapidly became one of the most prolific, if unlikely, SOES bandits, and the number one consumer of Island data. Instead of sweaty-palmed traders staring bug-eyed at their Watchers, however, ATD's computer was clocking the market and zipping in and out of stocks at high speeds. The ATD system was completely automated, far quicker off the mark than any human.

Eventually, several ATD employees joined up with Island before going on to work at other high-frequency firms, spreading the technique. Within a few years, automated traders such as ATD would make up the bulk of Island's volume. Eventually, they would make up the bulk of all stock trading in the United States.

ONE of the most successful and notorious automated traders would be a secretive, highly successful hedge fund based on Long Island, called Renaissance Technologies. At first, Renaissance's programmers—the firm was entirely run by mathematicians, scientists, and computer wonks—were dubious of Island. The reason: Datek. They were suspicious that the Datek bandits were secretly watching Island's flow and front-running it.

But Island proved too big to ignore. One day in the late 1990s, several of Renaissance's top executives, including a pair of AI experts who'd formerly worked at IBM, Peter Brown and Bob Mercer, paid a visit to 50 Broad. They were bemused by the giant lizard, the pool full of turtles, the trash. Renaissance's headquarters in East Setauket, Long Island, were as pristine as an Ivy League campus. More than anything, Brown and Mercer were deeply impressed by Levine, whom they instantly realized was a programming genius with a profound understanding of the market's plumbing.

Like ATD, Renaissance deployed cutting-edge AI programs to build its models and guide its trading. But Renaissance's AI was an evolutionary leap beyond what any other firm had ever attempted, creating a strategy that would turn Renaissance into the most profitable trading machine in the world, with annual returns averaging north of 40 percent a year. Island's high-speed platform was an ideal match for its strategies.

The Island-ATD-Renaissance fusion was a vision of the future in which high-speed AI-guided robots would operate on lightning-fast electronic pools, controlling the daily ebb and flow of the market. The AI Bots poured their valuable liquidity into Island, which, in turn, made it possible for the Bots to operate at high frequencies. They fed off one another, creating a virtuous cycle that would become unstoppable. Little-known outfits such as Timber Hill, Tradebot, RGM, and Getco would soon start trading on Island, forming the emergent ganglia of a new space-age trading organism driven by machines. Tricked-out artificial intelligence systems designed to scope out hidden pockets in the market where they could ply their trades powered many of these systems.

In the process, the very structure of how the U.S. stock market worked would shift to meet the endless needs of the Bots. The human middlemen, though they didn't know it, were being phased out, doomed as dinosaurs. And the machines were breeding more machines in an endless cycle of innovation, as programmers pushed the boundaries of speed more ruthlessly than Olympic sprinters. Trading algorithms would mutate, grow, and evolve, feeding off one another like evolving species in a vast and growing digital pool.

In the 1990s, that future had been inconceivable to all but a few visionaries—such as Levine, who had a bird's-eye view of the market as it evolved. By late 1996, roughly *half* of all of Nasdaq's SelectNet trades came from Island—from a single Dell computer sitting in a garbage-cluttered office on 50 Broad (Island trades that didn't cross internally were routed out to SelectNet). Between July 1 and September 31, 1996, orders to trade 5.6 billion shares flowed through Island's pipes, resulting in transactions valued at $22.1 billion.

The irony was rich. Island had become Nasdaq's biggest customer.

# CHAPTER NINE

# THE GREEN MACHINE

A whisper of a smile played across Janet Reno's face as she stepped to the podium inside the Justice Department's Washington, D.C., headquarters. Now and then the flash of a camera reflected off the pear-size lenses of her glasses.

Bill Clinton's attorney general was thrilled. It was July 17, 1996. The massive settlement Reno was about to announce was pure political gold, a strike against the fat cats on Wall Street in the name of the little guy. Twenty-four major Nasdaq securities firms had been charged with inflating spreads in Nasdaq stocks, picking the pockets of mom-and-pop investors, just as the Christie-Schultz study on odd-eighth spreads had first revealed in 1994.

"American investors had to pay more to buy and sell stocks than they would have if there had been true competition," Reno said in her flat-toned voice. "We have found substantial evidence of coercion and other misconduct in this industry."

It had been a two-year investigation, one aided behind the scenes by SOES bandits such as Harvey Houtkin and Shelly Maschler. Firms named in the settlement (none of whom ever admitted their guilt) included Wall Street titans Lehman Brothers, Goldman Sachs, Bear Stearns, Morgan Stanley, Smith Barney, and PaineWebber. A

class-action lawsuit swiftly followed, resulting in a $1 billion settle-
ment. It was the largest antitrust settlement in history at the time.

Soon after the Justice Department issued its findings, the SEC
lowered the boom. Released on August 7, 1996, the SEC's report was
a fatal blow, the result of Leo Wang's tireless investigation into Nasdaq's shady operations. "The investigation uncovered a number of
matters of fundamental concern about the operations and structure
of the NASD and Nasdaq market," the report read. "The Commission
believes that significant changes to the NASD and Nasdaq market are
warranted."

Aside from its most damaging find—price-fixing on a massive
scale among market makers—the report drew a bead on one of
Levine's biggest complaints: the practice of backing away. "Certain
market makers at times did not honor their quotations for those
with whom they preferred not to trade and 'backed away' from their
quotes," the report found. What's more, dealers routinely ignored
complaints about backing away (many of which came from Levine).

While the NASD frequently ignored such complaints, the SEC
discovered that many NASD officials seemed obsessed with one particular group of traders: SOES bandits. Going after SOES traders became an "enforcement priority for the NASD," the report stated.

The report was a smashing victory for the bandits. Aided by the
landmark Christie-Schultz study that showed that Nasdaq market
makers ignored odd-eighth quotes, as well as a small band of allies
inside the SEC and the Justice Department, the scrappy bunch of
traders had won a major battle against the NASD, a giant organization that oversaw more than 5,400 securities firms and half a million
brokers.

There was more to come—much more. Soon after the SEC released the report, it proposed a set of rules that would strike at the
heart of the Nasdaq market-making monopoly and set the table for
the rise of the machines—and Island.

Dubbed the Order-Handling Rules, a reference to how market makers "handle" customer orders, the new SEC rules forced Nasdaq to post quotes from competing firms alongside quotes from market makers on their national system.

If a Datek trader put up an offer to buy Intel for $22, and the best market maker quote was to buy for $21.90, the Datek quote would appear on Nasdaq's system for the entire market to see. In the past, the Datek orders not executed on SOES would go to market makers, who could simply choose to back away from them. No one outside the closed Nasdaq circle could see the orders, denying investors the opportunity to purchase Intel at a lower price or sell at a higher price.

The rules created more competition for Nasdaq market makers and brought more discipline to the overall system. But there was another target: Instinet, the private market Levine had tried to cut a deal with before creating Island.

The largest venue for trading Nasdaq stocks—next to Nasdaq—Instinet had become a private playground of institutional investors and market makers, a dark pool where dealers swapped stocks, often at prices better than those offered to the public. Market makers could use Instinet to their advantage in a myriad of ways. They could buy a stock for a client while offering to sell the same stock over Instinet at a better price. To the rest of the market, the Instinet side of the offer was invisible—it was dark.

More creative market makers could sell a stock they actually wanted to buy on Nasdaq or the NYSE in order to trick other traders into selling, pushing down the price. Meanwhile, they'd snap up big chunks of the stock on the sly on Instinet. It all worked very nicely . . . for the Wall Street insiders.

Instinet quotes were available only through a private computer known on trading floors as the Green Machine due to its iridescent green screen. Unless you had a Green Machine, you couldn't get Instinet's quotes. Most Nasdaq market makers, of course, had the machine, as did many institutional investors. Regular investors didn't, and couldn't get it, since the system was designed to be exclusive — that was its selling point.

The SEC was out to stop these games and force Instinet's quotes into the open. To that end, the commission designated an entirely new trading entity called an electronic communications network, or ECN. Anyone who had the technology could create an ECN, which essentially would be a hub for computer traders that would either match trades internally or send quotes to Nasdaq. Bids and offers on ECNs that didn't match internally would appear directly alongside market maker quotes on the Nasdaq system.

Instinet just so happened to meet all of the technical qualifications of an ECN — an electronic communications network over which stocks are swapped — so Instinet quotes would no longer be secret.

Island happened to meet those technical qualifications as well.

The rules weren't just a game changer — they created *a new game*. The market would be transformed. Before the rules, Nasdaq dealers controlled the markets' ebb and flow. With the Order-Handling Rules, the entire Nasdaq marketplace would shift toward an electronic platform wide open to computer-driven trading. Quick-draw day traders using electronic systems like Island could suddenly compete head-to-head with big market-making firms such as Goldman Sachs and Morgan Stanley. It was as if minor-league pitching prospects were thrust into the majors with the stroke of the regulator's pen.

The monopolistic stranglehold the big dealer firms had on the stock market was about to be cracked. The phone-based system of human dealers would quickly become a screen-based cyberpunk network of computer jockeys born and bred in electronic pools such as Island.

With the good-old-boy market makers sidelined, AI-based trading systems would become viable. Math and computer whizzes had been toying with AI on Wall Street for years, but the effort largely had been a failure. At Hull Trading in Chicago, Haim Bodek would tinker with machine learning, but the plumbing for such trading wasn't in place yet. To be sure, Renaissance and ATD used AI to *generate* trading models—but AI wasn't part of the actual trading process itself, the implementation of the order in the market (at least until the ECNs came along). The split-second precision demanded by dynamic AI algos that could instantly shift gears as the market changed wasn't possible with people in the mix. Those quirky market makers were simply too human, prone to mistakes, delays, or pure, old-fashioned greed.

Another factor that would fuel AI: flowing streams of digitized data. Through its ITCH feed, Island spit out far more machine-readable data—information coded in a way that computer programs could make sense of it—about stock transactions than Nasdaq and the NYSE combined. The latest trades, bids and offers, volumes, depth of book—it was all available in digital form. For a computer with the bandwidth to crunch it all, it was like seeing the market in 3-D Technicolor compared with an ancient black-and-white cathode-ray tube with bad reception.

The human dealers didn't stand a chance against the rising warehouses of supercomputers armed with the latest advances in AI. Just as IBM's Deep Blue was beating the world chess champion, Garry Kasparov, scientists on Wall Street were hard at work designing trading machines that no human could match—not even Warren Buffett.

Many of these advances remained well in the future. But a major victory for the machines had been won. With the Order-Handling Rules, the upstart electronic pools would be going head-to-head with the big boys.

And there was no pool as swift and surrounded by as many undulating waves of liquidity as Island. While Instinet was the largest alternative network, it was stuck in the past just like Nasdaq and NYSE, relying on human dealers to match trades.

Behind it all: the reclusive computer genius Josh Levine, who kept tap-tapping away on his Dell computers in his cluttered office at 50 Broad.

■ ■ ■

IN the days after the release of the Order-Handling Rules, Levine worked day and night, feverishly upgrading Island's code. It was a race against time—against the planned rollout of the rules in January 1997.

To keep Datek's traders up to speed, Levine sent a series of e-mails with instructions on how to download Island's software and use it.

"How do I get my Island?" he wrote. Simply send an e-mail containing the text "ISLAND IS GONNA MAKE ME RICH!" Levine quipped that the e-mail "must be heartfelt or I may not respond."

He came up with a slogan for Island: "The Power to Move the Market." The message was clear: With Island and the SEC's new rules, everyday investors could put up bids and offers that could compete directly with Nasdaq's market makers and, by doing so, actually *move the market.*

Nasdaq wasn't sanguine about the market's future—or its own. Behind the scenes, it was telling the SEC that the new rules would be a disaster. If every trader on the planet could go head-to-head with market makers, chaos would rule—and the market itself could crash due to an overflow of data from the new electronic systems.

Mark Tellini, one of the chief architects of the Order-Handling Rules at the SEC, was skeptical of Nasdaq's claims of impending disaster. Soon after crafting the rules in early 1996, he'd heard about an upstart band of tech heads at a place called Island who were matching trades electronically on a single Dell computer. Nasdaq market makers were nowhere to be found. He soon discovered that Island wasn't a *band* of tech heads at all. A single computer programmer in his mid-twenties was behind it.

Tellini called up Levine to learn more. He told Levine about Nasdaq's claims that the new rules would crash their market. The programmer replied flat out that Nasdaq was blowing smoke, delaying for the sake of delays. The threat about the market crashing was a pure scare tactic if not a bald-faced lie, Levine said. If Island could match orders electronically, why couldn't Nasdaq?

A meeting of all three sides was set up. On October 23, 1996, at the SEC's Washington, D.C., office, Levine met with the NASD chief economist John Wall and Nasdaq's senior technology guru Mark Denat, as well as Tellini and several other SEC officials.

The conversation quickly became heated. Wall, a clean-cut, fatherly figure in thick-framed glasses, had seen what Island could do. Nasdaq had been flooded time and again when Island had been turned on full throttle, pounding it with orders and overflowing its pipes. He said he was concerned that Island would crash Nasdaq's computer system on a daily basis if given carte blanche to blast away.

Levine scoffed, his eyes narrowing as he turned his intense gaze on Wall and Denat. He knew from personal experience that Nasdaq could create a network to handle the traffic. "You wouldn't have any problems if you'd automate your system," he said. "Just execute all the orders on SelectNet that match. Simple."

"It's not that easy," Wall said.

"Why not?"

Wall didn't have an answer. Nasdaq tech guru Denat, for his part, didn't trust Levine. He'd had his own battles over SOES with Shelly Maschler through the years and felt the whole operation was simply out to make a fast buck. Denat didn't believe for a second that Levine was actually interested in *making the market better.*

Tellini was convinced, however. He and the other SEC staffers looked at one another in amazement as Levine proceeded to break down Nasdaq's arguments piece by piece. It was a virtuoso performance. Quickly, it was apparent that the baby-faced programmer understood Nasdaq's plumbing far better than Nasdaq's own experts.

At bottom, Levine was making a simple argument: Nasdaq should simply become *like Island*—automate the system. Execute all orders that match instantly. There was no reason *not* to do it, except greed.

It was a nonstarter, a conversation killer. What would all the market makers do if Nasdaq were computerized? It was heresy, an idea Nasdaq would fight for years.

More important, Levine's deft attack on Nasdaq's stonewalling convinced the SEC that it was on the right track. Without Levine—and without Island as a clear example of how an electronic network could seamlessly match buy and sell orders—Nasdaq might have chipped away at the new rules until they were toothless. Nothing would have changed.

Instead, everything changed.

EVEN while Nasdaq's old guard stuck their heads in the sand, a number of younger Nasdaq employees could see the world shifting beneath their feet. The ECNs were there to stay. In a scramble to prepare, Nasdaq organized a group of experts to study the impact the new rules—slated to go live January 10, 1997—would have on its business.

An economist named Dean Furbush led the group. Ever since Black Monday in 1987, when he was an economist at the SEC, Furbush had been knee-deep in arcane market structure issues. After leaving government work in the early 1990s, he'd spent three years at Economist Inc., a Washington, D.C., think tank. One of his first jobs was to consult for Nasdaq on the Christie-Schultz study. Eventually, Nasdaq hired him to work full-time on SOES issues.

Soon after landing at Nasdaq, Furbush hired a young researcher from Economist Inc. named Jamie Selway. Furbush told Selway he wanted to form a back-channel liaison with Island. Selway would be his point man.

"Be careful," Furbush told him. "It's highly sensitive. We've been at war with these guys for years."

Selway first contacted Josh Levine in August 1996. But Nasdaq's head-in-the-sand honchos got wind of the move and told him to back off. They still hoped to convince the SEC to shift course. By November, the gag order on Selway had been lifted as it became clear to everyone that the Order-Handling Rules were a fait accompli.

On November 21, Selway shot off an e-mail to Levine.

"A while back you and I spoke briefly," he wrote. "Dean and I are very interested in learning from you/getting your input on some issues, some of which are pretty hot as Jan 10 nears (and some pretty sweeping changes take place). I think this could be valuable to you too; I get the impression that you haven't quite had a positive experience with our organization, and I think that's no good for either party."

Selway said he wanted to meet. "I'd like to do something outside the normal channels, if you know what I mean. I'd love to work something out, if you're up for it."

Levine responded—somewhat ironically—the next day.

"Hey Jamie, I love the NASD. I would love to talk to you. Just let me know what you need to know."

They set up a meeting for early December. Selway and Furbush caught a train to New York to meet with Levine and Jeff Citron at 50 Broad.

While there were practical issues to work out, the initial meeting was more about sizing one another up. Citron, as usual, did most of the talking. Levine sat slumped in his chair, mute and bleary-eyed.

"I'm beat," he told Selway. "I've been up thirty-six hours writing code."

After the meeting, Selway and Furbush got a look at Levine's office. Turtles scrambled in a swimming pool. A bazooka leaned in a corner. Amazed that Island's ragtag operation could have caused such a headache for a giant like Nasdaq, Selway wondered, *What kind of wacked-out place is this?*

Citron showed off Island's "data center," the baker's racks stacked with Dell towers crammed side to side, a dizzying tangle of cords winding into their CPUs from all directions. Compared with Nasdaq's state-of-the-art center in Trumbull, Connecticut, where employees had to badge in to its sealed rooms full of massive Sun Microsystems servers, it seemed laughably primitive. Cables jutted out of the wall and through holes in the ceiling. Wires snaked across the floor. Was that *a lizard*?

"I could trip on this wire and unplug your market?" Furbush asked.

While it seemed as if Island was little more than a science fair project held together by bubblegum and Scotch tape, Levine's system was in fact far more robust than Nasdaq's. He was exploiting a relatively new technique in computer science known as *distributed computing*. Rather than centralize the network on a single massive mainframe, he'd spread Island's system across multiple hard drives. If one drive got fried, it might briefly impact a customer or two, but the network would remain up and running. Furbush could trip on several wires at once, and Island would keep cranking away. And anytime he needed more juice, Levine simply bought another computer and plugged it in. If a computer had a hardware problem, he'd swap it out for a new one.

Nasdaq's space age Trumbull network, despite its bleeding-edge hardware, was far more exposed to systemwide crashes and data bottlenecks. If one server went down, the whole system could crash. It was large, clunky, complex, and slow. Island was simple, easy to fix, massively scalable, and blazingly fast. (Word about Island's next-generation durability spread well beyond the world of finance. David Filo and Jerry Yang, the founders of Yahoo!, once visited Island to learn about how Levine's system worked.)

Furbush was impressed with Levine. Citron, he thought, was a fast-talking player piggybacking on Levine's genius. "Josh was incredibly open and wicked smart," he recalls. "Here was this kid who'd figured out this awesome system. He saw that the world was moving in the direction of where it is now."

Selway also hit it off with Levine, as well as with Levine's friend Peter Stern. Earlier that year, Stern had launched Datek Online, one of the first PC-based day-trading platforms for regular investors. Levine and Stern had met at Carnegie Mellon in the late 1980s. In

1995, Levine convinced Stern to move to New York from Washington, D.C., where he'd worked for a military contractor that designed helicopters, to join him in hacking the market. Datek Online charged $9.99 per trade, making it the cheapest online trading service in the country. It was also the fastest, and the growing ranks of day traders using it added to that precious liquidity sloshing through Island.

A few weeks after Selway's visit, Levine and Stern invited him to a New Year's Eve party they were throwing at a Stratton, Vermont, ski lodge. Selway and his girlfriend traveled to New York and met the two programmers at a downtown helipad. Citron, hearing about the trip, had offered up his helicopter.

As the copter swerved away from the jagged skyline of downtown Manhattan, Stern, drawing on his time with the helicopter designer, explained how it was something of a miracle that helicopters could actually remain airborne—striking terror into the heart of Selway's nerve-racked girlfriend. At the lodge, Levine kept serving up Mudslides, a mix of Baileys Irish Cream and Kahlúa.

It was a strange experience for Selway, a straight arrow who'd spent the first part of his professional career as a loyal worker bee operating inside the system. But there was something seductive about these young, rich, rebellious outsiders who were taking on the powers of the market—and seemed to be winning.

It wouldn't be long before Selway joined their side.

EVEN as Island was poised for its greatest victories, dark clouds were forming over Datek. In late 1996, the SEC fined Shelly Maschler $675,000 and dinged Jeff Citron for $20,000, for violating SOES rules. Maschler was suspended from association with any NASD member for a year. He stepped down from his lead role at Datek, though he remained a constant presence in the office. Citron, for his part, fiercely held on to his top spot at Datek—and for good reason. Profits at Datek were booming. In 1996, it made $95 million, up from $3.8 million in 1992.

Island powered relentlessly forward, propelled by Levine's nimble brain. The challenge was epic. All of Wall Street seemed lined up against Datek and Island. But Levine was convinced he was working for the forces of good. In his mind, the market was designed to rip off the individual investor and line the pockets of fat-cat bankers and traders. It was a rigged game.

Island was going to blow it up. Island was going to *change the world*.

Compensation for revolution was nothing to smirk at, of course. In 1996, Datek Securities paid Citron and Levine nearly $145 million for the use of software and services such as Island and the Watcher (as CEO, Citron pocketed most of those revenues).

There were, to be sure, competitors lining up. In time, one of the most successful—one that would compete head-to-head with Island—emerged from the trading Mecca of the Midwest, Chicago. In a tip of the hat to Levine & Co., as well as an open challenge, its name was Archipelago: a cluster of islands. Its creator was a mercurial entrepreneur who would rise to become a kingpin of the stock market in the following decade. Like Maschler and Levine, he would butt heads with Nasdaq, the NYSE, and a host of other entrenched powers on Wall Street. And he would win—big.

# CHAPTER TEN

# ARCHIPELAGO

J erry Putnam picked up the phone in his office on 100 South Wacker Street in downtown Chicago. On the line: an Instinet representative, Island's Josh Levine, and Eugene Lopez, director of market services for Nasdaq. It was late December 1996. The discussion concerned the nuts and bolts of implementing the Order-Handling Rules and certain technical aspects surrounding the new electronic communications networks, or ECNs.

Putnam could barely contain his excitement. Tall, stocky, with a friendly wide-open face, quick with a laugh or a bawdy joke, Putnam had been scrambling for years in the back warrens of high finance to hit a home run. And he thought he'd finally done it. He'd developed a new electronic trading network called Archipelago Holdings, which he believed could go toe-to-toe with Island and Instinet. While the new rules implied that practically anyone could build an ECN and plug into Nasdaq, few had picked up on the fact. Putnam that fall had figured it out and cobbled together his system in a matter of months. In fact, Archipelago was in many ways more of a thought experiment than a piece of technology.

But Putnam was in for a rude shock. Toward the end of the call, Lopez said, "Jerry, I need to talk to you."

"Sure, no problem, Gene," Putnam replied.

Lopez had bad news. Nasdaq had previously indicated that the new ECNs would need to pony up a quarter-million dollars for an account to cover their trading activities. If a trader using the ECN lost a huge chunk of money and couldn't cover it, the ECN would have to help foot the bill.

"We've changed our minds," Lopez said. "We need a million."

Putnam's stomach quaked.

"I don't have that capital and you know it, Gene," he said.

"That's too bad," Lopez replied flatly and hung up.

Putnam felt faint. In just a few weeks, the SEC's Order-Handling Rules would go into effect for fifty of the most active Nasdaq stocks—heavy hitters like Microsoft, Oracle, and Whole Foods—allowing just a few ECNs to post their quotes alongside established market makers. Putnam worried that the SEC would put a freeze on their ECN experiment after its initial test run. The only way to get in on the game was to be ready at the starting gate.

Nasdaq wasn't going to make it easy. Lopez was telling Putnam he needed more money—three-quarters of a million more. It was chump change for Instinet; Island, backed by the likes of Jeff Citron, also had deep pockets. Putnam, however, had tapped himself out just getting Archipelago started. He was livid. *They're trying to destroy me at the last minute.*

Right after the call, he rushed to his clearing firm, Southwest Securities, just down the block on South Wacker Street. He explained that unless he had the extra cash immediately, Archipelago would never get off the ground. To his immense relief, Southwest agreed and provided a $750,000 loan in exchange for a 5 percent stake in the company.

Finally, after weeks of foot-dragging, on January 20, 1997—a tenday delay from the initial target date—the Order-Handling Rules went into effect. Putnam flipped the switch on his machine and quotes generated through its system went live alongside Island, Instinet, and another ECN called Bloomberg Tradebook.

Putnam had barely made it—but he had a toehold in the market, and he wouldn't let it go.

ALL his life, Putnam had chased his vision of the American Dream. In other words: He wanted to be rich. Very rich. But until the Order-Handling Rules came along, it looked as if he'd never succeed. The son of a career army officer, Putnam was born in 1958 and grew up in the middle-class neighborhood of West Philadelphia, home of *American Bandstand*. As a student at West Catholic High School in the 1970s, Putnam excelled in his accounting class, but his true passion was sculling. A rower for a private club team, he competed in national championship matches in his junior and senior years of high school.

Putnam's early years in finance were less than auspicious. After earning a bachelor's degree at the University of Pennsylvania's Wharton School in 1981, he took a job at Dean Witter. After failing to pull in much business, he was let go. During the following decade, he worked at firms ranging from PaineWebber to Prudential Financial, with middling success. Along the way, he met Paul Adcock—Paulie to his friends—a skilled trader of futures contracts tied to commodities such as oil or sugar. A farm boy from central Illinois, Adcock would prove to be one of the most loyal and longest-lasting members of the Archipelago team.

By 1994, Putnam's career had hit dead end after dead end. He was running low on cash and had just bought an expensive house. His back against the wall, he decided to launch his own brokerage, called Terra Nova Trading. The name, a Latin term meaning "new land," marked Putnam's vision for the future—and a desperate hope that his luck would turn.

But luck didn't seem to be on Putnam's side. Soon after Terra Nova's launch, a big hedge fund client he'd hoped to sign up shut its doors. Putnam had a broker dealer, and hardly any business.

His career in finance seemed doomed. Talking it over with Adcock, who had joined Terra Nova, Putnam joked that he was thinking about opening up a bait shop in Wisconsin, where he liked to fish. Adcock talked about going back to work on his father's farm.

Then Putnam met Stuart Townsend, founder of a trading-software development firm called Townsend Analytics. Townsend had created a real-time Windows-based stock-quote system called RealTick, software that tracked the up-and-down "ticks" of security prices. The software was quickly gaining ground on trading floors across Wall Street. Akin to Josh Levine's Watcher, RealTick gave traders the ability to track bids and offers for stocks using raw Nasdaq data. Since it was Windows-based, it had the potential to become widely adapted as PCs, loaded with Microsoft's software, made their way into more and more trading rooms.

Putnam became convinced that RealTick had massive potential. Markets were becoming increasingly electronic. Computers were transforming trading in ways few could imagine. RealTick could be at the vanguard of the revolution—and hold the key to limitless riches.

Then Putnam learned that a number of traders in Chicago had started using a computer system to buy and sell small chunks of stocks in rapid-fire fashion on Nasdaq. The system, of course, was SOES.

It went back to Harvey Houtkin, the New Jersey trader who'd first introduced Maschler to SOES. Chicago had been one of the first cities where Houtkin had opened a SOES trading operation, for good reason. The Windy City was fast becoming a hub of electronic trading. The Chicago Mercantile Exchange had developed automated systems to trade futures contracts linked to everything from the price of gold and oil to stock indexes such as the S&P 500. The Chicago Board of Trade was implementing systems to electronically track and trade stock options.

Word about SOES had been spreading in Chicago, and Putnam and Townsend started to discuss opening a SOES trading outfit of their own. It was a way to put Terra Nova to work, and it could spur demand for RealTick.

To learn more about SOES, Putnam and a few colleagues traveled to New Jersey and attended Houtkin's SOES training program in February 1995. Rather than learning the Xs and Os of how to trade on SOES, Putnam was more interested in learning how to start his own trading outfit. What equipment do you need? How do you hook up with Nasdaq? What kind of fees can you charge?

Soon after, Putnam set up shop on the fifteenth floor of an old AT&T building on 318 West Adams in the Chicago Loop, blocks away from the Chicago Board of Trade. He wired up computers equipped with Nasdaq Level II Workstation software and RealTick and took out ads in trade publications for the operation. He called the firm Chicago Trading & Arbitrage.

---

**POINT, CLICK & TRADE!**

*Have you thought about becoming a*

**DAY TRADER?**

State of the art executions including SOES
Proprietary momentum & search algorithm software
cTa . . . Chicago Trading & Arbitrage, LLC

318 W. Adams
Chicago, IL 60606
Call us at: 1 (888) U-SELL-HI

---

About a dozen traders signed on. The operation was primitive compared to Datek's trading machine at 50 Broad, armed with Levine's Watcher and Monster Key. Traders seeing opportunities on their screens had to shout out orders to a clerk—at times Putnam himself—who would enter the order through the Level II Workstation. It was tedious and time-consuming.

Putnam and Townsend thought there had to be a better way. The orders, they realized, could be entered far more quickly if RealTick had point-and-click mouse functionality. The traders could be quicker on the draw—and it would generate more fees for Chicago Trading, since there would be more orders. Following that line of thought, Townsend turned RealTick into a direct-access order-entry system.

In place by July, the system was a hit. Chicago Trading was soon routing hundreds, then thousands, of SOES orders to Nasdaq a day. But Putnam wanted more.

That meant opening up new trading rooms outside Chicago. There was one major obstacle: Each trading room needed a Nasdaq Level II Workstation to process the trades. That was expensive. Putnam didn't have the money.

Then he had an idea: Since Chicago Trading was routing orders to the Level II Workstation from computers programmed with point-and-click RealTick software in the West Adams office, why couldn't trading rooms elsewhere link through the Internet to *the same machine*? He wouldn't need to purchase new gear. He simply needed to set up a routing system between the satellite trading rooms and the Chicago office.

Putnam quickly established ties with roughly five day-trading branch offices in cities ranging from White Plains, New York, to San Jose, California. Orders were routed from the "trading salons," as Putnam called them, to the central computer at 318 West Adams, generating fees for Terra Nova.

Putnam was working like a mule, putting in weekends, staying late at the office, coming in at the crack of dawn—if he left at all. But the money was good, and by mid-1996 he felt as if he were back on his feet again.

But he was exhausted, worn ragged by the furious expansion of his day-trading empire. In August, he came down with a virus and was bedridden for days. While recovering, he started combing through a three-hundred-page document just issued by the SEC: the Order-Handling Rules.

As Putnam plunged into the rules—reading the proposal beginning to end several times in growing stages of excitement—he began to see the incredible potential of the electronic communications networks the rules created.

One question on Putnam's mind was whether Nasdaq planned to build an ECN of its own. Rather than letting outsiders take away its business, Nasdaq could simply build its own electronic matching system. If it did, most traders would simply route their orders to Nasdaq's pool. Some might continue to use Island and Instinet, but there was little hope for new contenders. It made perfect sense. Indeed, Nasdaq would be *insane* not to do this, Putnam thought. But he'd heard nothing about a Nasdaq-owned ECN.

Then he learned that Nasdaq was giving a presentation about the Order-Handling Rules in downtown Chicago. Sitting in the audience, Putnam didn't hear any mention of a Nasdaq ECN.

He shot up his hand.

"You're going to create one of these networks, right?" he asked.

"No, we're not," the Nasdaq presenter said.

Putnam was stunned. After the presentation, he pushed to the front of the room.

"I don't understand," he said. "Why wouldn't you do this?"

"If you've got a problem with it, write your congressman," the Nasdaq official quipped.

Putnam quickly realized that Nasdaq was protecting a vested interest—its market makers. It was the same head-in-the-sand attitude Levine had encountered. Nasdaq didn't want to encourage electronic trading. It wanted to maintain its phone-based system in which dealers controlled the ebb and flow of the market. That was a mistake, Putnam thought. And it made Nasdaq vulnerable.

"Well, maybe I'll just start my own," he said.

"I guess you could try," the official replied.

Putnam knew it was a long shot. He was well acquainted with Island, since Chicago Trading had linked to it. Like Datek, he'd cobbled together a group of day traders who could provide liquidity for his own pool. But he didn't have remotely the same amount of volume that Datek generated. Island also had powerful outside users such as Automated Trading Desk. Chicago Trading simply didn't generate enough liquidity to provide consistent, reliable matches for fast-moving traders.

Putnam's solution was counterintuitive — and ingenious. Why not create an electronic routing system that could send orders to *other pools*? If a Chicago Trading client put in an order to buy Intel for $20, the system would first check to see if it had an internal match. If it didn't, it would instantly route the order to the pool that had a match, whether it be Nasdaq, Island, or Instinet.

The system would be a conduit, tapping into the volume generated by the *entire* market. Putnam's pool wouldn't be an isolated "island" of liquidity, it would be *a chain of islands* connected electronically — an *archipelago* of linked pools. Other pools, including Island's, only matched orders internally before routing out to Nasdaq.

Putnam acted fast as the implementation for the new rules closed in. Scrambling to figure out the code, he repeatedly called up Levine and grilled him for information. The Island programmer proved helpful, even going so far as to e-mail pieces of Island code to Putnam. Levine even showed Putnam how he could build a direct link between Island and Archipelago to avoid having to go through Nasdaq's antiquated system.

On December 27, 1996, Putnam and Townsend founded Archipelago Holdings. Each held a 50 percent stake in the company. Putnam filed the appropriate papers with the state of Illinois and the SEC and set up a brokerage account with Nasdaq.

That same day, Levine sent Putnam an e-mail in reply to Putnam's inquiries about testing the connection between their systems before the new rules went live. Levine told Putnam he would "build the link" between Island and Archipelago, thereby erecting the plumbing, connecting what would one day become key parts of two of the biggest exchanges in the world.

"I'd love to meet you live and in person," he added. "To be honest, I don't see myself in Chicago anytime soon, but if you are in NYC, I would be honored to take you to dinner and give you the mandatory office tour."

# CHAPTER ELEVEN

# EVERYONE CARES

The SOES bandits were spreading, growing, mutating. First there was Shelly Maschler, Houtkin's partner when Black Monday struck. Maschler's hothouse genius Josh Levine built the Watcher, then Monster Key, then Island. Then Jerry Putnam took Houtkin's SOES trading class, leading to Archipelago.

Then there was Block Trading, a Houston-based SOES firm set up in 1992 by ex-Lehman stockbrokers Chris Block and Jeff Burke. Block and Burke, like Putnam, had taken Houtkin's SOES training class in New Jersey. Their trading software: the Watcher.

Realizing that there could be a gold mine in trading software, they launched an effort to build their own. Working out of Block Trading's Houston headquarters, an Irish computer programmer named Philip Berber started writing code for a trading system that was remarkably similar to Watcher. Out of that program was born CyberTrader. In the next few years, CyberTrader would become one of the most widely used day-trading programs in the country, wielded by stay-at-home dads, doctors and housewives, teenagers and bored retirees, providing the rocket fuel for the coming dot-com bubble. After Charles Schwab purchased Berber's company for nearly half a billion in 2000, Cyber-Trader became a household name synonymous with online investing.

CyberTrader and its ilk, such as Datek Online, marked an evolution of the day-trading phenomenon. Instead of popping in and out of positions in seconds, trying to scalp a fleeting spread, traders using CyberTrader were surfing on *momentum*. They'd follow charts, hunt for patterns, plot graphs, run formulas and programs to capture stocks moving sharply up or down, before piling in, often using a hefty dose of leverage. These were not weekend warriors buying shares of IBM and Intel for their retirement funds from their clunky E*Trade accounts. These traders were wagering tens of thousands in huge one-way bets—often on small-cap stocks that could be pushed around by a single trade.

Other day-trading firms started mimicking the style, which became more and more popular as the dot-com bubble took off—and drove that bubble to new heights.

Unlike SOES bandits, who always ended the day with no money in the market, the momentum jockeys often rode positions for days. Many kept pressing their bets at night as the new electronic markets offered after-hours trading.

As more day traders piled in, volatility, the lifeblood of momentum trading, exploded. Tech stocks like Intel, Cisco, and eBay made massive moves, gaining momentum that would draw in even more traders surfing the waves.

These new gunslinging *mo-mo* jockeys piling into dot-com stocks and IPOs turned Nasdaq into a frenzied Wild West, pushing stock values to levels that had no relation whatsoever to fundamentals. The profits didn't matter—it was all about the digits flashing on the screens of their CyberTraders, their Watchers and RealTicks, the price of the stock, how much it had moved, how much it was going to move.

And so the market turned into a massive online casino, an electronic lottery holding out fantastic riches to the few, the lucky. Even risk-averse, staid fund managers began piling in, since the exploding dot-com prices made their ho-hum 10-percent-a-year returns look ridiculous. Before long, it became a nationwide mania rumbling headlong toward disaster.

■  ■  ■

BACK in New York, Levine had been feeling the strain of almost single-handedly running one of the fastest growing trading centers in the country. All the twenty-hour days, the hard work keeping Island humming, were wearing on him. For the first time, he was experiencing enough fatigue and stress to give him a glimpse of what it might feel like to burn out. He didn't want to go there. He needed help.

Luckily, he was about to get it in spades. Indeed, the small cadre of traders, programmers, and lawyers that Island would hire in the next few years would form an elite vanguard who would spread Levine's gospel of electronic trading throughout the market. They would rise to the top echelons of the U.S. exchanges and work behind the scenes at the most advanced trading operations the world had ever seen.

Levine's first hire was a downsized clone of Levine himself. In the summer of 1995, an eighteen-year-old student from the University of Texas named Will Sterling took a job at Block Trading's Houston headquarters. Sterling had planned to go back to school in the fall, but when Block offered him the chance to run its first branch office in Tyler, Texas, he dropped out of college and never returned.

At Tyler, Sterling started working with Philip Berber to develop CyberTrader. While doing so, he frequently spoke on the phone with Levine, since Island was one of Block's primary trading pools. One day during a trip to set up a Block satellite office in New York City in the summer of 1997, he gave Levine a call.

"Guess what, I'm in New York," he said.

"Awesome," Levine said. "Want to meet for dinner?"

They met at Tortilla Flats, a small West Village Mexican restaurant. The two felt almost as if they were staring into a slightly distorted mirror. They were both short, trim, and had sandy-brown buzz cuts. But their personalities couldn't have been more different. While Levine was laid back and prone to practical jokes, Sterling was far more businesslike—more "Wall Street." Over tacos and salsa, they discussed how the new Order-Handling Rules had changed the game for day trading, and for Island. Levine was seeing more orders flow into his pool every day.

He could see that Sterling clearly knew the business end of electronic trading and had a strong grasp of the technical details.

"You should come meet with us," Levine said. "You should meet Jeff," he added, referring to Citron, at the time the manager of Island (Levine didn't have a formal title). Sterling smiled and nodded. He knew what Levine was saying—it was tantamount to a job offer.

"I'd love to talk to you guys," he said.

A few weeks later, Sterling became Island's first full-time employee aside from Levine and Citron. Island's next hire proved to be one of its most important: an ambitious, fast-talking, charismatic trader named Matt Andresen.

As a student at Duke, Matt Andresen had little time for his studies. Six-four, beanpole thin, he spent most of his time fencing, making the all-American team all four years of his college career. After graduating in 1993 with an economics degree, he moved to New York to pursue a spot on the 1996 Olympic fencing team. Living with friends from college in a tiny, dank apartment on 77th Street on the Upper East Side of New York, he fenced at night at the New York Athletic Club while working days as an assistant trader for Lehman Brothers, where he got more experience making coffee runs than actual trading. He quickly grew frustrated with the job. He wanted action and Lehman wasn't giving it.

In 1995, Andresen landed a trading slot at Datek. He proved adept at the gunslinging, manic trading style typified by SOES bandits. As a fencer, he'd honed his ability to concentrate in short bursts and think tactically several moves ahead. When he saw a trade opening up, he didn't waste a moment before he was hitting the offer, scooping up a stock on the cheap and then selling it back seconds later. While his shot at the Olympic fencing team faded, his future as a trader looked bright.

Eager to improve, Andresen started buttonholing a quiet figure who worked in a clutter-filled room off Datek's trading floor: Levine. Andresen quickly discerned that Levine was the brains behind the operation and often swung by the programmer's computing lair after trading hours to ask questions about Watcher or the broader structure of the market. Levine's chaotic, garbage-filled office could be panic-inducing for Andresen, a fastidiously clean and ordered person. The wires jutting from walls, cords snaking through obscure piles of junk, the turtles, the lizard, the *bazooka* . . .

Levine always patiently answered Andresen's questions, and he quickly realized that Andresen was much more than yet another pesky and bothersome day trader. He'd become one of the captains of the trading room, teaching other traders—some far more seasoned—the ins and outs of Watcher. The twenty-seven-year-old Andresen was a born leader, and Levine needed someone he could trust. A reclusive hacker who loved working alone, tinkering, solving problems, Levine had no desire to take on the duties of a chief executive or a pitchman.

Citron, for his part, was embroiled in legal issues as the SEC bore down on Datek's trading operation. Will Sterling was street smart and knew his code, but he was just twenty years old and a college dropout. By comparison, Andresen, with his Duke degree and year at Lehman, was a polished Wall Street veteran. That he was bald as a cue ball didn't hurt, making him appear more mature.

One day in late 1997, Levine asked Andresen into his office. "Island needs a CEO, someone to take it to the next level," he said. "I really think you can do it, Matt."

Andresen was stunned. "But Josh, I don't have any management experience, nothing," he said.

"That's OK," Levine said. "You're a smart person who cares."

"C'mon, Josh," Andresen said. "Everyone cares."

Levine shook his head. He'd seen enough of the dark side of Wall Street in the last few years to know better.

"No, they don't," he said.

ANDRESEN didn't waste any time putting his stamp on Island. Soon after taking over management, he started hunting for programmers. One of his first hires was a Russian-born computer programmer named Mike Lazarev—the same programmer who years later would go to work for Haim Bodek at Trading Machines. At the time, Lazarev was working for a high-tech communications firm while studying humanities at Rutgers University. After seeing a job posting on an Internet site, he applied for a programming slot at Island.

His first interview with Andresen put him on notice that Island wasn't an ordinary company. After a few questions, the Island CEO offered him the job.

"Right here, right now," Andresen said. "Do you want it?"

Lazarev was confused. "Isn't there some kind of HR process?"

"Fuck that!" Andresen said. "Forget the process! Let's do it!"

Within days, Lazarev found himself working alongside Levine, whom he hadn't met during the interview process. (Levine didn't do interviews.) He had little idea that Levine was the brains behind Island. Sterling and Andresen appeared to be in charge of the show. Levine would stroll in every morning in his ragged jeans or cargo shorts, plop in front of his computer, type, crack a few jokes, hand out bagels, then get to work. With his ripped socks, soiled sneakers and old sandals, his ratty cardigans and torn T-shirts, Levine seemed incredibly laid back, certainly not the force behind a firm that was shaking Wall Street.

But whenever thorny questions about Island's system arose, Lazarev could see that everyone came to Levine. It steadily dawned on him that the quiet, diminutive programmer he worked beside was in fact the man in charge of the whole show.

■  ■  ■

By 1998, as Levine continued to improve Island and train a cadre
of young programmers, it was becoming clear that the gold mine at
Datek was no longer the trading operation. It was the technology
infrastructure.

There was Island, of course. There was also Datek Online, which
was fast becoming one of the most popular online trading venues in
the country, with nearly a hundred thousand customers trading about
$2 billion in assets. Users were blown away by its lightning execution,
helped by its direct access to Island's pool.

But there was a dark shadow looming over the firm. The SEC
had already handed out hefty fines to Maschler, Citron, and others
at Datek, and there were plenty of signs that more trouble was on the
way. The SEC was looking into the fixed rates Datek paid its "nominees" in order to trade under their names, a potential violation of anti-
fraud provisions.

In the spring of 1998, a decision was made to reconstruct the company. A new company called Datek Online, containing the online
trading site and Island, was launched. Citron was CEO. Levine, as
usual, had no title.

The SOES trading operation was stripped out into a separate firm.
Maschler's eldest son, Erik, and several partners formed a company
called Heartland Securities, which took its name from Heartland Village, the Staten Island neighborhood where the Maschler clan lived.
Heartland purchased the day-trading business, which continued to
operate out of 50 Broad. A wire cage was built around Island's racks
of computers to cordon them off from Heartland's.

Island, meanwhile, continued to grow at a staggering rate. By 1998,
it already accounted for one-tenth of the volume of all Nasdaq stocks.
Fueled by a small army of frenetic, momentum-chasing day traders as
well as cutting-edge computer-driven outfits such as ATD, Island had

become the number one Nasdaq dealer of hot Internet stocks such as Yahoo and Amazon.com.

Island was facing a mad rush into the ECN space. Jerry Putnam's Archipelago was growing fast in Chicago. In November 1997, Spear Leeds & Kellogg, one of the biggest specialist firms, rolled out the REDIBook (short for Routing and Execution Dot Interface Book). Harvey Houtkin launched his Attain ECN the following February, based on the trading network and volume created by his day-trading legions.

In April 1998, future Nasdaq CEO Robert Greifeld, then chief of financial software giant SunGard Data Systems, started an ECN called BRUT that capitalized on volumes traded through SunGard's computer system for trading Nasdaq stocks, BRASS (BRUT was short for BRASS Utility). An operation called Strike Technologies leveraged the high-speed trading volumes of Chicago quant-trading behemoth Hull Trading (which had recently employed data-mining expert Haim Bodek). Future Ponzi schemer extraordinaire Bernard Madoff, head of Bernard L. Madoff Investment Securities, helped develop Primex Trading, backed by firms such as Merrill Lynch and Goldman, whose electronic trading tentacles were suddenly everywhere. Bloomberg, the financial-data firm owned by the future New York City mayor Michael Bloomberg, had jumped in with Bloomberg Tradebook, called B-Trade for short.

Big money—the *biggest* money—was rolling into the pools like monster waves on Hawaii's North Shore. Giants such as Charles Schwab, Lehman Brothers, and Bank of America backed REDI-Book. Goldman was gearing up to plunge millions into Jerry Putnam's Archipelago. Madoff had deep-pocketed backers across Wall Street.

Other ECN investors included Bear Stearns, Morgan Stanley, Salomon Smith Barney, PaineWebber, and Credit Suisse First Boston. Wall Street's giants, the very firms that ran the biggest Nasdaq market-making operations, were pumping hundreds of millions into the upstart trading networks.

The electronic pools, aided by the Order-Handling Rules, were clearly changing the game. The easy money in market making was evaporating. Suddenly, there was a furious race to the new frontier of electronic trading. For those who got there first, piles of riches awaited. The SEC in 1998 rolled out a new set of regulations called Reg ATS (short for Alternative Trading System) to bring a semblance of order to the growing horde of electronic pools, which had to either register as a broker with Nasdaq, become an official exchange, or stay under a specified trading volume.

The largest ECN remained Instinet, with about 70 percent of the over-the-counter market in 1998. Island was rising fast at number two, with about 20 percent, while Jerry Putnam's Archipelago controlled about 6 percent; the remaining scraps were divided up among BRUT, REDIBook, Bloomberg's B-Trade, and Houtkin's Attain.

But Instinet still employed dozens of brokers who traded the old-fashioned way: over the phone. Fees were high, roughly 2 cents per share traded, compared with fractions of a cent at most ECNs.

Instinet was blinded by its size and huge cash stockpile. At corporate dinners, the sky was the limit. "You took out clients, and no one asked about the bill," recalls one former Instinet employee. "We'd go to Morton's Steakhouse and rent a side room out. Take the wine list, do what you wanted. No one gave a shit."

The Green Machine that tracked Instinet orders had become omnipresent on Wall Street trading floors. But the system was notorious for glitches and crashes. Traders expecting instant results loathed it.

Indeed, most Wall Street brokerages *hated* Instinet because it took business away from their own market-making desks. Mutual funds that wanted to buy a hundred thousand shares of IBM were increasingly going straight to Instinet instead of giant banks such as Merrill Lynch, Goldman Sachs, or Morgan Stanley. (The three firms' market-making interests were so closely aligned that they were collectively known on the Street as MGM.)

For years, Instinet had a lock on the dark market for stocks. It had the liquidity, and liquidity breeds and controls other liquidity (traders have to go where the action is whether they like it or not). Its salesmen would show up on trading floors brandishing Frisbees and stress balls and launch them into the crowd of traders, who cheered and booed them at the same time.

When the ECNs appeared on the scene, MGM saw an opportunity. If enough trading flow could be channeled through the electronic networks *that they owned*, Instinet could be neutralized. All that precious liquidity would flow elsewhere, shrinking Instinet's pool. The banks wanted to control the flow—the rivers of orders sloshing through the market every day.

A fierce power grab began. Instinet was in the crosshairs.

Doug Atkin, Instinet's newly appointed, glad-handing CEO, seemed oblivious to the threat he was facing. He spearheaded efforts to throw money at one initiative after another, from retail brokerage services to fixed income trading. He spent a fortune on an advertising campaign and rolled out a new logo for the company (which had never had one), a matador waving a cape around. He even let CNBC broadcast from the Instinet trading floor, an alarming move for a company that had long thought of itself as the best-kept secret on Wall Street. Atkin spent wads of money on everything—everything but Instinet's bread and butter, stock trading. The firm's pockets seemed so deep, and it had dominated its market for so long, that it was blind to its own vulnerability.

The firm seemed to have little idea that its business was under assault. At a company-wide meeting at Instinet's midtown headquarters in late 1998, Atkin addressed the troops. He talked about all the new initiatives—the brokerage, the bond trading, the new logo. Times were good and getting better, he said.

Then he whipped out a pair of scissors.

"We're going casual!" he announced, grabbing his tie and snipping it off. The room erupted in cheers.

Instinet's troubles came as little surprise to Levine. In 1995, he'd given the firm a chance to team up with Datek and pool their liquidity together. He'd been laughed out of the room. In response, he'd built Island, which was eating up more of Instinet's business every day.

Archipelago — or "Arca," as it had become known among traders — was also rising quickly. While Putnam and Levine had exchanged dozens of e-mails and spoken many times on the phone, they'd never met. Then one day in 1998, as Levine was typing away at his computer at 50 Broad, a man he'd never met before stepped into his office.

"Hi, Josh," he said, "I'm Jerry Putnam," offering his right hand for a shake.

To Putnam's surprise, Levine didn't shake his hand. Instead, he bolted from his seat, bear-hugged Putnam around his waist, and lifted him into the air. Putnam, a stocky six-one compared with Levine's elfin five-six, was shocked. He considered Levine a competitor, and yet the programmer was treating him like a long-lost brother. Levine, in fact, saw Putnam as a close ally in his effort to take down the entrenched interests on Wall Street. The more electronic trading options, the better, he felt.

After Levine let him go, Putnam looked around the room. He took it all in: the turtles, the giant lizard. Electronic gear tossed about like discarded toys. The stacks of Dells, spaghetti tangles of wires all over the place.

He was impressed.

Few knew better than Putnam how powerful Island was becoming—Archipelago, in fact, was one of its biggest customers, since it directed most of its flow to outside pools through its order routing system. Levine, Andresen, Sterling, and their small team of twenty-something übernerds had been working all hours to ramp up Island's speed and bring in more users—and more profits.

These were heady times. So much cash was fizzing through Island's pipes that the office was literally rolling in gold—gold bars. Levine had taken to bringing bars of gold and platinum to the office and then leaving them there untended. Will Sterling or Matt Andresen might stroll into the office in the morning and find a glittering bar of bullion on each of their desks, left there the previous night by the absentminded programmer.

NEVER content to sit still, Levine had another trick up his sleeve— one that in future years would alter in a fundamental way how the U.S. stock market worked.

Island made money by charging users $1 per order executed on its platform. While that was far less than the $2.50 charged by Nasdaq for SelectNet trades, it had a few holes. For one thing, it didn't provide any scale—a single trade could amount to a hundred shares, or a thousand, or ten thousand. Each cost a dollar.

It also didn't provide any incentive to big-volume traders—firms like ATD and Renaissance—to use Island. For those firms, which conducted thousands of trades a day, that $1 per order could quickly add up. To be sure, they still used Island—it was cheaper than Nasdaq or Instinet. But it still cost money.

What if Island *paid* them to trade? Levine thought.

Liquidity could *explode.*

So in 1998, Levine began to ponder a way to lure the big traders into his pool by offering them what amounted to a legal kickback. He thought back to an e-mail he'd received the previous year from an Island subscriber who'd suggested that Island *pay* firms that execute certain kinds of trades on its system.

Levine had dismissed the idea out of hand. But now he started to reconsider. Soon after, he was sitting on an airplane leafing through *Reshaping the Equity Markets*, the Robert Schwartz market-structure textbook he'd used as a touchstone since the early 1990s. In chapter eight of the book, he came across a description of the "cost of ignorance" for market makers. Schwartz describes the cost of ignorance as "the cost to a dealer of trading with better informed investors."

While market makers have far more information than mom-and-pop investors, they're often outgunned by more sophisticated traders, hedge fund aces or Warren Buffett types. Making a market for such traders can be hazardous. They may know something the market maker doesn't, such as a likelihood that Intel is going to come out with blowout earnings or Sears is going to put up horrendous sales numbers. Stepping in front of such orders can mean big losses.

In response to the chance of getting winged by a well-armed gunslinger, market makers typically widen their quotes, providing a lower bid or higher offer.

The result: wider spreads. And there was little Levine hated more than wide spreads. Why not *pay firms* a small amount per share traded to offset the cost of ignorance? The idea amounted to a way to lure firms into Island's pool and step in front of the gunslingers.

The model would come to be known as "maker-taker," part of the market plumbing quirks that more than a decade later would be one of the key factors in the destruction of Haim Bodek's Trading Machines. Recall the apple that a grocer is offering to sell for $1. Not wanting to pay that much, you bid 95 cents. If the grocer gives in and sells it to you for 95 cents, he pays the "take" fee while you earn a "make" fee. It's a system that rewards patience—whoever waits the longest before agreeing to a deal wins the prize.

After bouncing the idea off of Sterling, Andresen, and Citron, Levine decided to give the maker-taker idea a trial run. On June 1, 1998, Island instituted a payment of 1 cent for every hundred shares of an order that provided liquidity—that *made* a trade. Customers who *took* the trade paid 2½ cents for every hundred shares. Island pocketed the 1½-cent difference. (Taking was determined by crossing the spread to *take* an order.) It was a way to feed liquidity providers for swimming in Island's pool, while charging the firms that wanted to eat there.

The amounts seemed fleetingly small on the surface. If a firm made one hundred thousand trades, it would earn a mere $10 in rebates. A firm "taking" those orders—crossing the spread to get the trade—would pay $25. In the late 1990s, volumes weren't substantial enough for such sums to add up to much.

That would change with the rise of high-frequency trading in the 2000s. Speed traders juggling hundreds of millions of shares a day became adept at capturing the rebate, creating a whole new class of "rebate traders." Trading for many firms became a race to capture the trade, to get in the front of the queue to buy and snap up the rebate, only to pivot in a fraction of a second and sell, capturing another toll. Speed was paramount, and so was high volume. The more trades, the more speed, the more rebates.

Soon, nearly every other electronic pool would copy the model. Maker-taker would go on to dominate the stock market, deployed by giants such as the NYSE and Nasdaq and other large exchanges around the globe. Of course, all the *takers*—fund managers and regular investors—would be paying through the nose.

The irony of maker-taker: One of the primary reasons why Levine created Island in the first place was to *push out the middlemen*, letting everyday investors interact directly. With maker-taker, Island helped create a new class of middlemen, high-frequency traders. Levine would come to regret the maker-taker model in later years. "We feel that we created a monster," says one of Levine's former colleagues at Island.

But it worked well enough at the time. More and more quick-draw traders started sending orders Island's way, creating a boom in liquidity—and *liquidity breeds liquidity*. At bottom, it was the law of supply and demand. The pools needed buyers and sellers to work. The more buyers, the more sellers.

In ways, it was like the battle of the social networks in the 2000s. Whichever site pulled in more users would win the game—friends would go to where other friends were members. At first there were several networks: MySpace, Friendster, Facebook. In 2006, MySpace dominated, with seventy million users. Facebook had only seven million. But then something changed: More people started switching to Facebook, helped by innovations such as allowing friends to write public messages on a user's "wall" and allowing others to comment, or providing a way for friends to play Scrabble against one another, in turn pulling in an older audience. Those friends were the liquidity Facebook needed to dominate the competition and eventually become the largest social network in the world.

For Island, it was innovations such as maker-taker that were leaving most of its competitors in the dust, pulling in more buyers *and* sellers.

Levine, of course, was no Mark Zuckerberg. He had no grand designs on becoming a power mogul with private jets and sprawling mansions (that was Jeff Citron). Levine was a true believer on a singular mission—to make the market free. Wealth was simply a by-product of the mission. Even if the money hadn't been there, he would have done it all anyway.

It was a force of will and idealism that Levine's competitors on Wall Street couldn't fathom. Nasdaq was fighting rearguard actions, trying to protect its turf. The NYSE remained a dominant monopoly. Island seemed little more than an annoying gnat buzzing in its ear. Instinet, too focused on going casual, proved flat-footed, unable to adapt to the new hyperelectronic reality.

Before long, it would suffer the same fate as Nasdaq: dwindling market share as Island surged ahead.

# CHAPTER TWELVE

# PALACE COUP

On a chilly November day in 1998, a young couple strolled along the windblown beach of Coney Island. Far away on the horizon loomed the gray shadows of the World Trade Center. The park rides had been stilled, and there were few people queued up before Nathan's Famous hotdogs. But there was plenty of excitement on the beach as Josh Levine, dressed to the nines for once in a black suit and tie, married Meredith Murrell, a petite, dark-haired woman from Portland, Maine. Levine had somehow found time to date Murrell between fighting Nasdaq and running Island.

Coney Island was one of Levine's favorite places in New York City. He loved the idea that he could simply hitch a ride on the subway to the beach, the hazy outline of Manhattan in the distance. He liked to take his little black dog Mosa along and run up and down the shoreline or the vast boardwalk, often going during off-season when there were no tourists in sight.

Levine had begun to discover life outside of his hermetic lair at 50 Broad. There were also indications that Levine was losing his love of the game. In early 1999, Levine, Citron, and Peter Stern became the focus of a lawsuit filed by an individual who'd lost money trading on Datek Online. The suit, which proved frivolous, shook Levine. He removed all relevant trading information from his website, josh.com.

"This website used to contain what I think was some useful and entertaining information about such fun topics as SOES, ECNS, and day trading," he wrote. "As the person who wrote the software that handles a significant portion of the trades that happen in the NAS-DAQ marketplace, I think I have a unique perspective and some valuable insights to offer on these topics. But recent events have convinced me to give up. And I have. It's just not worth it."

One of Levine's most effective moves to extricate himself from Island's day-to-day grind had been hiring Matt Andresen as CEO. Bit in mouth, Andresen was charging ahead full speed. In the process, Island began a steady shift from a nerdy hothouse start-up to a focused, buttoned-down corporation.

Meanwhile, big trouble was brewing for Levine's longtime partner, Jeff Citron.

In July 1999, Datek Online was hit with subpoenas from the Justice Department seeking records of trading activities going back years. It was serious. The investigation had the potential to lead to criminal charges. While Datek Online had spun off its SOES trading operation to Heartland, the companies remained uncomfortably tight-knit. Heartland was located on the eleventh floor of 50 Broad, several floors above Island and Datek Online, and had a direct line into the Island matching engine.

In early 1999, Datek Online had already made a move to spiff up its image by hiring a banking veteran named Ed Nicoll to be president and chief operating officer. The tall, dapper forty-six-year-old co-founder of Waterhouse Securities—renamed TD Waterhouse after its purchase by Toronto Dominion Bank in 1995—fit the mold of a staid, steady-as-she-goes Wall Street executive to a tee.

Nicoll's business career had been idiosyncratic in the extreme. A former sheep farmer and commodities broker, Nicoll was the first person in history to gain admittance to Yale Law School without a college degree. Two years after graduating from Yale in 1997, he landed at Datek Online, hoping to get in on the boom in online trading.

Nicoll moved fast to consolidate his power. A believer, along with Federal Reserve chairman Alan Greenspan and many other financiers on Wall Street, in the free-market philosophy of the novelist Ayn Rand, he was a cool operator who quickly realized he'd stumbled on a gold mine at Datek. Even with a team blessed with zero business background at the helm, Datek Online was proving to be hugely successful. Island was in control of a huge chunk of the trading of Nasdaq stocks. The online trading site was growing rapidly. With an experienced executive on top, the firm's potential was limitless, Nicoll believed.

Big money had already been flowing in the door. Vulcan Ventures, a Seattle investment firm controlled by Microsoft mogul Paul Allen, had made a commitment to invest as much as $100 million in Datek Online. Groupe Arnault, the family holding company of French banking mogul Bernard Arnault, and TA Associates, a Boston venture-capital firm, had agreed to invest as much as $250 million.

Like many before him, Nicoll was deeply impressed by Levine, who shared many of his free-market views. Both were firmly convinced that there were few markets that needed more shaking up than the stock market. But Nicoll worried that Datek Online had a potentially mortal flaw in its ties to Shelly Maschler and his notorious SOES trading operation. Nicoll knew that no brokerage firm in history had survived a criminal indictment. After Datek Online was hit with the subpoenas in July 1999, he acted fast to contain the damage.

First, he decided the investigation amounted to a "materially adverse event" regarding the investment commitment from Vulcan, Groupe Arnault, and TA. Such events give investors the right to exit a deal with no consequences. Citron disagreed, but Nicoll overruled him. A criminal indictment would clearly cripple Datek Online. Vulcan, Paul Allen's firm, quickly pulled out. TA and Groupe Arnault slashed the maximum amount they'd invest to $195 million from $250 million.

Nicoll decided that Datek Online had to make a clear statement that its days as a renegade trading operation were long behind it. And the clearest way to do that was to cut the snake off at the head.

That meant Citron had to go. Quickly. Nicoll knew it would be painful. Citron was a founding father of Datek. He was smart and aggressive and had boundless energy that could be extremely useful to a hot young tech start-up.

But the risks were too great. So he arranged a meeting with Datek Online's senior executives—all except Citron. (Levine wasn't officially an executive at the firm and never involved himself in business decisions.) On a hot August morning, Nicoll met with Peter Stern and Alex Goor, Datek Online's chief strategy officer, in a conference room at 50 Broad. He laid out the case: Citron was a liability and could destroy the company if the investigation got serious.

"There's too much at stake," Nicoll explained. "Jeff has to go."

Stern and Goor agreed. With the rest of the team behind him, Nicoll didn't want to waste any time. He called Citron, who at the time was working out of a Datek Online office in Edison, New Jersey.

"We need to meet, Jeff."

"OK, when?"

"Today."

Nicoll, Stern, and Goor piled into a car and drove out to the Edison office. They were nervous and quiet during the drive. Stern's stomach was churning. For years, he'd worked side by side with Citron in that cramped room at 50 Broad. But he also felt that Citron could destroy all of the work he'd put in for years, the hundred-hour weeks, the sleepless nights, to build what he believed was the best online trading platform in the world.

The meeting was tense from the start. Citron knew that Nicoll had been agitating against him. But he had no idea what was about to go down. Sitting in on the meeting was Datek Online's chief financial officer John Grifonetti, who also worked at the Edison office.

Nicoll took the lead.

"Jeff, we're all agreed," he said. "You have to step down. And you need to hand over the voting control of your shares. You keep the shares, but you won't have any control of the company. It's over."

Citron's face turned white. He was stunned. He couldn't believe the company he'd personally helped create was shoving him out the door. By giving up his voting control, he'd have no say in its future.

Citron started talking, and kept talking, in his notorious *ratatat* blue streak. He conceded that he should leave, but he wanted to go on his own terms. "I'll go, but not like this," he said. "Give me time, let's wait this out, let it blow over, and then I can go on my own terms."

He tried to convince Goor and Stern to come over to his side, but they refused. When the meeting was over, Citron stormed out of the room in a fury.

During the next few days, the two sides squared off. Nicoll got word that Citron was putting in calls to Stern and Goor, so he corralled everyone into a single room at 50 Broad so he could keep an eye on them. Management lawyered up; so did Citron.

Nicoll decided he couldn't wait any longer. If word got out about the split in the firm, it could spark a media firestorm. On the morning of October 6, he sent Citron two press releases. One of the releases would hit the newswires at 4 P.M., he explained. Citron would decide which release that would be.

One stated that Jeffrey Citron, CEO of Datek Online Holdings Corp., was resigning, and that Edward J. Nicoll was taking over as CEO. The other release stated that the entire upper management of Datek Online — except for CEO Jeffrey Citron — was stepping down due to philosophical differences with the current CEO, Jeffrey Citron.

It was a palace coup. Nicoll had orchestrated it to perfection.

Citron had no choice. Against his will, outraged at Nicoll, he agreed to sign off on the first press release. His meteoric career on Wall Street had come to an end.

Citron was hardly washed up. He was just twenty-nine and owner of 30 percent of a company worth more than a billion dollars on paper. Looking for a new industry to tackle, he soon trained his attention on another up-and-coming disruptive technology: telecom. Several years later, he would help launch Vonage, the Internet-based phone service he believed represented the same kind of game changer for the telecom industry that Island had been for the financial markets. "It will change the world," he told *Bloomberg News*, echoing Levine's boasts about Island.

Maschler and Citron eventually decided to cash out of Datek Online. Nicoll helped put together a giant club deal between the firm's private-equity investors to buy them out. Together, the investors shelled out $700 million for the pair's 52 percent stake.

ISLAND, meanwhile, continued to plow ahead with initiatives that would have a deep impact on the broader market. In September 1999, it introduced a twelve-hour trading day, lasting from 8 A.M. to 8 P.M. Eastern time. Because trading was conducted electronically, it made little sense to restrict trading hours to the traditional six-and-a-half-hour trading day that still held at the NYSE. Because of Island's move, Datek Online became the first online broker to provide the extended hours to its customers. Competitors quickly followed.

Fueled by the growing legions of Datek Online day traders, Island's volume continued to boom. In the first quarter of 1999, an average of ninety million shares a day traded on Island, up from seventeen million in late 1997. Archipelago, by contrast, was handling seventy million shares *a month*. For all of 1999, twenty-seven billion shares traded on Island, with a total dollar amount of $1.6 *trillion*.

Volumes surged again in 2000. In the first quarter of the year, even as the dot-com bubble started to burst, trading volume jumped past twelve billion shares, accounting for more than $800 billion in total dollar volume. On April 4 alone, 126.8 million shares traded on Island, for a dollar volume of $18.3 billion.

Finally, in December 2000, Island was spun off from Datek Online as a separate company. Nicoll was named chairman. Andresen remained president and CEO.

Levine had no title—and he didn't want one. At Datek Online, CFO John Grifonetti had once given Levine the title of executive vice president. When Levine found out, he called Grifonetti and asked him to take it away.

"I don't want a title, I don't want to manage anyone," he said. "I just want to do my own thing, OK?"

Dumbfounded, Grifonetti agreed.

IN February 2000, the news service Knight-Ridder ran a profile of Island. The article's focus: Matt Andresen.

"If there is a ground zero for the revolution sweeping through the U.S. securities industry, it's probably located in the spartan Manhattan offices of Matt Andresen," it began.

The reporter seemed dazzled by Island, amazed that an upstart such as Andresen and "his tech-savvy cohorts are transforming the way stocks are traded in America."

Andresen escorted the reporter to the basement of 50 Broad, where all the Dell computers had been moved, and pointed to a computer no bigger than a briefcase. "That is Island," he said.

Andresen explained that Island was "democratizing" stock trading and eliminating "middlemen profiteers." There was no mention, of course, of the fleet-footed computer traders populating Island's pool, the new breed of electronic middlemen. The article referred to Levine once, in passing. The reclusive computer programmer continued to shun the spotlight even as he watched his creation emerge as a world-changing force in the market—just as he'd predicted.

Skeptics, however, were pouring cold water on Island and the ECNs. Erik Sirri, a finance professor at Babson College who later became head of the SEC's division of market regulation, said people like Andresen were "fooling themselves if they think they will one day replace Nasdaq. The Nasdaq's market makers and the NYSE's specialists are critical components to maintaining a liquid market."

Island also had several close calls with its computer system. In early 2000, the stock market started to buckle as the dot-com mania collapsed. Trading volumes surged to record levels, especially on Nasdaq, full of massively inflated tech outfits from America Online to Pets.com to eBay. By then, nearly 15 percent of all Nasdaq stocks were flowing through Island's pipes.

The Nasdaq index peaked at 5049 on March 10, a Friday. The following Monday, before trading started, a wave of sell orders for bellwether tech stocks such as Cisco and Dell swept into the market. Many flowed through Island, a haven of before-hours trading. When Nasdaq opened for business at 4879, the 170-point drop stunned investors around the country. Within a few days the Nasdaq had cratered by nearly 10 percent.

The selling intensified. Day traders scrambling to salvage their winnings from the past year dumped stocks in a panic. Island's trading volume surged, topping fifteen billion shares a day on a regular basis.

On March 24, 2000, as the pressure grew, Island experienced a catastrophic hardware failure, taking out half of its backup computers. With its backups down for the count, the system was on thin ice. Any problems in its primary system, and it would have crashed.

Making matters worse, the air-conditioning system in the basement at 50 Broad broke down, threatening the computers. Temperatures topped one hundred degrees. An eighteen-wheeler truck equipped with air-conditioning units was called in to funnel a hose into the basement as Island's tech team scrambled to get the backup system online.

Despite what might have been a perfect storm, Island continued to trade smoothly—and users were deeply impressed. They'd watched as nearly every other ECN choked and wheezed through the turmoil, even as Island kept humming like a jet engine.

Andy Madoff, Bernie Madoff's oldest son and an executive at Bernard L. Madoff Investment Securities—a big user of Island—lavished Levine's system with praise in an April 7, 2000, e-mail. "Every day that goes by without your system going down builds my respect," he wrote. "REDI, ARCA, B-Trade have all been plagued with almost continuous problems at crunch times during the last 2 weeks."

Island was building a reputation as the most reliable pool in the stock market. When traders needed immediate action, they knew there was one place to go. Without question, the answer was *not* the NYSE or Nasdaq. In the race to win the new high-speed trading merchants, the twin stock market titans had been passed, then lapped. None were more aggressive than Island.

But rapidly coming up from behind: Archipelago.

# CHAPTER THIRTEEN

# BAD PENNIES

Jerry Putnam sat in a room facing a gathering of Archipelago's board of directors. He could see his future right there in front of him.

It had a name: Goldman Sachs.

It was the summer of 1999, near the height of the dot-com bubble. The board had assembled in an expansive Goldman conference room on the forty-eighth floor of Chicago's Sears Tower. Looking around the room, Putnam allowed himself a moment to relish it, to embrace the idea that the huge home run he'd been striving for his whole career was coming true. He'd been on the edge of failure so many times. Now, he felt, success was within reach.

He gave a wink to John Hewitt, Goldman's electronic-markets guru. Known as "Spock" at Archipelago due to his uncanny resemblance to the brainy Vulcan on *Star Trek*, Hewitt had been charged with preparing Goldman's electronic trading systems for the twenty-first century. He'd handpicked an unlikely ally to help accomplish that goal: Archipelago. Earlier that year, he'd spearheaded a $25 million investment in Putnam's pool, giving it not only much needed capital but a stamp of approval from one of the most respected banks in the country.

Also representing Goldman was Duncan Niederauer, a sharp,

gray-eyed electronic-trading expert and fast-rising star at Goldman. Niederauer would go on to become one of the most powerful figures on Wall Street, eventually taking the helm of the New York Stock Exchange itself. In the late 1990s, he was working behind the scenes to transform the entire market into a tech-driven speed machine. And there were few better places to effect that change than Goldman, which was rapidly extending its tentacles into every last corner of electronic trading. That same year, it purchased Hull Trading for half a billion dollars. The forerunner of Goldman's vaunted high-frequency-trading platform, and employer of Haim Bodek, Hull had been a pioneer in sophisticated, computer-driven trading strategies.

Goldman was spending billions on investments in technology firms and on its own computer infrastructure. By the end of the decade, it had more than twenty thousand personal computers and workstations backed by eighty trillion bytes of storage. About eighteen thousand miles of cable and thirty thousand phone lines snaked through its Broad Street headquarters, linked to a fiber network that could sling data to its offices around the world at 6.1 gigabits a second. With Goldman on board, Archipelago would be an end recipient of much of the liquidity spun out by its own market makers as well as Hull's high-octane trading desk. For the ECNs, such constant, steady flow was crucial. It was the new mantra: *Liquidity breeds liquidity.*

It was a fundamental law of markets, like gravity. The bigger the flow of trades, the stronger the pull.

Hewitt and Niederauer's presence in the room was like a warm security blanket for Putnam. They made him feel *safe*.

But others in the room had visions far beyond anything Putnam could imagine. After he gave a short speech and thanked everyone for coming, he surrendered the floor to Niederauer.

Niederauer, a tall, heavy-limbed man with close-trimmed salt-and-pepper hair, stepped to the front of the conference room and picked up a dry-erase Magic Marker. After a few introductory words, he walked to a whiteboard, wrote "NYSE," and drew a circle around it.

"We're going to be the electronic trading arm of the New York Stock Exchange," Niederauer said.

The room let out a collective gasp.

Just as Levine had used Datek to upend Nasdaq, Goldman was going after the NYSE—using Archipelago as its Trojan horse.

The trouble for Putnam was that the NYSE was not only seen as Enemy Number One at Archipelago, it was seen as an impenetrable force. The Big Board *was* the establishment—that's why it was the *Big* Board. The idea that the NYSE would have any interest in aligning itself with Archipelago, still a tiny upstart, scrappy as it was, with roughly five thousand subscribers who transacted a few million shares a day, seemed nothing short of delusional.

But Niederauer knew the future was shifting toward fast computer trading. And Archipelago was drawing some heavy backers and fetching valuations, albeit on paper, north of $200 million. As Niederauer's presentation in the Sears Tower that day showed, Putnam & Co. were beginning to have grand visions of a future dominated by electronic networks.

That's why Putnam decided to make one of his biggest moves yet. Rather than continue life as a plain-vanilla ECN, Archipelago was going to become a full-fledged exchange, giving it the ability to trade blue chips such as General Electric and IBM.

That meant only one thing: It was time to go head-to-head with the eight-hundred-pound-gorilla itself, the New York Stock Exchange.

PUTNAM didn't know which he hated most, Nasdaq or the NYSE. His disdain for Nasdaq was visceral. Within Archipelago, Nasdaq was the subject of constant ridicule. A Nasdaq towel—a Christmas present to Nasdaq customers—was used as a throw rug in the office. Archipelago employees loved to wipe their dirty shoes on the towel, which eventually became pitch-black with Chicago street grit.

But Putnam had a deep, stomach-level hatred for the NYSE. Once, in a phone conversation with an NYSE official, he called the exchange a monopoly.

"Don't say that," shot back the NYSE official.

"You're a monopoly!" Putnam shouted.

"Stop saying that."

"You're a monopoly!" Putnam shouted again. "You're a monopoly! A monopoly!"

He loved pulling their chain—and he was also convinced he was right.

A brash propaganda campaign against the Big Board broke out. Archipelago rented a Brink's armored car, parked it in front of the NYSE on Broad Street, and handed out rolls of pennies. The company put up signs around the exchange saying DON'T GET PENNIED, a reference to the allegation that specialists would front-run their customers by buying stocks cheap and selling them pennies higher. It hired fake protesters to march around the NYSE with signs that said DON'T GET PENNIED! Eventually, the New York Police Department forced them to stop.

Putnam even contemplated dropping rolls of toilet paper stamped with the Archipelago logo on top of the NYSE from a helicopter, a locker-room joke on the Big Board's archaic ticker-tape past. He called up Archipelago's marketing guru Margaret Nagle and asked her to check into the legal implications of such a stunt.

"Can you find out if it's a felony or misdemeanor to TP the New York Stock Exchange?" he asked.

"Excuse me?" Nagle replied.

While he eventually scotched the plan to TP the Big Board, Putnam relentlessly hammered the vision of the floor of the NYSE as a mysterious world where insiders took advantage of the little guy.

Archipelago adopted mottos such as "Everything Out in the Open" and "The Market Is Open."

The implication, of course, was that the NYSE was closed—and had something to hide.

Putnam had a strong ally fighting alongside him in his battle against the NYSE: none other than his toughest competitor, Island.

ON July 3, 2000, Matt Andresen mounted a platform in front of the Rayburn House Office Building in Washington, D.C. Behind him loomed the sharp-cut profile of Abe Lincoln on an eight-foot copper-toned cardboard penny.

"Investors will no longer have to settle for industry-established increments that limit their ability to obtain the best possible price," Andresen told a gathering of reporters and onlookers, including several congressmen. "When the U.S. Congress told our markets to be decimal-ready by July 3, we took that deadline very seriously."

He was talking about one of the most controversial and most feared changes coming to the stock market: decimalization.

For years, regulators and congressmen had been pushing Nasdaq and the NYSE to start trading stocks in penny increments—or decimals—rather than the fractions they'd always used, a convention that went back to the use of Spanish pieces of eight as a common currency. Nasdaq and the NYSE pushed back, hard. If stocks were quoted in pennies instead of fractions—the smallest slice was one-sixteenth of a dollar, or 6.25 cents—spreads would narrow, crimping profits. Rather than buying a share of Intel for $20 and reselling it for $20 1/16, they might be forced to buy Intel for $20.05 and resell it for $20.10, a meager 5-cent spread.

It was a change Levine had foreseen as far back as the mid-eighties when he was peddling software to Wall Street firms as an eighteen-year-old high-school dropout. Why could he buy a box of cereal for $2.45 but could only buy a stock for $2.50? Clearly, he thought, market makers had a nice scam going.

The SEC had been mulling a shift toward penny quotes since the mid-1990s. In March 1997, Congressman Mike Oxley, a Republican from Ohio and the powerful chairman of the House Energy and Commerce Committee, introduced a bill dubbed "Common Cents Stock Pricing Act" to force the SEC to mandate a shift to pennies. The bill was dropped after the NYSE, to preempt any moves from Washington, pledged to shift to pennies by the year 2000; Nasdaq followed suit.

But both the NYSE and Nasdaq had been dragging their heels. By early 2000, it was clear that neither the NYSE nor Nasdaq would start quoting stocks in pennies unless Big Brother did some serious arm-twisting. In due course, the SEC mandated that Nasdaq stocks would start listing in decimal form on July 3, 2000. Predictably, the agency postponed the move after a major pushback from Nasdaq.

Andresen was there in Washington to give the market notice that Island wasn't going to wait any longer. It was moments away from a historic event: the first penny trade in the history of the U.S. stock market.

The move went back to Levine, who'd been enraged by Nasdaq's constant delays on decimalization. To demonstrate how easy it was to trade in pennies, he decided to beat Nasdaq to the punch: Island would start quoting stocks in pennies *on its own*. Of course, penny-priced trades could only take place on Island, since other venues didn't price stocks in pennies. But Island had more than enough liquidity to make it happen.

The move angered many in the industry who thought Island was going rogue. Andy Madoff told Levine in an e-mail that "the message sent to the world was that anybody who isn't ready to move forward . . . is basically dragging their feet. If Congress in their infinite wisdom forces Nasdaq to implement decimals before they're ready, it will be a disaster for all of us, including Island."

Levine's response was terse.

"As far as I am concerned," he wrote Madoff, "NASDAQ has

relegated themselves to nothing more than a last sale data aggregator and vendor. It's hard to imagine anything that could make the situation worse."

To drum up publicity for Levine's plan, Andresen traveled to the nation's capital to stage a press conference — and the first penny trade.

The honor fell to Virginia Republican Tom Bliley, who placed an order to buy shares of Nextel Communications, the Virginia-based telecom provider, using penny increments.

Within the next few months, more than 10 percent of all Island orders were submitted in decimals.

The pressure worked. In the next year, the entire U.S. stock market shifted toward decimalization — and spreads started to narrow dramatically. Traders going head-to-head kept upping the ante a penny at a time, until at last the spread between a buy and a sell for heavily traded stocks was . . . one penny. One market maker would offer to buy Intel for $20.10 and sell for $20.20, the next would offer to buy for $20.11 and sell for $20.19, until at last the bid was $20.15 and the offer was $20.16. Such hyper-progressive trading proved extremely hard for human traders. Computers, however, could easily juggle the load.

Levine, of course, was pleased that progress was being made — but he didn't think that the regulators had gone far enough. He believed that markets should be so malleable that stocks would trade in increments measured in *fractions* of a penny per share. In a December 2001 letter to the SEC, he recommended that stocks trade four decimal places out from a dollar — instead of trading at $20.01, a stock could trade at $20.0099. At the time, the SEC restricted such subpenny trades (it still does for the most part).

"As designer of Island ECN's market structure and system software," he wrote, "I think my experience with sub-penny trading may provide insight into these issues."

Levine argued that the rule was arbitrary. It was as if the government passed a law forcing car dealers to sell cars at $1,000 increments. The SEC wasn't convinced.

But the ball was already rolling, and the change to penny quotes was going ahead full throttle. The shift would cap the work begun by Levine in the late 1980s. The result: Human market makers started to drop out of business in droves. Specialists on the floor of the New York Stock Exchange began to close shop, their profits eroded so ferociously that most simply began to look for a new line of work. Taking their place: high-frequency traders.

# CHAPTER FOURTEEN

# DUMB MONEY

Matt Andresen sat perched at his desk at 50 Broad Street leafing through the latest volume report for Island. It was a Monday, early 2000. A chill breeze pierced into the room, even though his window was shut. The windows in the office were like paper, useless against the harsh winter blasts that whipped up Broad off the Hudson River. It was so bad that several of Island's programmers had taken to wearing gloves with the tips cut off.

Andresen didn't care about the cold: He was rapt. He loved his weekly volume-report ritual, a moment to pore over the hard data showing the exponential growth of Levine's electronic pool. As he scanned the list of users, a startling figure made his eyes pop open. A new subscriber had started pouring a Niagara Falls of orders into Island, millions of shares a day.

He'd never heard of this particular user. His only clue was the firm's identification code: IBKR. Still, he was thrilled. Whoever it was, they were more than welcome. Millions of new shares a day were flooding into its system. All that Island had to do was open up an OUCH port like a hungry mouth and swallow as quickly as it could.

As Andresen well knew: *Liquidity breeds liquidity.*

His elation didn't last long. The following Monday, as he

scanned the next volume report, he noticed that IBKR had virtually disappeared.

Andresen was stunned. What could have happened? He thought it might be a technical issue, so he asked his client team to investigate. The problem, they learned after checking with IBKR, wasn't technical. "It's a business decision, Matt," he was told. "Why don't you go pay them a visit?"

The name of the firm, he learned, was Interactive Brokers. Based in Greenwich, Connecticut, Interactive was a giant brokerage firm for regular and sophisticated investors. It also owned a little-known, though highly successful, electronic trading outfit called Timber Hill.

Andresen made an appointment. Several days later, he drove up to Greenwich, about forty miles north of New York City. He'd never been to the small, tony town of Greenwich and didn't know that it was the home base of hundreds of powerful hedge funds. In the following years, he'd return many times.

He stepped through the front doors of Interactive's headquarters at One Pickwick Plaza, a nondescript office park located in the center of downtown Greenwich, and was ushered into a waiting area. After several minutes, he was escorted into an expansive, low-ceilinged corner office with sparse furnishings. It was dimly lit, aside from the radiant glow of a large computer monitor. Hundreds of quotes in a microscopic font flooded across the screen. Andresen grew dizzy with a glance at the buzzing stream of numbers.

Before the monitor sat a trim, silver-haired man sporting a close-cut beard and black turtleneck. He stood and introduced himself.

"I am Thomas Peterffy, CEO of Interactive Brokers," he said in a thick Hungarian accent. "Eet is nice to meet you."

Peterffy returned to his seat behind a broad mahogany desk and motioned for Andresen to take a chair. The Island CEO had little idea that Peterffy, a Hungarian immigrant who'd come to America in the 1960s virtually penniless, was a legend in the electronic trading world.

He was among the first traders in the world to use computers to price stock options in the 1970s. In the 1980s, Peterffy had been the first to use handheld computers on a trading floor, the Amex. He'd installed a complex device to flash trade signals using colored lights on the floor of the NYSE, a mysterious machine competitors called HAL, after the maniac AI computer in the movie *2001*. Peterffy had created a vast global trading empire worth billions, all of it run by sophisticated, lightning-fast pricing systems he had personally designed. In other words, Timber Hill was the exact kind of client Island was built for: smart, tech-savvy, and bloated with liquidity. But for some reason, Peterffy had shut Island off.

Like Haim Bodek at Trading Machines, Peterffy specialized in trading options. Hull Trading, where Bodek cut his teeth in finance, was one of Timber Hill's top competitors. As an options trader, Peterffy often had to dip into the stock market to hedge his bets (the activity that years later would plague Bodek's firm). He'd recently given Island a test drive. But something went wrong.

Andresen launched into his sales pitch. He emphasized Island's speed and its blue-light special rates.

"We're ten times faster and cheaper than our competitors," he said.

Peterffy nodded.

"Yes, Matt," he said. "Island is faster and less expensive."

"So why did you stop using us?"

"Because on Island I *do not make money*!"

Andresen was dumbfounded. He had no response and left Peterffy's office in confusion. On the drive back to the city, he tried to make sense of what he'd just heard. What did Peterffy mean when he said he didn't make money on Island?

With a sinking feeling in his stomach, he realized that Peterffy was saying that the traders he was going up against on Island were *too good*. They were so good that there was virtually no way to make a reliable buck, especially for an options firm such as Interactive that didn't specialize in stocks. It was pros against pros. Watcher gunslingers. Superfast hedge funds like ATD. Bank trading desks. A rising new breed of high-frequency robot traders.

It was a revelation. Andresen realized that Island had made a simple, though profound, mistake. By being the fastest, cheapest, and most reliable electronic network, it appealed to the fastest and most sophisticated traders.

The result: Island was a pool full of sharks devouring one another.

Andresen's solution was a harbinger of important changes in the market to come in the next decade. Island would no longer simply court the savviest investors—the sharks, the cheetah-fast hedge funds. It would start going after what on Wall Street is known as *dumb money*.

In other words, *retail* investors. That meant clients of E*Trade, Charles Schwab, Ameritrade—and even Interactive Brokers. Day traders or mom-and-pop investors who, more often than not, placed relatively unsophisticated orders into the market that the computer aces gobbled up.

It all went back to the "cost of ignorance" problem Levine had grappled with, which eventually led to his creation of maker-taker. Market makers often didn't know who was on the other side of their trade, whether it was a tipped-off hedge fund manager who knew a stock was about to rocket higher (or plunge) or a dumb-as-dirt day trader making a reckless gamble. Because of that ignorance, market makers often would only buy the stock at a low price, or sell at a high price, in order to protect themselves.

The equation is different with retail orders from a discount broker such as Ameritrade. Market makers know they aren't dealing with a wicked-smart hedge fund who can rip their faces off. Rather, they're typically dealing with fairly uninformed—or *dumb*—investors. Aunt Millie taking a hundred-share flyer on Microsoft. Panicky Uncle Joe dumping his fifty shares of General Electric because of an article in *BusinessWeek*.

That dynamic *reduces* the cost of ignorance, making it easier for market makers to earn a buck. And many of the sophisticated firms using Island were in many ways acting like market makers, buying stock and then selling it in a matter of minutes or even seconds. But Andresen realized, after meeting with Peterffy, that the sharks were starving. They needed food to survive. Of course, the solution amounted to nothing less than feeding Uncle Joe and Aunt Millie to the sharks.

Andresen didn't realize it at the time, but his revelation was a new twist in the evolution of a computer-driven market that would transform trading in the next decade. It was the start of the Algo Wars. The stock market—and almost all other markets—became a hunter-seeker battlefield of computer firms hunting for dumb money, or trying to detect the fat whale orders placed by a mutual fund. In time, the funds started fighting back, by creating their own smart algos or by hiding in dark pools.

Soon after returning to 50 Broad, Andresen got in touch with Chris Nagy, head of trading for Ameritrade in Omaha, Nebraska, home also to Warren Buffett's Berkshire Hathaway. A sharp-dressing clean-cut midwesterner, Nagy was in charge of some extremely *juicy*—i.e., dumb—order flow at Ameritrade, one of the largest online brokers in the country. In other words, lots of Uncle Joes and Aunt Millies.

Andresen wanted Ameritrade to start routing some of its flow to Island. It was a hard sell. Ameritrade had a deal to send most of its orders to Knight Securities, a computer-savvy broker dealer based in Jersey City. Knight paid Ameritrade for the orders, in return promising to provide a good execution for the trades. In the industry, this was known as payment for order flow, a practice none other than Bernie Madoff had pioneered years before.

Island didn't play the payment-for-order-flow game (though maker-taker was similar in that it provided a sweetener for traders to post orders), so Andresen had little to offer aside from promising fast execution. For Nagy, execution speed wasn't enough to trump the hard dollars and cents Ameritrade got from Knight.

Island would have to get its juicy order flow from somewhere else.

Andresen, meanwhile, continued to court sophisticated traders — including the most dangerous shark of all.

ANDRESEN was in the middle of his well-rehearsed pitch, ticking off all the benefits that Island brought investors who thrived on blinding speed and nosebleed volumes. The instant execution. The gobs of streaming data. The dirt-cheap fees. And if anyone was in the market for speed, data, and low fees, it was the hedge fund he was pitching to: Renaissance Technologies.

But the reclusive, white-bearded chieftain of Renaissance, Jim Simons, didn't seem to be listening. In fact, it seemed as if Simons had *dozed off* in the middle of Andresen's presentation in a conference room at Island's 50 Broad headquarters, his Merit cigarette burning to a cinder in an ashtray before him. Was Simons actually *snoring*? Disconcerted, Andresen muddled on, addressing his speech to the other Renaissance executives in the room, Peter Brown and Bob Mercer, the former IBM AI experts who'd turned Renaissance into an invincible trading machine. They were familiar with Island — they'd been dabbling on it for the past few years. But they were still skittish. Andresen was trying to convince them to route more flow his way.

The distinctly cool reception from Simons wasn't inspiring confidence. After his pitch, he wrapped it up. "Any questions?"

Simons's eyes popped open. He yawned, lit a fresh Merit, took a slow drag, then proceeded to reel off every single one of Island's major weaknesses. Island was largely shut out of the largest stock market in the world, the New York Stock Exchange. That seemed like something of a problem, no? You can't trade IBM, you can't trade General Motors. Institutional clients such as Fidelity and Vanguard weren't using the ECN. Why not? What if regulators did anything to upset the model?

Andresen was shocked—and deeply impressed. He realized not only that Simons had been listening to every word, but that he had an incredibly nimble and perceptive mind. That caused him to want Renaissance's business more than ever.

He soon got it.

THE fund structure at Renaissance was something like a Russian matryoshka doll, with funds concealed inside of funds. Inside Renaissance was another fund called Medallion, which Simons had launched in 1988. Inside Medallion was Mercer and Brown's fund, Nova. Its strategies were completely automated and involved lightning-fast moves in and out of stocks that were rising or falling.

Nova got a not-insignificant boost from Island's appearance on the scene. The human market makers and specialists it had had to deal with in the past could throw a wrench into its fine-tuned models, which required fast and flawless execution. It was the same problem that would help scuttle Haim Bodek's efforts to build an AI trading system at Hull in Chicago.

On Island, human middlemen weren't a problem. What's more, the high speeds and low transaction costs—as well as the reams of data Island spit out—blended perfectly with Nova's strategies, which were driven by cutting-edge AI systems that went back to Mercer and Brown's days developing AI-driven language-translation systems at IBM in the 1980s and early 1990s.

Renaissance's relationship with Island wasn't perfect. Pathologically secretive, the firm was wary of sending orders to any outfit that might be able to peer into its complex strategies. It was suspicious of Island, for instance, because of its ties to the former Datek trading outfit. Inside Renaissance, the theory was that Island had been created to let Datek traders avoid the "uptick rule," a regulation requiring traders to wait for a stock to tick higher before selling it short, hoping to profit from a decline. The uptick rule had been created in the 1930s to stop bear raids, when short sellers piled onto a stock and sold share after share in order to crack it. Traders using Island could simply ignore the uptick rule, since no regulator was monitoring exactly when each trade was made, at least according to Renaissance observers.

An even worse fear: What if those Datek bandits opened up the hood at Island and started looking at Nova's orders? The risk seemed too great—at first.

But it was clear that electronic trading was the future, and there was no fund more about the future than Renaissance. Initially, Renaissance had formed a relationship with Bloomberg Tradebook, known as B-Trade. Part of Michael Bloomberg's media and technology empire, B-Trade's hope was to transform Bloomberg's ubiquitous data machine, which sat on virtually every trading desk on Wall Street, into a tool that firms could use as a trading portal. B-Trade's aim was to capture orders from the big boys such as Fidelity and Vanguard, which had largely eluded Island.

Brown and Mercer wanted to have a shot at trading against that flow, which they naturally thought would be easy pickings for their space-age systems—to them, a fund manager at Fidelity or Legg Mason was about the dumbest money on the planet.

But there was a problem: B-Trade wasn't getting the flow. The major institutions remained wary of the electronic pools and were sticking with more traditional broker dealers, who operated directly on the NYSE or Nasdaq. Almost all of the orders coursing through the ECNs were coming from hedge funds, day traders, and sophisticated bank trading desks—the sharks at Island who'd alienated Thomas Peterffy.

That left Renaissance exposed. Eventually, it became the largest user of B-Trade, accounting for about one-quarter of all of its volume.

Brown and Mercer started to worry that savvy competitors would deconstruct their strategies simply by watching what was happening on B-Trade.

They needed to start spreading their trades around to other ECNs, including Island. While Island didn't have the juicy Fidelity or Legg Mason flow Renaissance craved, it at least had enough volume to help it cover its tracks. Eventually, despite Simons's initial concerns, Renaissance became one of the most prolific users of Island.

It was perfect timing.

"We remain optimistic," Simons wrote in a 1999 letter to Renaissance investors. "An inexorable trend towards electronic trading in . . . equities is having the effect of increasing liquidity and decreasing transaction costs."

The Bots were growing, flexing their muscles, and becoming increasingly powerful. Timber Hill and Renaissance, along with electronic traders such as ATD, were at the vanguard of the Algo Wars, designing programs that could trade automatically, with little or no human intervention.

It was just the beginning. The automated firms flocking to Island represented the first generation of computer-driven trading. The next generation would transform the structure of the market so dramatically that it would become virtually unrecognizable even to electronic stalwarts such as Levine. While outfits such as Timber Hill and Renaissance were fast, they didn't trade remotely as manically as the new breed of high-frequency trading firms, which would blast thousands of orders into the market every second. Many rose up outside of New York and environs—in the prairies of the Midwest, the deserts of Texas, the suburbs of Los Angeles—and would escalate the Algo Wars to a fevered pitch, in turn threatening the very stability of the market itself.

In Austin, Robbie Robinette, a physics professor at the University of Texas, and Mark Melton, an AI expert who also taught at the university, teamed up with local attorney Richard Gorelick to form a computer-driven trading firm called RGM Advisors. Operating out of Robinette's living room, they designed an automated stock-trading strategy that jumped in and out of stocks at high speeds, the AI program guiding its moves. Striking a deal with Datek Online, they programmed the Watcher software to automatically execute their orders. Heartland, the former Datek Securities operation, acted as the broker dealer to mainline their trades directly into the Island computers through a cable that snaked down the stairs to 50 Broad's basement, where Island had moved its computers in 1999.

Chicago's Getco, another high-tech player, started to send microbursts of orders for stocks through its broker dealer, Octeg. Datek Online's Ed Nicoll once paid a visit to Getco's ragtag office at the Chicago Mercantile Exchange and noticed that the sign on the glass door read OCTEG GETCO, like a mirror image. Immediately, he knew there was something unusual about the small group of ex–floor traders running the company. And he was right. In the next few years, Getco would grow to become one of the most hyperactive trading firms in the world. Highly secretive, Getco became a prolific user of AI techniques that could learn and react to shifts in the market at the blink of an eye.

Another high-frequency trader closely allied with Getco, a North Kansas City outft called Tradebot, would become so consistently profitable that in the late 2000s its founder would tell people that his firm hadn't lost money in *a single trading day since 2002.*

# CHAPTER FIFTEEN

# TRADE BOTS

G rowing up in the middle-class town of Weatherby Lake, Missouri, a small suburb on the north side of Kansas City, Dave Cummings became fascinated with computers while hanging out at a computer software store that his father, a Trans World Airlines pilot, ran as something of a hobby. At Purdue University, the future high-frequency-trading kingpin studied computer programming and electrical engineering. After graduating in 1990, he took a job with Cerner, a Kansas City health-care software firm, where he worked for about three years.

Then Cummings caught the trading bug. He quit Cerner and soon found himself swapping future contracts for hard red winter wheat (the primary ingredient of bread) and stock indexes on the floor of the Kansas City Board of Trade. Each day, he'd don a forest-green jacket and dive into the sharp-elbowed crowd of traders and scream out orders to buy and sell, buy and sell. It was tiring, stressful, sweaty work.

Long-limbed and rangy, Cummings had the meaty build of a floor trader. He had a pumpkin-size head and steel-plow jaw, his close-trimmed black hair prone to stick out at odd angles. Quick with a laugh, he also had a whiplash temper.

But Cummings also had the brains of a serious egghead. When his analytical mind spotted openings—such as strangely wide spreads—

he started jumping ahead of the pack by offering better deals, cutting the spread.

It was exciting, energizing, and challenging, but it wasn't the life Cummings wanted. While he was making about $100,000 a year, he wanted more. One day, while reading about how IBM's Deep Blue program had defeated the world chess champion Garry Kasparov, the kernel of an idea began to form in his mind: Could a computer program beat the market?

Since Cummings's specialty was pit trading, he naturally imagined a computer program that could replicate the actions of a pit trader. A robot could buy and sell contracts just as well as a human being, and much quicker, he thought.

So in January 1999, Cummings quit the floor. Settling down in front of his computer in a spare bedroom in his home, he started to bang out a robot trading program. Like a broker, it would post buy and sell orders, making money on the spread. Best of all, Cummings wouldn't have to spend all day jostling in the pit. He could sit back in his office and watch his robot do the hard work.

In October, with an initial investment of just $10,000, he launched Tradebot Systems.

His first task was to find a broker to execute his orders. That posed a problem. The system he'd designed had unusually high turnover— so high that typical brokerage fees could eat away all of its profits. While the holding times usually averaged several minutes, it was still far greater turnover than most investors saw. He needed a partner who'd cut him a deal in return for the high volumes he'd deliver.

Cummings started pitching his idea to dozens of firms. Fund manager American Century seemed like a natural fit. Also based in Kansas City, it boasted the tech-savvy investment team that had been among the first institutional firms to use Archipelago. But while the American Century team thought Cummings's strategy was ingenious, they also thought there was little way it could ever make enough money to matter to the firm, which managed billions.

Other reactions were less polite.

Cummings would fly to Chicago on Southwest Airlines and take the Orange Line downtown to pitch his idea. But Chicago's seasoned brokers laughed out loud at his computer demos. It was nice in theory, they told him, but no computer could account for all the chaotic factors a floor trader had to deal with. Tradebot would get smashed to bits trying to pick up nickels and dimes in front of a steamroller.

The clock was ticking. If Cummings didn't convince a broker to take him on, he'd have to give up his dream of building a robot trader. He'd have to get a normal nine-to-five job and slug it out like all those everyday schmoes he didn't want to become.

Then Cummings heard about Getco.

ONE day in early 2000, during one of his Chicago trips to pitch Tradebot, Cummings picked up a copy of *Futures* magazine, a trade publication popular in the city's trading circles. Deep inside its pages he came across a tiny ad for a broker dealer with the bizarre name of Getco LLC.

Cummings made an appointment at Getco's office at the Chicago Mercantile Exchange, a forty-story skyscraper on South Wacker Drive known among traders as the Merc. Soon after, he met Getco's founders, Stephen Schuler and Dan Tierney, in a hot, tiny, computer-lined office. As Cummings explained his strategy using his much-maligned computer demo, he started to notice something odd: Schuler and Tierney weren't laughing.

Instead, Schuler and Tierney were becoming increasingly excited. Almost immediately, they'd realized Cummings had discovered something amazing.

Schuler and Tierney sparked to Cummings's strategy for a good reason: They were also disillusioned floor traders who'd come to see electronic trading as the future. Schuler had been a pit trader on the Merc, juggling futures contracts linked to the S&P 500. Tierney had been a floor trader at the Chicago Board Options Exchange. They'd only recently launched Getco and were looking for partners.

Schuler had begun his career in 1981 as a runner on the floor of the Merc. In the mid-1990s, he grew increasingly concerned about his future at the helm of his small brokerage firm, Schuler Group. He had watched in frustration as electronic giants such as Timber Hill and Hull Trading grew more and more powerful. He started to envision a world in which human dealers had become obsolete, a world where all trading was controlled through a computer screen.

That worried him. His wife was pregnant, and he began to wonder if he had a future as a trader. Computers were pushing into every corner of the market. To catch up, he started reading everything he could get his hands on about how electronic markets worked.

Then he met Tierney, a young, cerebral floor trader more given to perusing works of philosophy and economic theory than the latest edition of *The Wall Street Journal*. Tierney, who'd started trading on the floor of the CBOE in 1993, had been doing his own research into electronic trading and had become convinced it was the future. The floor would one day be a relic of history—all trading would be handled through screens in isolated offices in a global electronic money grid.

On a Friday afternoon in 1999, the two founded Global Electronic Trading Company, or Getco, over a handshake. They quit their jobs and set up shop at the Merc in a tiny office of about one hundred square feet. They installed floor-to-ceiling computers that at times became so hot the room temperature topped a hundred degrees. Ethernet cables snaked along the floor. Computer monitors blinked along the walls. It looked like a wild experiment by a couple of mad scientists. To process their orders, Schuler and Tierney also launched a broker dealer called Octeg.

Their strategy was a basic "pit to screen" approach—trading on small, fleeting differences between contracts traded on the pits of the

Merc and the computer screens in their offices. They focused on the S&P 500 futures contract that changed hands on the floor of the Merc and its much smaller cousin, a contract known as the E-mini that was more easily traded on a computer screen. A Getco broker worked in the S&P 500 pit, taking orders over a headset. Schuler and Tierney traded on the screen. But their strategy, while profitable, wasn't as successful as they'd hoped. Since Schuler and Tierney weren't experienced computer programmers, they struggled to design systems that could handle screen-based trading.

Then Dave Cummings walked through their door talking about a revolutionary new computer-driven trading strategy. Cummings's high-speed trading robot was the system they'd been looking for— one that could replicate the actions of a market maker.

They struck a deal. Getco's broker, Octeg, would also act as Tradebot's broker. Since Cummings was strapped for cash, Schuler and Tierney fronted him $500,000 for a stake in Tradebot. They also "rented" the trading program's source code in exchange for a slice of their profits.

Cummings used the windfall to crank up Tradebot's operation, setting up shop in a small storefront office on Armour Road in North Kansas City.

In short order, Getco and Tradebot started gunning an open fire hydrant of orders into the stock market. And the high-frequency streams flowed directly to one destination: Island.

Cummings's strategy was simple, but it required massive bandwidth. Tradebot would post a two-sided quote—a bid and an offer—for several stocks and exchange-traded funds. For Intel, it might offer to buy for $20 and sell for $20.03, a 3-cent spread. Meanwhile, it constantly monitored the S&P 500 futures contract trading in Chicago for a clue as to whether Intel might make a move (often the futures contract moved slightly *before* the underlying stocks). If the S&P 500 futures did tick up sharply, the algorithm would aggressively buy Intel while canceling its sell orders, simultaneously placing new sell orders a few cents higher, say $20.10. If Intel continued to rise, the algorithm would become less aggressive. If the stock finally rested at $20.17 bid and $20.20 offer, the algorithm would only bid around $20.10 while selling at $20.20, trying to unload the shares it had just scooped up in order to cash in on the move. Tradebot was also very quick to sell if a stock moved against it, a strategy that went back to Cummings's roots as a floor trader swapping futures contracts at the Kansas City Board of Trade. A tried-and-true floor-trading strategy was to dump losing positions quickly in order to be able to trade another day—a lesson learned by many successful SOES bandits, as well. (The strategy was essentially the very same scalping technique deployed by the bandits.)

Unlike the bandits, Tradebot was fully automated. It was mind-bendingly fast and juggled massive volumes, putting up hundreds of thousands of orders a day, far more than the first generation of electronic traders, like Renaissance or ATD. ECNs such as Island loved Tradebot's flow because it provided rivers of precious liquidity.

Island's competitors were soon dying to get a taste of the heavy Bot flow. But Island was the only electronic network that could handle that industrial-strength volume. Other ECNs, such as BRUT, the network launched by Robert Greifeld, or Archipelago, were far too slow and clunky. They didn't have the computing capacity to process the orders. When they let Getco and Tradebot plug in, it was like touching a hot wire—and they were burned badly. "The younger ECNs, not Island, would beg us to turn on our models," says Keith Ross, Getco's CEO in the early 2000s. "We'd turn them on, and they'd call us back in five minutes and beg us to turn off."

"We were getting overwhelmed," recalls Bill O'Brien, a former executive at BRUT, who would later go on to run Direct Edge. "We'd call them up and say, 'If you don't slow down, we're going to crash.' "

One of Island's technical advantages was that it never—or hardly ever—paused during the trading day. Other ECNs were constantly hitting the spin cycle because they were downloading the day's trading information onto a hard drive in order to store the data. They had to do this periodically in order to open up memory for more trades. Island's system, through Levine's programming alchemy, didn't need to save its data during the trading session. It simply kept gobbling up the new orders and asking for more, without pausing for a millisecond.

And the Island team *loved* the gushers of orders from their frenetic new clients. Indeed, Island began to depend on them like a junkie getting a fix. One day, Getco's morning meeting ran long, past the start of trading in New York, and they were late turning on their systems. About five minutes after the bell, they got a frantic call from an Island official asking them what the hell was wrong.

Island was hooked. The rest of the market wouldn't be far behind.

TRADEBOT in its early days certainly didn't seem to be at the vanguard of the new market elite. Its trading room sat in the basement of the small, dingy storefront office in North Kansas City, a dilapidated industrial no-man's-land just east of the Missouri River. A team of five or so traders—associates, as Cummings called them—constantly monitored their trades on stacks of monitors piled high on their desks. The carpeting was gray, the walls were gray, and there were no windows or televisions. Water leaked through cracks in the walls during heavy storms. Cummings set up his office on the second floor, where he had several computers for trading.

Each computer came armed with software called a "tradebot," a program that showed which stocks the computer traded and the parameters that controlled its strategy, such as momentum or leverage. Traders could adjust variables such as the amount of money they were betting, and they had the option of pulling the plug when the market was behaving strangely. Mostly, the system ran on automatic pilot, like a jet liner cruising at high altitudes.

For a time, traders could pick and choose which stocks they'd trade. Eventually, Cummings started assigning traders specific stocks. The plum assignment was the Qs, the Nasdaq 100 ETF. The only catch was that Cummings expected Qs traders to be the cream of the crop, at times making as much as $15,000 a day (the amount, naturally, changed from month to month). Other traders were expected to make between $2,000 and $8,000 a day.

Losses were unacceptable. Whenever a model started losing money, the system would start scaling back. Cummings became so adamant about *never* losing money that on days when Tradebot's daily profit-and-loss was approaching zero, he'd simply shut the whole operation down and tell everyone to go home.

By 2002, roughly one hundred million orders a day were flowing out of Tradebot. As many—or more—were streaming from Getco. Combined, they accounted for roughly 10 percent of all trading in Nasdaq stocks just two years after launching.

Cummings's robot was tap-dancing in and out of stocks at rates never before seen. Tradebot would buy a small chunk of a stock, then turn around and sell it in seconds—or less than a second. Just as the SOES bandits used the Watcher to hop in and out of stocks at a rapid clip, Tradebot was picking off trading opportunities in the blink of an eye, able to make money on nearly every tick of a stock, up *and* down.

Decimalization turbocharged Tradebot. Once penny trading kicked in, the ticks grew smaller and smaller. Spreads for the most heavily traded stocks narrowed to pennies—often a single cent. Tradebot could buy Microsoft at $27.69 a share and flip it for $27.70 in a flash.

As spreads narrowed, Nasdaq market makers began to fall by the wayside. Penny spreads were simply too thin for them to make money. Into their place stepped the speed traders such as Getco and Tradebot, the new market makers of the digital age.

Their presence altered the very structure of the market. Much like the SOES bandits of old, the high-speed, algo-driven firms often traded in small chunks of a few hundred shares at a time, since they were easier to buy and sell—they were *more liquid*. As a result, by the mid-2000s, the average size of a trade on Nasdaq had shrunk to about five hundred shares from about fifteen hundred in the mid-1990s.

Trading in ETFs such as Qs (the Nasdaq 100) and Spyders (the S&P 500) fueled the mania, since firms could trade the funds as well as most of the underlying stocks, often hundreds at a time.

TRADEBOT and Getco parted ways in January 2002. Schuler and Tierney were interested in branching into Europe, while Cummings wanted to continue his focus on the U.S. stock market. To regain his independence, Cummings bought back Schuler and Tierney's stake in Tradebot in exchange for a royalty-free copy of the source code.

Getco, still using Cummings's code, quickly branched out from stocks into Treasury bonds, futures, and currencies. As they expanded, they snapped up computer equipment from busted Internet companies and started poaching math and computer wonks from the Illinois Institute of Technology, a breeding ground of techheads.

Since neither Tierney nor Schuler were experts in computer programming, they didn't hesitate to pay top dollar for the best programmers and traders they could find. One of their earliest coups was Dave Babulak, a former trader at Hull who'd worked alongside Haim Bodek (and had even attended Bodek's bachelor party). Babulak left Hull in 1999 to form a futures-trading operation called Blink Trading, which Getco purchased in 2002. With Blink, Getco had tapped into the Hull diaspora that was spreading sophisticated computer-trading strategies across Wall Street.

Like Automated Trading Desk, RGM Advisors, and Renaissance before them, Getco started recruiting AI programmers skilled in machine-learning techniques. Highly sensitive programs would monitor reams of data coming from all corners of the market, learning dynamically on the fly which strategies worked best under a variety of circumstances.

Getco soon became one of the most active trading firms in the world, in control of as much as 20 percent of the daily volume of blue chip stocks such as General Electric and Google. It was a dominant player in Treasuries, currencies, futures, and ETFs, pumping massive volumes into markets across the globe. A fringe benefit of all that trading was that Getco was armed with vast, highly sensitive market radar. Able to detect the smallest shift in market direction in the blink of an eye, across multiple assets around the world, Getco could then predict the future in a way few competitors could match. It was as if the firm had deployed hundreds of thousands of real-time sensors throughout the atmosphere to determine weather patterns, while competitors were staring at a rusty weather vane.

Getco soon moved out of its cramped offices at the Merc into several floors directly above the trading pits of the Chicago Board of Trade. Rooms packed with cutting-edge servers alternated with rooms full of programmers, quants, AI experts, physicists, and even video-game programmers, perched before stacks of massive digital screens that reached to the ceiling.

The firm became a steady presence in Washington, D.C., hiring ex-SEC hotshots and top lobbyists. Former SEC chairman Arthur Levitt was an adviser. Getco in its public statements repeatedly said it stood behind open markets and a "level playing field" for all investors.

But Getco, with its technological prowess and its hoards of money, had become one of the new kings of Wall Street. Its founders, Schuler and Tierney, said to be worth hundreds of millions each, remained shadowy Oz-like figures behind the curtain. For years, not a single photo of either founder was publicly available.

It was a deep irony: A firm that beat the drum of open markets and transparency was in fact one of the most secretive trading operations in the world.

TRADEBOT also kept growing. Soon after he broke away from Getco, Cummings devised an entirely new strategy. It focused squarely on capturing maker-taker fees — that model Josh Levine had first rolled out in 1998 to reward firms for posting bids and offers. By 2002, nearly every pool paid firms to provide liquidity, typically 20 cents per hundred shares. At the same time, they charged firms that "took" liquidity 30 cents per hundred shares.

By late 2003, as more and more high-speed traders jumped into the market and spreads narrowed, it was increasingly hard to make money through simple scalping strategies. But with maker-taker, even if Tradebot didn't make money on the trade itself, it could collect fees for posting trades. If Tradebot could pump enough quotes into the market and snap up enough "make" fees, it could have a strategy that was akin to an ATM machine — as long as every other high-frequency trader in the universe wasn't doing the same trade.

The strategy had an ideal candidate for a test drive: WorldCom. In late 2002, shares of WorldCom, the telecommunications company that went bankrupt after an accounting scandal, were trading for less than 10 cents apiece. Some traders, including Cummings, quickly realized that a golden opportunity had opened up. The reason: maker-taker rebates. Tradebot could place an order to buy a thousand shares of WorldCom for a paltry cost of $100. But if it got the rebate, it *made* a dollar on the trade (that is, one dime per hundred shares). While a dollar doesn't sound like much, it added up because the volumes in WorldCom were massive, with millions of shares changing hands every day. In other words, *a lot* of dollars were there for the taking, with very little risk involved. And since the market was so large, such trading was massively scalable. In high-frequency trading, it was all about the *volume* of trades, not the profit per trade.

Of course, the frenetic trading sparked by such strategies served zero purpose for investors. The mania around WorldCom showed how the market was evolving into a giant electronic slot machine for high-speed traders plugging it for dollars . . . *millions* of dollars. Maker-taker was becoming algorithmic steroids for high-speed firms, pumping them full of a steady flow of income for posting orders (while collecting fees from firms that *had* to trade, such as hedge funds and mutual funds). And all that high-frequency liquidity wasn't going into stocks to simply "make markets," as its practitioners claimed. It was methodically hunting down every last hole in the market's plumbing to make a very fast buck.

As Cummings continued to push his machine to the limits, he started noticing that at times competitors such as Automated Trading Desk were beating him to the punch on Island. ATD had placed its computers right beside Island's baker's racks of Dell computers in the basement of 50 Broad, giving it a huge advantage over Cummings's firm, based more than a thousand miles away in North Kansas City.

Those miles meant money. In the world of automated speed trading, it was like racing a Ford Model T against a Lamborghini Testarossa. Because Tradebot often popped in and out of stocks in seconds, a fleeting sliver of time could mean the difference between a profit and a loss. Just as floor traders had an advantage by being at the heart of the action, proximity to a trading network's computer systems gave certain firms an edge over competitors in the race to grab a trade.

Speed was doubly important for Tradebot because of the nature of its strategy. Since it was responding in real time to rapid moves in the market, the firm had to constantly update its orders. If it bought a stock and the price started to fall, it had to get rid of it *instantly.* Speed—speed in entering new orders, in canceling old orders, and in receiving constant updates about the market through Island's ITCH feed—was crucial. If Tradebot was responding to stale information— in the Formula One world of high-frequency trading, a half-second delay made data Paleolithically stale—it could lose money.

That's why Cummings realized he needed to move his computers as close to Island's matching engine as possible. He jumped on the phone and called Matt Andresen.

"This is unfair, Matt," he said, explaining his concern.

"It's true," Andresen conceded. "Our customers outside of New York are at a big disadvantage. We agree, it should be a level playing field."

Andresen explained that Levine and Will Sterling had been working on a model to let a much larger number of firms place their computers directly next to Island's computers. That way, no one would have an advantage over anyone else. Heartland Securities, the former trading arm of Datek, had already mainlined into Island's computers through a cable that snaked down the stairway to the basement at 50 Broad. Broadway Trading, the sister day-trading operation to Heartland, had a similar setup. So did ATD.

Cummings could tell. He knew that no one had faster systems than Tradebot. But other firms were putting their quotes up before him, beating him to the punch. He could see it on his screens every day. As he saw his competitors beating him on trades he was used to winning, he realized he was facing a new obstacle: the speed of light.

To overcome it, he needed to put his own computers directly where the battle was being fought—right next to Island. The practice came to be known as "colocation," *colo* for short, in which trading outfits were "colocated" with exchange computers. Colo would form the backbone of high-frequency trading and eventually become the model for how securities were traded everywhere, with giant server-packed data centers rising up around the world.

It wouldn't be free, of course. Island charged a small fee—a few thousand dollars a month—for firms to place their computers beside Island's matching engine. Cummings readily agreed.

It was money well spent. The difference in performance was dramatic: With his computers next to Island, Tradebot could execute twenty orders during the one-fiftieth of a second it took an order to travel from Kansas City to New York.

After plugging into Island's computers, Cummings set his sights on cozying up to Archipelago. While he wasn't thrilled about trading on Archipelago, which he saw as achingly slow compared with Island, he liked to have all options available. Tradebot also frequently exploited discrepancies between prices on Island and Archipelago. Intel might be selling for $20 on Island and $20.02 on Archipelago. Tradebot could buy on Island and sell on Archipelago for a quick 2-cents-a-share profit—as long as the execution happened instantly. On Archipelago, delays of several seconds could wipe out that profit and at times result in a loss. Losses, to Cummings, were unacceptable.

Frustrated with Archipelago's technology, Cummings rang up Jamie Selway, who'd recently become Archipelago's liaison with the high-speed traders. Selway, who'd been Nasdaq's point man for the ECNs, had joined Goldman Sachs in the late 1990s. But he felt stifled by the winner-take-all culture of the bank and in 2000 jumped ship to join Archipelago, where he worked closely with computer-driven out-fits such as Tradebot and Timber Hill. There was no one Selway would spend more time with than Cummings.

Cummings complained that Archipelago was too slow. Tradebot often had to throttle back as Archipelago's computers hit the spin cycle, making a hash of his fine-tuned models. "I can't manage that risk," he told Selway.

Cummings pushed Selway to make fixes, constantly comparing Archipelago to Island—usually unfavorably.

He became so demanding that Selway began to worry that Archi-pelago would become the plaything of big-volume traders such as Tradebot while overlooking the needs of regular buy-and-hold inves-tors. It marked the beginning of the dynamic that years later would lead to the very problems that Haim Bodek faced at Trading Ma-chines, a market in which exchanges catered to the every whim of high-speed traders, eager to win their business. Selway could sense the market forces shifting. *Fear the Bot*, he told himself.

It was a losing battle. Cummings paid a visit to Archipelago's offices on the twentieth floor of the Hartford Plaza North building in Chicago's Loop, where he met Jerry Putnam. He was eager to move his computers alongside Archipelago's. Putnam pushed back. Unlike

Island, Archipelago hadn't set up colocation capabilities for anyone else yet. Putnam was worried that other clients would get wind of the deal and complain. He wanted Cummings to wait until Archipelago finished a new data center in Weehawken, New Jersey, just across the Hudson River from Manhattan. The center would have plenty of space for Tradebot's computers and any others that might want a piece of the action.

Cummings wasn't in the mood to wait. He moved his computers to a spot roughly a mile from Archipelago's Chicago headquarters. When Archipelago finally set up its center in Weehawken, Tradebot was first in line to "colo" alongside it.

CUMMINGS had more tricks up his sleeve. Around 2004, he began to develop a strategy to make money trading in dark pools, a rising force in the early 2000s. While institutional traders were running from the lit markets such as Nasdaq into dark pools, in order to get away from the new breed of high-speed traders, like Tradebot, the speed traders devised methods to swim in the dark as well. Known as "latency arbitrage," the strategy involved gaming the difference between the price of a stock in a dark pool and its price in the lit markets. Tradebot was effectively exploiting the "latency" of the system, a measurement of the time it takes for information to move from place to place in a closed system, such as a market.

Behind the difference: dark pools that priced stocks based on an electronic feed called the Securities Information Processor, or SIP. If the price of Intel rose to $20.02 from $20 on Nasdaq, many dark pools would get that price through the SIP feed. The trouble with the SIP was that compared to the microsecond speeds of Tradebot's world, it was punishingly slow. For firms practicing latency arb, that amounted to a gold mine. Trades that occurred on Island would occur a split second before the information reached the dark pools. Tradebot had a direct line into Island through its colocated ITCH feed, which provided data on the trade *before* it reached the dark pools. If Intel rose to $20.02 on Island, Intel would still be trading for $20 on the dark pools. Tradebot could buy up shares of Intel milliseconds before the new price reached the dark pools through the "slow" SIP feed, and then sell Intel for a profit once the new price arrived. As usual with such strategies, the amounts were fleetingly small, just pennies per share, but done thousands of times a day they could add up significantly.

It was as if most investors were watching the Kentucky Derby on a delayed feed, while Tradebot and high-speed firms like it were at the track and able to make bets all the way to the finish line. The SEC didn't prohibit such trades—in fact, they were seen as making prices more efficient.

UNLIKE Getco's Schuler and Tierney, who hired experts from other firms or graduates from top universities to build and design their trading machines, Cummings was the primary model builder and big thinker at Tradebot. He rarely hired experienced traders and instead poached rafts of fresh brains from local universities in Missouri and Kansas, who came far cheaper than the Ivy League quants many top Wall Street firms were going after. Cummings liked to call it his "Halfway to India" strategy.

Working at Tradebot had its perks. The dress code was business casual. Ties were a rarity. Cummings himself preferred jeans, polo shirts, and sneakers, and in the summer he liked to wear shorts. Lunch was on the house, keeping workers busy at their desks. Most employees were out the door by 5 P.M.

But the environment was a pressure cooker. Cummings was a demanding boss. If he wasn't satisfied with an employee's performance, he didn't hesitate to push him out the door. Whole batches might be let go in a single afternoon. Cummings favored Fridays for his mass cullings. "There was a constant fear that you could lose your job, especially on a Friday," says one ex-employee.

After the closing bell every day, Cummings held a meeting

with the whole company to dissect how the day went. It could be nerve-racking, but it also kept everyone sharp and focused—the traders knew they'd have to explain every move to the boss at the end of the day. You didn't want to screw up. Few did.

Sometimes Cummings simply cut himself off from the company, taking "think weeks" by traveling to a quiet place where he could avoid interruption. When he started writing the code for a trading program, he would work like a fiend, spending eight- to ten-hour sessions of furious coding. One week, when he was in a particularly inspired stretch of coding, he slapped a sign on his door that read DON'T EVEN THINK ABOUT KNOCKING.

And it was all paying off. Eventually, Cummings moved out of the dingy Armour Road office into a gleaming new building in North Kansas City. Then, as a sign of his growing wealth and status, Cummings, who had a private pilot's license, purchased an eight-seat twin engine Cessna Citation luxury jet for the firm the year he turned forty years old.

THE Bots were taking control, pushing their favorite trading networks for more capacity, more speed, more creative ways to make money.

The tail was wagging the dog. While plain vanilla mutual fund companies couldn't care less about microsecond quirks in the plumbing of exchanges, high-frequency firms fixated on such information. They designed strategies that required maximum speed, and pushed the electronic networks and exchanges to provide it. And they did.

"It became about meeting the needs of that specific HFT community," says a technologist who worked for several top ECNs and exchanges in the 2000s. "The game changed. Firms like Getco and Tradebot wanted to know everything about our system so they could manage their orders accordingly. We spent a tremendous amount of money trying to meet their needs. They trained us to be fast. It's all about what functionality can I offer the HFT that they can take advantage of. We're going after *guaranteed economics*."

High-speed firms worked hand in hand with the trading networks to create exotic order types that would behave in very specific ways. The firms wanted orders that would never go to the NYSE or Nasdaq, or that would only go to other ECNs. Orders that would post a bid or offer, then immediately cancel if they weren't filled.

Archipelago proved to be a master at this game, which kept the speedsters coming back for more. While Archipelago couldn't match Island for speed, it proved more than willing to provide customized orders to meet the whims of its most important customers.

"We created all these different order types to accommodate how they wanted to trade," recalls one former Archipelago employee. "We tweaked how the order would interact with our book according to what they wanted. A lot of the unique orders were created at the request of a customer, typically a high-frequency customer. You had to be a sophisticated customer to learn how to use it. They'd send it in and we'd respond. It was a happy little circle."

The result: By the mid-2000s, just four firms—Automated Trading Desk, Renaissance, Tradebot, and Getco—accounted for roughly 25 to 30 percent of all stock trading in the United States. All along the way, they worked closely with the electronic pools, from Island to Archipelago to BRUT, to customize the plumbing of their systems to meet their needs. And the ECNs seemed to have little choice but to comply with their every demand. If they were going to survive in an increasingly competitive space, they had to cater to the best customers, the firms that filled their pools with liquidity.

Other high-frequency traders were getting in on the act, installing computer servers beside market-matching engines, setting up ultra-fast links between New York and Chicago. Traditional investment firms and banks weren't far behind. Banks ranging from Merrill Lynch to Goldman Sachs to Deutsche Bank to J.P. Morgan would soon co-locate with the matching engines of major market centers. The firms were adapting to the new algo-driven Formula One market pioneered by the likes of Cummings, Schuler, Tierney—and, of course, Levine.

Outfits most people have never heard of started to launch in diminutive offices in downtown Manhattan and Chicago, or places distant from the centers of finance—such as Austin, Texas; Southern
California; or the suburbs of New Jersey—where the electronic pools
were building their next-generation data centers.

In 2000, Mark Gorton, a math expert with degrees from Yale,
Stanford, and Harvard, launched Lime Brokerage. The firm was created primarily to cater to Gorton's high-speed trading outfit, Tower
Research. One day in late 2001, programmers at BRUT noticed a sudden surge in orders. More than the three million orders from a single
firm flowed through their pipes. The origin: Lime.

Hudson River Trading, located near the shore of its eponymous
river in downtown Manhattan, started up in February 2002, founded
by a trio of math and computer experts from MIT and Harvard. Chicago's Sun Trading was founded that same year by Jeff Wigley, an
options market maker on the CBOE.

More would come. In the next few years, the small band of computer traders would become a dominant force in nearly every market
imaginable, from stocks to currencies to commodities. Many of these
firms deployed advanced AI systems that controlled the trading and
adapted instantly to shifting market conditions.

Speed was the key.

In the early 2000s, it was a matter of milliseconds, or thousandths
of a second—two hundred times the average speed of human thought.
By the end of the decade, high-speed firms would be measuring executions in microseconds, or one-millionth of a second. There was talk
of trading in nanoseconds, one-billionth of a second.

It was a fevered race to zero, trades that moved so fast they took
place instantaneously. Concerns mounted about whether high-speed
trading would also mean high-speed crashing. And there were doubts
about whether all the frenetic trading actually improved the quality of
the market. A 2001 study of Island's system found that more than 25

percent of orders submitted to Island were canceled within two seconds or less. "The extensive use of these 'fleeting orders' is at odds with the view that limit order traders (like dealers) are patient providers of liquidity," the study found.

In years to come, canceled orders would become even more popular as speeds increased and the number of trading venues exploded. It was an essential part of the high-speed strategy—as prices bobbed and weaved, firms would duck by canceling orders and resubmitting new orders a millisecond later.

There were other more questionable practices behind these phantom orders. Some firms were layering in orders to create the illusion of demand—orders that they canceled well before they could ever actually execute. Such orders could ignite bogus momentum in a stock, faking out other algos' hunter-seeker radar and giving the speedsters the perfect opportunity to bet against the stock as it rose into a bear trap of counterfeit demand. In the industry, this was known as "spoofing."

Like Getco, many of the speedsters were expanding well beyond stocks. They were dabbling in bonds, options, currencies, and commodities. As they did so, they were pushing aside human traders at an ever-accelerating rate. One currency operation at a large French bank was said to employ traders who would literally tape their fingers to certain keys on their keyboards so they could more rapidly enter orders, all day long. By the mid-2000s, the operation was shut down—humans, no matter what tricks they played, couldn't compete with the Bots.

A new Wall Street elite was emerging, a wealthy technorati that owned the massive computers and superfast cables that shaved precious microseconds off orders. Levine's dream of a market without middlemen had been turned on its head. Technology had created a new entrenched middleman: the high-frequency traders.

In Tradebot's and Getco's early years, it seemed as if a new paradigm for trading had been created—and it had. With the help of the electronic platforms, trading was cheaper, faster, and seemingly far more efficient than in the bad old days of human market makers and specialists.

But there were already rising signs of trouble. Along with the ascent of the high-octane traders came the dark pools. At first, they were electronic networks that allowed large investors to swap big blocks of stock away from the prying eyes of the lit market. Among the first was a pool called Liquidnet, launched in 2000. In 2004, Dan Mathisson at Credit Suisse built a dark pool called Crossfinder. Pipeline Trading, run by a nuclear physicist and a former president of Nasdaq, rolled out a dark pool for big block trading the same year. Goldman Sachs would build a dark pool called Sigma X. Even Getco would eventually launch a dark pool. As algorithmic trading grew, large investors were finding it harder to trade large chunks of stock. More and more trades were sliced and diced into small, round-numbered pieces—two hundred, three hundred shares—that algos could more easily juggle. The algos deployed complex methods to hunt out the large whale orders the big firms traded, such as "pinging" dark pools with orders that they canceled seconds later. Some used AI pattern-recognition methods to detect their prey. Relatively small at first, the dark pools would grow larger and larger as electronic trading expanded dramatically in the coming years.

The electronic traders and the Plumbers who built the pools they swam in didn't see anything wrong with the market they'd help create. They celebrated themselves as democratizers, cracking the insider machine that had picked the pockets of mom and pop for decades. They'd brought light to darkness.

And they were right in many ways. They had defeated their foes. They'd won.

Whether they knew it or not, they were on their way to becoming the new insiders of Wall Street.

And the new enemy.

# CHAPTER SIXTEEN

# CRAZY NUMBERS

S moke and ash poured through the air-conditioning intake ducts in the basement of 50 Broad Street. Island's data center, stacks of two thousand Dell computer towers that Levine & Co. had been cobbling together since the mid-1990s, was heating up as the air filled with toxic particles. It was the morning of September 11, 2001.

Matt Andresen, who'd arrived early at the office for an 8 A.M. meeting, had watched through his office window as a wall of ash barreled down Broad Street after the South Tower of the World Trade Center collapsed. The smoke was so thick that he couldn't see across the street. As the impossible nature of the situation sank in, he began to worry about his wife and two kids, who typically went to a Borders bookstore at the World Trade Center for morning story time.

The mood at Island was the same as everywhere else that morning in downtown Manhattan: disbelief, shock, fear. The Russian programmer Mike Lazarev was pouring extra-strong screwdrivers to help calm people's nerves. Levine was busy making sure Island's system was secure. John Hillen, Island's chief operating officer and a former army cavalry officer who'd served in the 1991 Gulf War, urged everyone to stay indoors.

Andresen was frantic. His apartment was just a few doors down from Island's office. Around eleven-thirty, he left the office alone, making his way through the ash cloud and firefighters to find his family huddled with a group of other stragglers in the building's first-floor office.

Several marines appeared on the scene and helped evacuate the families to Beekman Hospital near City Hall. It was a spooky scene, an emergency room full of doctors and nurses but few patients. Andresen began to wonder if there were any survivors at all from the collapse of the towers. Later that day, he and his family were ferried north out of lower Manhattan in an ambulance.

Back at 50 Broad, Will Sterling, Levine's first hire at Island, scrambled to air out the basement. Covering his mouth and nose in a bandana, he frantically tried to clear the ducts of the ventilation system. As soon as he cleared one, another clogged up. The smoke was unstoppable.

That could have spelled disaster for the computers if they kept running. So Sterling made the call and pulled the plug on Island, the first time in more than four years that it wasn't operational during the trading day. The Island team did everything they could to protect the computers, covering them with tarps and plastic sheeting, then they evacuated the building to join the stream of terrified workers and residents trying to escape lower Manhattan.

There was no time to rest. The following day, Sterling and his technology team went to Island's backup data center in Secaucus, New Jersey, a half hour's drive from New York. The center had been in the works for months, but it was still a few months before it was supposed to be ready for live face time with perfectionist customers such as Thomas Peterffy and Dave Cummings.

It would have to do. Sterling jumped on the phone and started calling the hundreds of firms that used Island, trying to cobble together a virtual private network, tricked out with encryption technology so authorized users could gain access to the new data center. A team of Island technologists worked furiously to get the system up and running as fast as possible. After ironing out the glitches, Island was ready to go back online again by Wednesday, September 13. The New York Stock Exchange, however, wasn't—and it wouldn't be ready until September 17.

To the Island team, it was yet another example of the superiority of a computer-based network. Since Island didn't really exist anywhere, other than on the motherboard of a Dell computer, it wasn't as vulnerable as a physical exchange to catastrophic events such as September 11.

IT had been a busy year for Island. The stock market had continued to plunge as the dot-com bubble deflated, but Island kept growing and taking huge chunks of market share away from Nasdaq. By the end of 2001, a larger share of Nasdaq stocks would trade on Island than on Instinet.

A rapid uptick in high-speed trading was powering Island forward. Volumes were exploding. Levine had built Island to be fast, simple, and supremely scalable. It could handle anything anyone threw at it. But when the high-frequency traders such as Getco and Tradebot started ramping up, testing their strength with massive order flows and never-before-seen speeds, even Island was pushed to the limit.

"The numbers got crazy," recalls Will Sterling. "We put in a lot of design effort to leave room for scale. I was shocked at how quickly people leaned into that scale. You'd see the numbers come in and it was just insane."

There were two pools the speed Bots never swam in: the NYSE and Nasdaq. The two primary markets for stocks had been left behind, and they didn't even know it yet. Their refusal to upgrade their systems as they catered to the human specialists and market makers had proved to be a crucial mistake as the rise of high-frequency trading created an entirely new liquidity source. It was all flowing to the electronic pools.

Nasdaq officials started noticing floods of orders for Nasdaq stocks—but they weren't happening on Nasdaq. The Bots were dominating trading in big Nasdaq stocks such as Microsoft, Intel, Cisco, and WorldCom.

"We were seeing massive volume coming from firms we'd never heard of," recalls Nasdaq chief economist Frank Hathaway. "It was coming from these high-frequency firms out of the Midwest that we had no experience with. We'd contact them, but they had no interest in us."

It was a problem for Nasdaq, since it wasn't getting paid for the trades—Island was. Island reported the trades back to Nasdaq, whose liquidity was draining rapidly, spilling over to Island.

The die was cast. Nasdaq had to change, fast. The speed traders, with their massive volumes, were in the driver's seat. Nasdaq would have to adapt to suit their needs if it wanted to survive. With decimalization, the established market makers were already dropping out in droves as their profits evaporated. For Nasdaq, it was kill or be killed.

Its solution: a computerized trading network that came to be known as the ECN Killer. They called it SuperMontage (the market's book of buy and sell orders was often referred to as a "montage" of orders). And it would spark an epic fight that spread from the trading floors of Wall Street to the halls of Capitol Hill.

Doug Atkin stormed out of a meeting at the SEC's Washington office. It was October 2001, and the fight over SuperMontage was heating up. The Instinet CEO whipped out his cell phone and hit the speed dial for Matt Andresen.

Andresen didn't pick up, so Atkin left a message.

"If you don't get your fucking ass down to Washington to help us fight SuperMontage," he said, "we're going to cut you off from Instinet."

It was a serious threat. If Island couldn't access Instinet's order flow, it would be missing out on a crucial part of the market. Watcher traders constantly checked Instinet, since it was a good indication of what the big boys—the Goldmans, the Morgans, the Merrills—were doing in their favorite stocks.

Atkin's threat revealed how worried he was about SuperMontage.

In design, SuperMontage was a giant electronic super-pool. It would aggregate the best bids and offers throughout the market—including those on ECNs such as Island, Archipelago, and Instinet—and post them in a single, super *montage* that all traders could access.

The trouble was, SuperMontage wasn't fair, at least according to the ECNs. It gave a preference to quotes from Nasdaq market makers. If a Nasdaq market maker and a customer using Island had the same quote, say, a bid to buy Apple for $20, the Nasdaq market maker would be first in line.

That was a major threat to the ECNs—and they fought back, hard, sending reams of letters to the SEC explaining why SuperMontage was a disastrous idea.

"SuperMontage would, if approved, impermissibly permit Nasdaq to build an *anti-competitive* matching facility," Atkin wrote in a December 2000 letter.

Nearly every ECN sent similar attack letters to the SEC, except for one: Island.

Levine had taken a hard look at the architecture of SuperMontage, and he'd come to a simple conclusion: It was a bust. It would never succeed because no ECNs would voluntarily participate. SuperMontage violated a principal rule of markets that had motivated Island's creation in the first place: It was anticompetitive. That meant it couldn't work. Competition drove markets, made them better.

*There was no need to fight it.*

SuperMontage would die of its own accord, Levine told Andresen. So rather than waste time trying to stop SuperMontage, Andresen crafted a strategy to operate independently.

"We saw that they were trying to kill us," recalls Andresen, who likened the market to a shopping mall. With SuperMontage, Nasdaq was trying to make all customers enter the mall through Nasdaq's own store before they could reach the other stores. "We were like, why don't we just leave the shopping mall?"

After SuperMontage had been proposed, the SEC set up a series of meetings between Nasdaq and ECN officials to hammer out their differences. Island decided to skip the first meeting and lay low while they crafted their escape plan.

Their absence infuriated Atkin, who wanted the ECNs to put up a united front. Island had been one of the strongest voices against Nasdaq abuses over the years. They absolutely needed to join in the attack against SuperMontage, Atkin felt.

And so, after the first meeting, he phoned Andresen and threatened to cut Island off if they didn't play ball.

There was one problem with his threat: Cutting off a competing ECN was a violation of federal regulations designed to create an open, seamless market. Atkin was threatening Island with anticompetitive behavior—and, for kickers, leaving the threat on a recorded message.

Andresen decided he could use Atkin's mistake to his advantage.

At the time, Island had been tangled up in a contentious billing dispute with Instinet. Every time an Island trade was executed on Instinet, Instinet charged a fee. Because Instinet saw Island as its number one competitor outside the NYSE and Nasdaq, it started charging Island a much higher rate than it charged any other ECN.

Island's response was simple: It stopped paying. By the time of Atkin's phone call, it had run up a bill of about $1.5 million.

Andresen set up a meeting with Atkin at Instinet's headquarters at 375 Third Avenue in midtown Manhattan to hash out the dispute. Atkin was belligerent, fuming at Andresen about SuperMontage. And he demanded immediate payment for all the fees Island had been skipping out on.

Then Andresen pulled out a transcript of the phone call and handed it to Atkin. He said that if he kept pressing Island for payment and didn't start charging it the same amount as every other ECN was charged, he'd go to the SEC.

The move forced Atkin to agree to a settlement in short order. Andresen walked out of the office chuckling to himself. Another victory for Island — and another defeat for Instinet.

JERRY Putnam, meanwhile, was also making a number of moves to push Archipelago forward. A big test came on November 28, 2001.

Putnam was wrapping up a meeting in New York when he got an e-mail from Archipelago's Chicago headquarters. "Check out what's going on with Enron," the message read.

Standard & Poor's had just announced that it was downgrading Enron's bonds to junk status as the company's book-rigging scandal came to light. The stock collapsed within minutes. Trading of Enron was halted on the floor of the NYSE amid a chaotic stampede for the exits.

But trading continued on ECNs such as Archipelago and Island without a hitch, with ten million trades executed. Twenty-nine minutes after the halt, trading resumed at the NYSE. The first print of a large trade on the Big Board was identical to the price it was swapping hands for on the ECNs.

It was a pivotal moment. The electronic pools were *setting the prices* for the NYSE, instead of the other way around. It showed that electronic trading could handle chaotic situations, while the Big Board tossed up its hands.

Putnam did a victory lap, appearing on CNBC, where he crowed that the Enron event proved the floor was superfluous — comments that infuriated the NYSE's charismatic CEO Dick Grasso. High-tech magazine *Fast Company* anointed Putnam the king of electronic trading. "Jerry Putnam is the face of Wall Street's future," the magazine said in a May 2002 article.

■  ■  ■

ISLAND, meanwhile, continued to craft its strategy to operate outside the SuperMontage shopping mall. Andresen brainstormed several plans, some of which seemed like desperate Hail Marys.

Plan A: Join forces with Nasdaq's biggest rival, the NYSE.

To that end, Andresen called up Roger McNamee, a board member of Island investor Silver Lake Partners. McNamee's brother, George, was on the NYSE's board.

"Do you think George can arrange a meeting with Grasso?" Andresen asked.

"Let me check," McNamee said.

There had already been informal contacts between Island and Grasso. Some even wondered whether Grasso, a staunch defender of the NYSE's hallowed specialist system, was quietly mulling buying an ECN. One day, Grasso had walked alone into Island's office and had a look around. As he'd toured the office, someone had handed him an Island baseball cap, which he slipped on over his glistening bald head. As he walked out the door, though, he took it off.

"I don't think I should be seen on the street in this," he quipped.

After some back-and-forth, a meeting for late 2001 was set up. Andresen walked over to the NYSE's headquarters, a two-minute stroll from Island's office. He was escorted to Grasso's office on the sixth floor of the exchange, quietly snickering to himself at the Big Board's ornate oak-paneled decor.

In Grasso's expansive office, replete with memento mori from the executive's years at the head of the Big Board, Andresen immediately began to perspire. The NYSE CEO famously kept his office piping hot, ninety degrees or higher, either because he had a cool metabolism or because he liked to watch his guests sweat.

After they shook hands, Andresen launched into his pitch. "How would you like to eviscerate your biggest competitor?" he said.

"I'm listening," Grasso replied.

"Island is executing about fifteen percent of all of Nasdaq volume, more than any other ECN," Andresen said.

"I know," Grasso said.

"What if Island printed its trades on NYSE?" Andresen said.

All ECNs were required to post their trades on a regulated market—typically either Nasdaq or the NYSE. The markets then sold the trade data to a firm that ran the consolidated ticker tape. For years, Island had reported its trades to Nasdaq, since it mostly traded Nasdaq stocks. Andresen was proposing switching sides.

That would allow Island to circumvent SuperMontage while bringing in roughly $20 million a year in extra revenue to the NYSE, since the NYSE would get paid for posting Island's trades on the consolidated tape. Better yet, that cash would be coming straight out of Nasdaq's pockets—and it would make the NYSE bigger than Nasdaq in Nasdaq's own stocks, a potentially deadly blow in the constant fight over listings.

Andresen said the move could even help the NYSE achieve one of its most cherished goals at the time: to attract Nasdaq stalwarts such as Microsoft and Intel, companies that respected electronic pioneers like Island.

Best of all, the NYSE wouldn't have to do anything beyond signing on the dotted line and agreeing to receive Island's trades.

"It's a great idea," Grasso said. "Give me some time to think about it."

But Andresen could tell Grasso wasn't interested. He was still the arch-defendant of the specialists and floor traders who dominated the NYSE. In their eyes, any tie-up with Island was a deal with the devil. They weren't ready to join forces with the electronic-trading crowd. Not yet.

In the meantime, Andresen needed to come up with a workable plan to circumvent SuperMontage. Plan A, the NYSE, was a dead end.

Plan B was even more audacious.

THE Cincinnati Stock Exchange, which was actually based in Chicago, had for years been the playground of Bernie Madoff, who had also been trying to circumvent Nasdaq and the NYSE, with little success. In 1980, it had been the first exchange to go entirely electronic. But the business had never taken off. By the early 2000s, it was on life support.

Andresen thought he could strike a deal with Cincinnati. He contacted the exchange and pitched it on the same idea he'd tried to sell to the NYSE. Instead of printing its trades on Nasdaq, Island would print them on Cincinnati. The exchange would reap the benefit of the market data fees, all for simply signing on the dotted line. Desperate for any kind of business, Cincinnati agreed.

Soon after, Andresen called Dean Furbush, who'd been spearheading SuperMontage, and explained that very soon Island's orders would disappear from Nasdaq.

"We're going to leave, Dean," he said. "It's what's best for us and our customers."

"When?" Furbush asked.

"We're looking at early 2002."

Furbush was flabbergasted. Nasdaq appealed to the SEC, claiming Island's move wasn't legal, but its plea was rebuffed. As the transfer date approached, Furbush arranged a meeting with Andresen at Le Bernardin, a posh French seafood palace in midtown Manhattan.

"Give us a chance to keep you," Furbush pleaded. He promised to work out a plan that Island would find acceptable.

Andresen was skeptical but he agreed.

"OK, Dean, we'll wait a little while," he said. "But not long."

Days later, at a quiet Italian restaurant near Times Square, Andresen met with Wick Simmons, who'd taken over the chairmanship of Nasdaq in late September. A gregarious, backslapping executive who'd spent most of his career at old-line investing houses such as Prudential Securities and Shearson Lehman Brothers, Simmons was all smiles. "I just got off the phone with Meg Whitman," he said, referring to the CEO of eBay, the online auction site. "I just sold a Porsche on eBay!"

Andresen smirked. *Who does this guy think he is?*

As they talked over steaming plates of pasta, Andresen explained that Island had no choice but to leave Nasdaq. He said Island expected to save about $20 million with the move, since it wouldn't have to pay the fees Nasdaq charged to use its system.

"You forced us down this path," he said.

"Here's what I'm prepared to do," Simmons replied magnanimously. "Of the twenty million dollars, I can get you seven million."

Andresen laughed. "I think you're thirteen million short, Wick."

Simmons left the meeting confident that Island couldn't do without Nasdaq. At bottom, he didn't think Island had the guts to go through with their plan, and the $7 million sweetener had sealed the deal. He returned to the office boasting that he'd staved off disaster.

"I got those Island guys," he told Furbush.

As word about Island's plans got around, market players who used it wanted to learn more about what would happen. Island had become a key link in the trading chain and any major moves by it could impact everyone else.

On January 2, 2002, as Island's planned shift to Cincinnati neared, Andy Madoff sent an e-mail to Josh Levine. Madoff, then director of Nasdaq trading at Bernard L. Madoff Investment Securities, wanted Levine to join the Security Industry Association's technology management committee, a group of top officials from exchanges, banks, and major hedge funds. With Levine on board, the committee would have better insight into Island's next move.

Levine said he was game.

"Count me in!" he wrote back. "Just tell me where and when the meeting is and I'll be there."

Levine's presence at the first meeting in late January, at the SIA's 120 Broadway office, was memorable—but not for what the committee discussed. As the industry bigwigs settled into their seats in an SIA conference room, Levine strolled in, doffed his jacket, and sat

down, handing out a few business cards (which would later expand
into brick-size sponges if they touched water). The dull buzz of the
room's conversation faded to silence as the committee members took
a gander at the reclusive boy genius of Island they'd all heard about.
Levine was wearing a T-shirt and jeans. Everyone else was fitted out
in their custom-made suits, their Armani ties, and their Thomas Pink
herringbones.

Madoff was scandalized. The morning before the next meeting,
on March 5, he sent an e-mail to Levine. Its subject line: "Meeting
Dress Code."

"I'm begging you," he wrote, "no t-shirt at the next meeting."

Levine didn't see the e-mail and, of course, showed up in a T-shirt.
After he returned to his office, he saw Madoff's note.

"I just got this email after the fact or I would have complied," he
wrote. "Sorry. I'm not sure I'm the right guy for the SIA committee.
You probably want a more normal business/tech guy from Island.
Right?"

Right.

On March 18, 2002, a few weeks after Levine's last SIA meeting,
Island began reporting its trades to the Cincinnati Stock Exchange.
Suddenly, Nasdaq's most active user had vanished.

The move was a blow for Nasdaq and SuperMontage. Without
Island's oceanic flow, a major chunk of the market had disappeared
from Nasdaq. Island was flexing its muscles. "It was like the New York
Yankees pulling out of Major League Baseball," recalls Andresen.

WITH electronic trading transforming the face of Wall Street, the race
to cash in on the bonanza began to heat up. In early 2002, Datek Online was put on the block by its venture capital investors Bain Capital,
TA Associates, and Silver Lake Partners. The fourth largest online
broker in trading volumes, behind Charles Schwab, E*Trade, and
Ameritrade, Datek Online handled about eighty thousand trades a day.

Back-of-the-envelope estimates valued the company at $1 billion, despite the drop-off in trading as the dot-com bubble popped. After a bidding war against E*Trade and TD Waterhouse, Ameritrade walked away with the prize, shelling out $1.3 billion. The deal made the Omaha-based discount broker the largest online trading site in the United States, with nearly three million customers (Ameritrade would later merge with TD, Ed Nicoll's old firm).

Bain, Silver Lake, and TA were also majority owners of Island, with a combined 90 percent stake. Potential buyers were everywhere—other ECNs, the big exchanges, even several large banks expressed interest.

A natural partner also seemed the worst: Archipelago.

Archipelago and Island had been fierce competitors since the Order-Handling Rules had been implemented in January 1997, and the idea of teaming up was anathema to both sides. But they were also well aware that a host of fierce rivals was hot on their trail. Instinet, BRUT, B-Trade, Attain, and others continued to maneuver to gain on the leaders. To compete, each ECN kept slashing the prices it charged or boosting the maker-taker rebates it paid. Either way, it was a hit to the bottom line.

The battle over liquidity became a matter of life or death. Despite all the chest-thumping about "competition" and "level playing fields" from the likes of Andresen and Putnam—a blatantly self-serving ethos since they primarily meant they wanted more competition with Nasdaq and the NYSE—consolidation seemed the only solution.

After a few feelers, the Island team seemed receptive to the idea of a merger with Archipelago, and Putnam said he was game. He'd secretly drooled over Island's technology, which he knew was light-years better than his own.

Things moved quickly—though not in the direction Putnam expected.

IN May 2002, the Archipelago and Island teams met for dinner at Gibsons Bar & Steakhouse on the north side of Chicago. They'd just shaken hands on a deal to merge, a combination that would create a powerhouse in control of nearly one-fourth of all Nasdaq stocks.

They high-fived and told ECN war stories: the fights with Nasdaq, the weird meetings with Dick Grasso, the crazy demands from speed merchants like Tradebot. Putnam and Andresen clinked glasses and congratulated each other on the deal.

Shortly after that dinner, however, Archipelago's general counsel Kevin O'Hara, an aggressive attorney who'd spent most of the 1990s in the halls of the SEC, spoke privately with Putnam. Something was amiss, he felt, but he couldn't put his finger on it.

"The music just doesn't feel right," he told Putnam.

SOON after the meeting, Putnam was riding the train into work and leafing through *The Wall Street Journal*. His eyes popped as he started reading an article reporting that Instinet and Island were negotiating a merger.

Rushing into his office, he grabbed the phone and called Ed Nicoll.

"What about this story in the *Journal*?" Putnam asked, his heart racing. "Is it true?"

Nicoll played possum and said there was no deal with Instinet, which technically was true since the deal papers hadn't been signed yet.

Putnam wasn't sure what to believe. Josh Levine had always seemed like such a straight shooter. He didn't realize that Levine had little say about how the company was run.

A few days after Putnam's call to Ed Nicoll, he received a call of his own. At about 3 A.M. on June 11, 2002, Nicoll dialed up Putnam's work phone and left a message on his voice mail. Island had just inked a deal with Instinet, he said.

Putnam felt blindsided. Island and Instinet had cobbled together the deal at the exact same time the talks with Archipelago had taken place. Island's private equity investors, Silver Lake and Bain, had taken the lead. They negotiated directly with Tom Glosser, chief executive of Reuters Group, Instinet's majority owner. Island's top attorney, a former SEC official named Cameron Smith, ran the negotiations on Island's side.

It was a blockbuster deal. Instinet agreed to purchase Island for $508 million. Doug Atkin, Instinet's current CEO, would be chairman. Nicoll would be CEO. Matt Andresen would be chief operating officer. The combined pools would be an electronic-trading juggernaut in control of nearly one-fourth of all Nasdaq stocks—nearly as much as Nasdaq's 30 percent.

Putnam couldn't believe it. He'd been suckered all along. He thought back to what Kevin O'Hara had told him that day after they'd written up the term sheet for an Island-Archipelago deal.

*The music just doesn't feel right. . . .*

Now Putnam had a new problem. One of his chief rivals had suddenly become massive. While Instinet was the purchaser in the deal, it was clear that the Island team was taking control. Suddenly, the renegade band of eggheads from 50 Broad was at the helm of a trading giant with markets in more than forty locations around the world. The barbarians weren't just at the gate—they'd smashed it down and were pouring into the palace grounds.

As the details unfolded, the feeling at Archipelago was of betrayal, bitterness, anger—and a thirst for revenge.

"We were lied to continuously through that process," recalls O'Hara. "After that happened, all bets were off."

# CHAPTER SEVENTEEN

# "I DO NOT WANT TO BE A FAMOUS PERSON"

Jerry Putnam's worst fear had been that the Instinet-Island merger would prove devastating for Archipelago, creating a rival with deep pockets and brains to match.

Instead, it proved to be a godsend.

As with most mergers, the reality didn't match the hype. Ed Nicoll, CEO of the combined company, quickly discovered that Instinet was a bloated monstrosity built on antiquated technology. His time rapidly became absorbed in the red tape of cutting costs — and jobs.

Nicoll tried at first to laugh it off. At a companywide meeting soon after the merger, he addressed the troops, acknowledging that there would be painful layoffs. "One way to save money would be for me to cut my bonus," he quipped. "But we all know that's not going to happen!"

A few chuckled. But the mood was grim. Island's leading lights started to slip away. Days after the consummation of the merger in October 2002, Matt Andresen resigned to become head of global trading at the New York bank Sanford C. Bernstein. (Soon after, Andresen would leave Sanford to join the Chicago hedge fund giant Citadel.) Will Sterling replaced him, before stepping away the following June to become head of electronic trading in U.S. stocks for the giant Swiss bank UBS.

The firm did pull in some new blood. In the late 1990s, Levine had started tinkering with a programming language called Java, which had top-grade graphics capabilities and was compatible with most computers. He created a stock-quote screen for Island users with Java as well as some other functions. In 2002, he'd started toying with the idea that the language could run the entire Island matching engine.

To help with the switchover, Island hired an expert in Java, a young programming whiz named Brian Nigito. Nigito had spent several years as senior engineer at an ECN called MarketXT, which specialized in after-hours trading.

Obsessive about market fairness, and not a little self-important, Nigito hit it off with Levine, who once called Nigito "a better me than me." Like many others who worked at Island, Nigito would go on to become a behind-the-scenes power broker, bringing his skills and knowledge of the market's plumbing to high-speed trading operations at Citadel and Getco. It would be a pattern that would occur many times in the next several years as Island insiders took jobs at banks, high-frequency operations, and hedge funds.

The chief architect of Island met a different fate. Levine didn't fit in with the rigid bureaucracy of Instinet, a firm he'd always despised. He was further disheartened when Island shut down its 50 Broad HQ and moved into Instinet's sleek headquarters in midtown Manhattan.

The final straw came from a longtime antagonist: the SEC. Levine's old ties with the SOES bandits, with Shelly Maschler, Jeff Citron, and the rest of the Datek gang, finally caught up with him. The SEC had been investigating Datek's operations for years. By 2002, the regulator had built an ironclad case against the firm, alleging widespread fraud. On January 14, 2003, the commission announced that Datek's chief figures would pay $70 million in fines for illegal trading and fraudulent bookkeeping. It was one of the largest securities fraud settlements on record, making headlines around the country. Citron and Maschler took the brunt of it, agreeing to pay $22.5 million and $29.2 million, respectively. They also agreed to walk away from the securities industry forever.

They weren't exiting the scene paupers. Each was worth hundreds of millions at the time of the settlement. A year before the charges, *Fortune* magazine estimated that Citron had a net worth of nearly $200 million. Maschler was well on his way to becoming a billionaire.

Levine, for his part, was slapped with a $1 million fine for bookkeeping fraud, but he wasn't barred from the securities industry. Levine told the SEC that he wasn't aware that Datek had been using the Wire — the computer system he designed to shuffle around trading assets — for fraudulent purposes, according to a former SEC official who worked on the case. None of the defendants in the case admitted or denied that they'd done anything wrong.

His reputation in tatters, Citron proved resilient, building a new career as a founder of the voice-over-Internet company Vonage. In 2006, Vonage had one of the most successful IPOs in years, pulling in about $2 billion (the stock struggled for years thereafter).

Maschler retired to Boca Raton, Florida, purchasing a sprawling mansion, investing in country clubs and cigar shops, and snapping up expensive toys such as a Lamborghini golf cart.

Maschler's eldest son, Erik, was also charged with fraud by the SEC and fined $6 million. In early 2003, when the charges were imminent, he sold out his interest in the remnants of the former Datek trading powerhouse, Heartland Securities, to Schonfeld Group, a New York outfit. Maschler's youngest son, Lee, remained at the helm of the trading operation, renamed Trillium Trading. While the firm was named after a delicate flower — a trillium is a lily with three leaves — it stayed faithful to its hard-charging push-the-envelope legacy.

LEVINE wasn't quite ready to stop trying to save Wall Street from itself, however. An inventor at heart, he was still determined to change the world through technology.

His next project concerned the computer system that disseminated trade data around the market, the Securities Information Processor, or SIP (the same SIP that high-speed firms such as Tradebot exploited for their latency arbitrage strategies). In the early 2000s, the SIP feed was notoriously slow—giving quick-draw firms opportunities to arbitrage a stock trading at slightly different prices on different pools. Levine submitted a proposal to build what he called the Big J SIP to a committee of market experts that was considering remaking the feed in 2002.

Levine proposed to do the work for $1. The next lowest bid was on the order of tens of millions. The process took more than two years of committee work and back-and-forth discussions. Market gurus such as Dave Whitcomb, founder of ATD, urged the committee to adopt the Big J Sip. They assumed that if it ran as well as Island, it would bring huge improvements to the broader market.

"Island is capable of handling an enormous volume of message traffic with extremely fast turnaround times and practically negligible down-time," Whitcomb wrote the committee in January 2002. "This is very important to ATD because it enables our automated algorithms to enter huge numbers of limit orders, which we revise continually. As a result, we do as much trading on Island as we do on all other ECNs combined."

By early 2004, Levine's proposal was among the last few under consideration. The programmer had by then stepped down from Island.

"I'll build a fast, simple, and reliable SIP system for $1. I'll run it for a year to prove that it works, then put it into a non-profit trust," Levine wrote a committee member in February 2004. "I'll deliver a working product within 6 months. I will guarantee that the technology operating costs will be [less than] $100,000 in the first year and will go down each year the system runs. I'll do it because I think a really good SIP would have really good side effects throughout the marketplace and the economy. I'll use the same sort of technology that I used to build Island."

Ultimately, the committee rejected Levine's plan even though it was strongly backed by experts such as Jamie Selway and Whitcomb. The firm selected was paid upward of $10 million to build a new SIP.

Why? Levine had spent years building a sterling reputation as one of the few people more interested in building a healthy market than a healthy bank account. Among insiders, he was widely seen as the world's most knowledgeable mind in the structure of the stock market. The SEC's charges, however, had left a stain that was hard to shake off. Even close friends remained unsure whether Levine knew about Datek's fraudulent activities. Given Levine's sharp mind, many found it hard to believe he was completely in the dark. They thought Levine justified Datek's actions because he believed Nasdaq's rules were unfair and deserved to be broken for the broader good.

Apparently embittered by it all, Levine decided to move on, quietly and without fanfare. No press release announced his departure. Many of the Island team that worked at Instinet didn't even know that Levine had left the company. They simply noticed that the elfin programmer wasn't around anymore to help them out when they got in a jam. Like one of General MacArthur's old soldiers, Levine just faded away to chase new dreams. He dabbled in wind power and created a computerized system to automatically create legal documents, called LawDact.

"I really think that it could change the world," he wrote on his website, josh.com, comparing LawDact to the formal logic of the *Tractatus Logico-Philosophicus* written by Austrian philosopher Ludwig Wittgenstein. It was an echo of the grand ambition of Island's glory days, but few were paying attention.

Levine's role as the chief architect of the most transformational technology in the history of Wall Street was unheralded, unknown to all but a few people who'd seen it happen. "Talking to Josh was like staring into the sun," says Matt Andresen. "He could tell you the grass is blue and the sky is green, and you're like, is that really true? You'd have to think about it."

Levine had never wanted fame. He'd always shunned the limelight, letting others such as Citron and Andresen take the credit for his innovations. In a 1999 e-mail exchange with a *Wired* reporter—the programmer would communicate with reporters only through e-mail, and he never consented to have a photo taken for a single article—he expressed a powerful aversion to celebrity.

"Any story about Island should not include a picture of me and any story about me will not enjoy my cooperation," he wrote. "I have learned the hard way that I do not want to be a famous person and I will do anything in my power to prevent it."

While Levine hadn't racked up the hundreds of millions pocketed by Citron and Maschler, he'd fared well enough. In 2004, he paid $3.75 million in cash for a vacant thirteen-thousand-square-foot five-story brick warehouse on historic Water Street in lower Manhattan. The 1830s Greek Revival building became his new home, doubling as a laboratory where he could pursue projects such as his solar-power system-in-a-box concept. In the next few years, Levine would construct a field of solar panels in the land surrounding an upstate New York retreat.

From the sidelines, he watched the market he'd helped create turn into a gigantic computerized speed machine. He found the race to zero deeply troubling. "People (machines) now have to race to be the first person at a fixed price level," he wrote in a July 2011 e-mail. "This has the effect of forcing marketplaces to compete in latency. You end up with exactly what you have now—people spending millions (billions?) of dollars to save milliseconds (microseconds soon?). What an expensive and needless mess. You could probably find a cure for cancer in a year if you just reassigned all the smart people who are now working on this artificially created and otherwise useless problem."

THE legacy of the Datek gang, while deeply controversial, was nothing less than astonishing. Maschler, Citron, and Levine had gone head-to-head with a corrupt, self-dealing network of Nasdaq market makers and helped destroy it. Island was a classic example of the massively disruptive computer technology that started sweeping across the world in the last fifty years, the epitome of Joseph Schumpeter's "perennial gale of creative destruction" behind capitalism. Fueled by Island, a new breed of dealers, quick-draw computer outfits like ATD, Tradebot, Getco, and Timber Hill were the new market makers. And Island's progeny fanned out across Wall Street, a technocratic vanguard of elite players.

And for a time, it looked as if Levine's vision of a seamless, nearly free market had come to pass. As the market makers and specialists fell by the wayside, trading costs plunged. It seemed as if the Plumbers had built a magnificent machine that was expanding the wealth of all Americans.

But somewhere along the line, the message was lost, co-opted by a newly enriched technorati. Levine's disciples would continue to pay lip service to the arguments Levine had made against Nasdaq and the NYSE in the 1990s, as a bulwark of their own newfound position as king of the hill. Any critic who complained of their push-button speeds, their machine-gun trades, their complex plumbing games that had turned the market into a video-game casino, was roundly dismissed as a Luddite who didn't favor *competition* or a *level playing field*.

But the field wasn't level. It never had been. The new hierarchy would be all about who owned the most powerful computers, the fastest links between markets, the most sophisticated algorithms—and the inside knowledge of how the market's plumbing was put together.

A revolution born from the idealistic belief that technology could shine a light on the dark forces of finance was being corrupted.

# PART III

IT IS OVER. THE TRADING
THAT EXISTED DOWN THE
CENTURIES HAS DIED. WE
HAVE AN ELECTRONIC MARKET
TODAY. IT IS THE PRESENT.
IT IS THE FUTURE.
—NASDAQ CEO ROBERT
GREIFELD, MAY 2011

# TRIUMPH OF THE MACHINE

CHAPTER EIGHTEEN

# THE BEAST

J erry Putnam stepped into the New York Stock Exchange through a back door in the western wing of the exchange's storied building. Archipelago's general counsel, Kevin O'Hara, and several other members of the Chicago firm's team were close behind.

It was the afternoon of April 20, 2005, a Wednesday. Putnam was sweating beneath his suit, from nervousness and the heat. Outside, it was pushing ninety degrees. The sky was dark blue. A few clouds floated far above the skyline and a cool breeze was blowing along the buzzing streets of lower Manhattan.

Putnam & Co., escorted by a team of handlers, walked through a labyrinth of dimly lit hallways, stairwells, and elevators, and finally entered a sixth-floor room adjoining a press bull pen. It was a surreal moment. As they sat waiting to face a gathering herd of financial reporters, they were tense, exhilarated, and exhausted.

O'Hara glanced at Putnam and smiled nervously.

"We're in the belly of the beast," he said. Putnam laughed. He could scarcely believe what he had accomplished in a matter of eight years since dreaming up Archipelago on a sickbed in Chicago.

The previous August, Archipelago had gone public. Earlier that morning, the boards of the NYSE and Archipelago had approved a blockbuster deal that would transform the U.S. trading landscape. A new public company, NYSE Group, would be formed, ending the Big Board's status as a not-for-profit concern. From then on, the NYSE would be driven by the bottom line. Its ticker symbol would be NYX.

The deal initially valued the combined entity—which would be the largest stock market in the world—at $3.5 billion. The NYX stock was the primary currency of the deal. The 1,366 NYSE seat-holders would receive stock and cash valuing the seats at about $2 million a piece, roughly double what they'd been selling for months before the merger was announced.

The merger had been hammered out in record time. Putnam held frequent one-on-one discussions with NYSE CEO John Thain, a former Goldman executive who'd taken the post in 2003, soon after Dick Grasso had been forced to step down amid a scandal over his massive pay package.

Since first meeting to discuss the tie-up at Goldman Sachs headquarters on January 20, Putnam and Thain had been surrounded by furious activity. Teams of lawyers, exchange executives, Goldman honchos, and Archipelago staffers worked around the clock as they worked out the details of the blockbuster deal with the utmost secrecy.

On January 28, Putnam had addressed Archipelago's board, revealing that he'd been in preliminary discussions with the NYSE about a merger. He urged everyone to keep quiet. If news of the talks broke, the whole thing could fall apart. Archipelago's stock price would skyrocket, and NYSE old-timers would scream bloody murder. To maintain secrecy, Archipelago was referred to in meetings as "Army"; the NYSE was "Navy."

By mid-March, the deal was ready. Top negotiators met on March 21 at Goldman's Broad Street headquarters. In attendance were Duncan Niederauer, John Thain, and Jerry Putnam. Goldman deal maker David Schwimmer joined by telephone. The biggest question concerned how to slice up the pie of the combined entity. Putnam pushed for a 40 percent allocation to Archipelago shareholders. Thain said

New York's seat-holders would accept nothing less than 70 percent, leaving a 30 percent slice to Archipelago.

After some haggling, Thain's plan stuck. Archipelago investors would get about one-third of the combined exchange, netting Putnam & Co. north of $1 billion. NYSE stakeholders would pocket the remaining 70 percent slice of the pie.

Conflicts of interest abounded. A particularly thorny issue concerned the status of Goldman Sachs, which was on both sides of the deal, as advisers to both the NYSE and Archipelago. It owned a 15 percent stake in Archipelago—and it held a block of NYSE seats through its ownership of the specialist firm Spear, Leeds & Kellogg (which Niederauer had run). Indeed, Goldman's ties to Archipelago were so strong that many viewed the exchange as Goldman's personal ECN unit.

The idea to get Goldman on both sides had been Putnam's. So concerned that word about the deal would leak, he felt that limiting the number of bankers involved could reduce the chances that someone would talk. He'd also know who to blame if there was a leak.

News of the merger hit the wires just after the market closed on April 20, a Wednesday, as Putnam and O'Hara were wending their way through the bowels of the exchange. It rocked the financial world. Archipelago's stock shot up 60 percent, to nearly $30 a share, in after-hours trading. Putnam marveled as he saw his stock surge on his BlackBerry while waiting for the press conference. In a flash, his net worth had dramatically improved.

At 5 P.M., Thain took the podium.

"I'm very excited to announce the transaction today, and I think it combines the best features of the New York Stock Exchange and our auction model with Archipelago's leading technology," he said. Thain went on to outline the details of the deal and how the NYSE management would look once it was consummated.

He handed the microphone to Putnam.

"I'm starting with Archipelago's goals slide," he said, opening up a PowerPoint presentation. "Our goals have not changed from what we've stated when we went public in August."

Putnam spoke as if this were business as usual for Archipelago — as if he believed Archipelago was taking over the NYSE, rather than the reverse. Putnam was a true believer. In his mind, the NYSE was little more than a strong brand name with a very bad business model.

Archipelago had the right model. Now it had the brand.

"We believe in order for us to be successful, we're going to have to build a strong brand," he said. "We've invested heavily in that brand and I think that this merger certainly gets us far, far, far along beyond anything that we've failed to do on our own."

With such brash talk, Putnam seemed convinced he was on the verge of taking over the front office at New York. But he was deeply conflicted. He'd seen the NYSE as the enemy for so long that it was hard to reconcile himself with his new position as a top dog at the Big Board — *the belly of the beast.*

Immediately after the press conference, Putnam grabbed a flight back to Chicago. He wanted to be in Archipelago's office the following morning to greet his team — and help allay any concerns that he was turning his back on his belief in open and fair markets.

It was a tough sell. But one factor helped ease Putnam's pitch: Archipelago's soaring stock price. Employees who'd been struggling for years in a business that often seemed on the edge of going under were suddenly much wealthier. Their consciences might sting a bit, but their fatter bank accounts eased the pain.

The NYSE-Archipelago deal was a watershed in U.S. financial history. It signaled that the storied floor of the Big Board, a symbol of capitalism known around the world, was no longer dominant. While Thain mouthed faith in the floor, he was well aware that it had become a prop, background color for financial news networks that advertised the NYSE brand. Computers would rule. Nothing could stop that.

No one was more aware of that shift than the man many credited as the secret architect of the NYSE-Archipelago merger, Duncan Niederauer. The Goldman Sachs executive had championed Goldman's 1999 investment in the ECN, and he'd been a behind-the-scenes force in putting John Thain in the top spot at the NYSE.

Soon after the deal was consummated, Niederauer received e-mails congratulating *him* on the deal. "Looks like your baby has finally grown up!" wrote one correspondent in an e-mail with a subject line that read "GS taking over the world . . . (or NYSE merges with ARCA)."

In fact, soon after the merger, traders coined a new name for the Big Board: the Goldman Sachs Exchange.

DICK Grasso, watching the details of the merger on CNBC from his home in Locust Valley, New York, was devastated, on the point of tears. His long, hard-fought battle to protect the floor was over. An American institution was dying. "This is a very sad day," he told friends.

Many at the NYSE were furious at the Arca deal. Floor traders and specialists, bitterly resentful of the shift toward electronic trading, started referring to Thain as "I, Robot" for his stiff, mechanical style — and his apparent allegiance to the Bots.

It was clear that the lion's share of trading at New York was going electronic. The floor of the NYSE was becoming little more than a showpiece. "The writing is on the wall for the floor," Jamie Selway, who'd left Archipelago in 2003 to form his own broker dealer, told the *Wall Street Journal* when the Archipelago deal was announced.

Putnam had achieved his dream. He was at the very center of the financial universe, the biggest pool of them all. Named copresident of the NYSE, he was in charge of the electronic trading arm of the exchange. His number two man was Paul Adcock, who'd been with Putnam from the beginning in the early 1990s. Along with an experienced team of technologists from Archipelago, they quickly started working on integrating the electronic system into the NYSE.

It would be their toughest job yet.

■  ■  ■

Two days after the NYSE-Archipelago deal was announced came
news of another blockbuster merger. Nasdaq had agreed to purchase
the trading engine owned by Instinet—the computer system formerly
known as Island—for $935 million.

It was a Friday afternoon. Nasdaq's CEO, Bob Greifeld, was convinced he'd pulled off a better deal than Thain had. Archipelago had
notoriously clunky technology. Instinet had the Island system—the
most powerful stock-trading machine ever created.

The deal had been championed behind the scenes at Nasdaq by a
onetime Island attorney named Chris Concannon. In 2003, Concannon had left Instinet to become executive vice president of market
operations at Nasdaq. His number one goal, as he told Greifeld from
the very beginning, was to take out the New York Stock Exchange.
With Island in his arsenal, he felt the odds had tipped dramatically in
his favor.

Levine, of course, was nowhere to be seen as America's leading
stock markets adapted to the grand vision he'd built as a nerdy teenager pounding the pavement of Wall Street in the 1980s, peddling
computer trading systems to banks and hedge funds. Not a single article in the major financial press mentioned the programmer.

But it was clear to insiders such as Concannon that Island had
always been the driving force behind the changes that were transforming Wall Street—decimalization, colocation, access to data, lightning
speeds, high-frequency trading.

Those changes were also moving overseas. When Instinet sold
the Island system to Nasdaq, it had agreed not to launch a competing technology in the United States. But the deal said nothing about
Europe. So Brian Nigito, the Island technologist who had rewritten
the system's code into Java years earlier, built a new electronic trading platform called Chi-X Europe, which Instinet would fully launch
in 2007. (The name derives from the Greek letter *chi*, written as X,

which represents the crossing of two sides of a trade.) Within just a few years, Chi-X Europe would account for more than one-quarter of all stock trading in Europe.

BESIDES advances in trading technology, there was a powerful force pushing the Big Board and Nasdaq toward modernization—a massive change to the structure of the market that was, metaphorically, a gun aimed squarely at the head of the NYSE. Designed by a small group of SEC eggheads, it was called Regulation National Market System, or Reg NMS—the very rule changes that eventually would spark the market-structure quirks that plagued Haim Bodek and Trading Machines.

In the works for years, Reg NMS mandated that any order to buy or sell a stock had to go to the venue that had the best price. If an investor placed an order to buy Intel at the NYSE, where it was selling for $20.01, and if there was a better price at Nasdaq, say, $20, the order would instantly route to Nasdaq. Such a system had become possible with the growth of electronic trading.

Reg NMS also proposed to alter a convention that had ring-fenced floor trading on the Big Board.

The NYSE's floor often took ten or twenty seconds to execute a trade, light-years compared with split-second trading on electronic venues such as Island and Archipelago. It was the problem that had stifled high-speed players such as Dave Cummings and forced them to stick with their bread-and-butter Nasdaq stocks.

Reg NMS would put an end to this regime by allowing firms to "trade through" human-controlled manual markets. If Cummings wanted to buy two hundred shares of IBM, an NYSE-listed stock, he could go straight to Archipelago or another ECN, because the NYSE's human dealers were too slow. He could do this even if IBM shares *were cheaper* at the NYSE.

Reg NMS, in essence, decreed that *speed* was more important than *price*. As such, Reg NMS represented a potential deathblow to

the Big Board, where price—along with human trading—was paramount. Suddenly, electronic traders would be able to swap NYSE-
listed stocks at will, bypassing the floor entirely.

For market centers that met the speed standard, Reg NMS meant
something else entirely. The basic rules still applied: Any order sent
to the market must trade at the best price. If IBM shares were selling
for $20 on Nasdaq, and $19.99 on Archipelago, a buy order would
*have* to route to Archipelago. Because the speed of the electronic
links between exchanges was nearly instantaneous, routing orders to
the best price in this way wasn't expected to cause any delay in getting
a fill.

The SEC, after mulling over Reg NMS for more than a year,
passed the rule in early 2005, although it wasn't fully implemented
until the summer of 2007.

For the NYSE, it was a matter of life and death. Unless it ramped
up its electronic trading capabilities, Reg NMS would shred it to
pieces. Its revenues would fall; its competitors would become stronger.
Nasdaq was also at risk, since its computer systems remained much
slower than Island and Archipelago. To compete, they had to tool up
double-time. Archipelago was the NYSE's quick fix. The Island system was Nasdaq's.

NASDAQ signaled that it planned to migrate all of its trading to Instinet (i.e., Island) within a year of the merger. SuperMontage, its own
attempt to compete with the ECNs, would be scrapped.

Soon after the Nasdaq-Instinet deal closed and the Island system
was officially running Nasdaq, Chris Concannon invited Levine to its
downtown headquarters to have lunch with CEO Bob Greifeld.

Levine showed up in his usual attire: tennis shoes, baggy shorts,
T-shirt. Dressed in a crisp suit and tie, Greifeld was bemused by the
programming wunderkind, whom he'd heard about through the years
but had never met. Levine expressed little interest in the merger, or
Greifeld's grand plans. Instead, he spent most of the time talking

about a solar farm he was cobbling together at his retreat in upstate New York.

Concannon shook his head. Levine seemed to have little interest in the fact that his creation was now the engine running one of the largest stock-trading platforms in the world. Now Concannon himself was helping run Levine's masterpiece. It would mark the most significant deal in Nasdaq's history up to that point. Almost immediately after the integration was complete, Nasdaq's market share started to improve.

The deal also started to fulfill Concannon's vision when he'd first come to Nasdaq: taking over a chunk of the trading of New York–listed stocks.

A different story entirely was playing out at the NYSE.

As the ink was drying on the NYSE merger, Putnam's team started combing over New York's technology. What they found startled them.

Walking through the exchange's floor, they'd hear the manic *clickclack* of typing, a noise that sounded like a forest full of crickets. The sound was emanating from the NYSE's DOT typists. Orders that flooded in through the DOT computer system—short for designated order turnaround—had to be matched by human beings. A printer published the orders *on paper.* A wall of typists would bang out matching orders at a frantic pace. It was impressive. They were the fastest typists Putnam had ever seen—*but this was 2005.* To Putnam, it was a symbol of just how far behind the Big Board had gotten.

It was absurd. The NYSE for years had boasted of huge investments in technology as it struggled to keep pace with competitors. But as Archipelago's computer experts dug into the spaghetti tangle of the Big Board's computers, they found a complete mess. A Rube Goldberg machine stood behind the world's most famous stock exchange. The latest software was running on computers installed around the time of Black Monday in 1987. *The New York Stock Exchange is held together by chicken wire and bubblegum*, Putnam's team thought.

Putnam and his partner Paul Adcock, along with Archipelago's top tech specialists, poured themselves into the job, working on the integration even before the merger was finalized in early March 2006. Putnam holed up in an apartment in New York, commuting on weekends—those he could spare—back to Chicago.

Resistance to the electronic herd remained fierce among the old guard at the NYSE, especially on the floor. Archipelago team members working to integrate the computer systems amid the hive-like activity during the trading day might suddenly take a painful thump on the shoulder or in the back. The action was so frenetic it was hard to tell where the blow came from—but the message was clear.

To break the ice, Putnam arranged to have breakfast with the top representatives of the NYSE floor at the private Stock Exchange Luncheon Club, a hallowed space reserved only for NYSE members and famed for its clam-juice-and-vodka cocktail known as a Red Snapper. As he walked into the room in the early morning hours, well before the opening bell, a steady chatter died to icy silence. Putnam sat down at his table, trying to avoid the cold stares directed his way from all parts of the room by some of the most powerful men in finance.

After breakfast had been served, he stood and cleared his throat. "As you all know, I'm a fierce competitor," he said. "Before the deal, this was a competition, and I did everything in my power to beat you."

He looked around. The cold stares were turning into fiery daggers.

"Now I'm on the team. I'm with you and I'm ready to do whatever it takes to win."

Despite such assurances, the NYSE specialists remained skeptical. They were keepers of the tradition, of the ways of the past. Putnam was the future. There was no getting around the contradictions.

Meanwhile, the IPO of the NYSE Group—which would occur when the merger was finalized—was moving up fast. It proved to be a huge media event, covered live by financial news network CNBC and Bloomberg. The date was set for March 6, soon after the merger received a thumbs-up from regulators. The company would have a market capitalization of about $10 billion, triple Nasdaq's size.

The morning of the offering, NYSE officials on the floor passed out silver bells emblazoned with NYX on the handle. Traders were told to ring them with abandon at the open. While they were billed as a shiny memento, their true purpose—to drown out the expected chorus of boos and catcalls from disaffected specialists—spoke volumes about the turmoil behind the scenes.

The IPO marked a crucial shift for the NYSE. As a publicly traded entity, it would see profits as paramount—and relationships with revenue-generating clients would become all the more critical.

Thain continued slashing costs, shutting down the NYSE's wood-paneled dining room where traders and Wall Street executives had gathered for decades to talk shop over steaming omelets and French toast before the start of the trading day. The floor started to shrink as specialists closed shop. In June 2006, Thain axed the exchange's beloved barber, a forty-three-year employee named Gerardo Gentilella who worked for a meager annual stipend of $24,000. Even after Gentilella asked to work for tips through the end of the year, Thain stood by his guns and sent the barber packing.

THE changes rocking the NYSE were the direct result of the computer-trading revolution sparked more than a decade before at 50 Broad. The upstart ECNs that had transformed the market now *were* the market. Fueled by the massive volume spawned by the high-frequency traders, the ECNs had been pulling in so much liquidity that the Big Board and Nasdaq simply bought out their competitors and integrated their technology.

One major player in high-frequency wasn't pleased with these recent developments: Tradebot's Dave Cummings. Cummings was furious that the major exchanges had swallowed up his favorite trading centers. He was certain that in short order the exchanges would boost fees, resulting in a direct hit to Tradebot's bottom line.

So, soon after the mergers, Cummings announced that he would launch his own ECN: Better Alternative Trading System, or BATS. Designed to be cheap and fast, BATS would put pressure on the big exchanges to keep their fees in check. There was little question that the BATS system was designed to mimic Island. Cummings had spent so much time on the phone with Island programmers that he knew its structure inside out. The likeness was obvious to insiders. For instance, Cummings dubbed the BATS market data feed FAST PITCH—just as Levine had called his data feed ITCH.

From all signs, BATS worked extremely well. By 2007, it had gobbled up more than 10 percent of all trading volume. And Cummings's high-speed colleagues in arms were along for the ride. A big investor in BATS, for instance, was Getco, his onetime partner in Chicago.

Cummings wasn't alone in setting up new trading centers. In 2005, Jersey City–based broker dealer giant Knight Capital Group purchased an ECN that had been languishing on the periphery of the trading world for years: Attain, the electronic trading platform created in 1998 by Harvey Houtkin, the original SOES bandit. Knight renamed it Direct Edge, and it soon became the fourth largest trading venue for stocks in the United States, just behind BATS.

A Direct Edge investor was Citadel, which operated one of the world's top high-frequency operations, called Tactical Trading. For a time, Tactical had been run by ex–Island programmer Brian Nigito.

Regulators didn't bat an eye. They didn't seem to question whether it was appropriate for several of the nation's most prolific electronic-trading firms—Getco, Tradebot, Knight, Citadel—to have such close ties with exchanges. Already, of course, the NYSE and Nasdaq had swallowed up Island and Archipelago, which had been the primary breeding grounds of high-speed trading.

The career direction could go the other way, as well. In 2007, Cummings stepped down from BATS to recharge Tradebot's engines. Industry gossip was that Cummings saw how powerful Getco had become while at BATS—which processed many of Getco's orders—and wanted to do the same for Tradebot. And some competitors were concerned that Cummings had been able to get a glimpse of their strategies while at BATS. Whether it was appropriate for the manager of a national market center to jump ship and run a powerful trading firm was, once again, not questioned by regulators.

It proved excellent timing, however. As Reg NMS rolled out in the summer of 2007, high-frequency traders were suddenly able to apply their strategies to many of the largest, most heavily traded stocks in the world: NYSE-listed stocks such as IBM, General Electric, and Alcoa. Before Reg NMS, it was difficult for fast traders to juggle NYSE stocks because of the slow response times on the floor of the Big Board. But Reg NMS stipulated that electronic venues could bypass the floor. The Bots were kids in a candy store—and their revenues fattened accordingly. Getco, said to have pulled in as much as $50 million in 2006, was suddenly making as much as $9 million *a day* in 2007, according to a person familiar with its operation. In 2008, when trading volumes spiked during the credit crisis (the result of lots of funds selling everything they could in a panic), the high-speed operation at the Chicago hedge fund Citadel, Tactical Trading, raked in $1 billion. Indeed, 2007 and 2008, a time when most of Wall Street was falling apart at the seams, would be the heyday for the Bots.

That would all change in the summer of 2009. In a matter of days, the computer-driven world that Island had helped spawn would come under a giant microscope.

# CHAPTER NINETEEN

# THE PLATFORM

From:  Mikhail Malyshev
Sent:   11:11 pm
To:     Sergey Aleynikov
Re:     let's move fast

It was nearing midnight as Sergey Aleynikov nervously clicked on the e-mail from his future boss. The subject line—"let's move fast"— said it all. Mikhail "Misha" Malyshev wasn't one to waste time. Speed was paramount, speed was everything.

"There's a huge amount of work ahead of us," the e-mail said. "Let's triple our focus. The future is ours and the game is already on."

The message was clear. Aleynikov, who'd emigrated from Russia to the United States in 1991, knew he had to act quickly.

He had to act *fast*.

It was May 31, 2009, and pressure was mounting. Speed *was* the game, in more ways than one. Aleynikov was a merchant of speed: a computer programmer for a secretive high-frequency trading operation run by Goldman Sachs. The operation was the heir of Hull Trading, the options-trading group that Goldman had purchased for half a billion in 1999 and that had employed such trading whizzes as Haim Bodek and Dave Babulak, head trader at Getco in Chicago.

Aleynikov's job at Goldman: write code that processed trades as quickly as possible. The code was the key.

Whoever had the best code, the *fastest* code, won the game. The algorithms were the futuristic space-age progeny of SOES bandit weapons such as the Monster Key—category-killing secret trading systems of the Algo Wars that generated massive profits.

That was why Malyshev had hired the thirty-nine-year-old Aleynikov—for his ability to write fast code. Malyshev, who sported a Ph.D. in physics from Princeton University, was a rising legend in the world of high-speed trading. He'd run Citadel's powerhouse high-speed outfit Tactical Trading, which had pulled in a stunning $1 billion in 2008, netting Malyshev alone $70 million for the year. Now he was launching his own trading machine, named Teza, after a river in his home country of Russia, and hiring top talent—math whizzes and computer geeks, like Aleynikov. Indeed, one of his first hires had been former Island tech guru Will Sterling.

After reading the e-mail at his home in the tony New Jersey township of North Caldwell, Aleynikov went to bed. But his mind was racing. He didn't have much time. He had only one more week at Goldman. He had to act—*fast.*

The next morning, he woke up early, caught a commuter train to New York, and calmly walked into Goldman's downtown office, at One New York Plaza. He hopped off an elevator, swiped a badge before the door that gave him access to a top-secret programming room, and went to his desk, busy with an array of computer screens flashing charts of markets from around the world.

Aleynikov, tall, with sapling-thin limbs, a jet-black goatee, and thin-framed glasses, felt lucky. With Teza, he'd finally caught his big break, the job where he could pull down the big money, the *fuck you* Wall Street money that would give him the freedom to do whatever he wanted. Not only was he going to triple his salary from $400,000 a year to nearly $1.2 million, he was getting in on the ground floor of an operation with seemingly limitless potential.

But he had to move fast.

Later that afternoon, after a full day of trading, Aleynikov looked around the office. No one was watching. At about 5:30 P.M., he began to type. He input a series of commands to copy and compress files from Goldman's high-frequency trading system. He encrypted the code using the password "thisisatest." He then accessed a computer server located in Germany and began downloading the encrypted code to the server. The process only took a matter of minutes. Finished, he slipped on his jacket and quickly left the building.

A few days later, working from his home computer on the night of June 4, shortly after 11 P.M., Aleynikov accessed the German server—designated SVN.XP-dev.com—and uploaded the code. The next day, his last at Goldman, he transferred more code at 7:07 A.M. Then, at 5:23 P.M., he ran a program to upload even more code to the German server. At last, hoping to cover his tracks, he swiped clean his computer's "bash" history, a record of activity on its hard drive.

He shut down the computer, said good-bye to his colleagues, and walked out of Goldman's office for the last time.

Aleynikov felt positive that he'd pulled it off. With the Goldman code, he'd have a cheat sheet to create new, even better code for Teza.

But he'd slipped. Goldman's security experts had detected the transfer of exactly thirty-two megabytes of data from its computer system to an outside server. They then traced the activity to Aleynikov's computer. After a sweep of the hard drive, they found everything. On July 1, the bank notified the Federal Bureau of Investigation.

Aleynikov was oblivious. He flew to Chicago on July 2 for a round of meetings with Malyshev and other members of the Teza team. The following day, a Friday, after more meetings, he packed up his laptop—loaded with secret Goldman code—and prepared to leave. Gazing through the tinted panes of a conference room on the thirty-seventh floor of the futuristic Smurfit-Stone Building in downtown Chicago, Teza's headquarters, the dark blue expanse of Lake Michigan stretching into the distance, he had no notion of the powerful forces of law and money marshaling against him eight hundred miles away.

They were all moving fast. The game was on.

Aleynikov smiled as he said good-bye to Malyshev, hopped on the elevator, and caught a cab to Chicago International O'Hare Airport. He was eager to get home to his wife, Elina, and their three little girls, all under the age of five.

At 9:20 P.M., as he stepped off his plane at Newark Liberty International Airport, six agents from the FBI were waiting for him in the terminal. Special Agent Michael McSwain, a stocky man with a salt-and-pepper buzz cut, approached, flashing a badge.

"Are you Sergey Aleynikov?" he asked in a raspy voice that seemed a dead-on impression of Clint Eastwood.

"Yes?"

"You're under arrest."

"This must be a mistake," Aleynikov said in a panic.

ALEYNIKOV was handcuffed, packed into an unmarked car, and taken to the Justice Department's Federal Plaza headquarters in downtown Manhattan. Several hours of intense grilling followed. In a state of shock, Aleynikov declined the help of a lawyer. Just eleven minutes into the interrogation, he agreed to let the FBI search his home. He readily confessed that he had taken code from Goldman's high-frequency trading platform. His excuse: He had intended to take so-called open source code—the kind available to anyone over the Internet and used by firms for basic computing functions—and had mistakenly grabbed bits of Goldman's proprietary code. He'd never shown it to Malyshev or anyone else at Teza, he said.

The FBI wasn't buying his story.

The interrogation ended at 1:45 A.M. Aleynikov spent the night behind bars.

Special Agent McSwain quickly got to work on his affidavit. He alleged that Aleynikov stole "proprietary computer code . . . and then uploaded the code to a computer server in Germany." Without naming Goldman specifically, he wrote that the code came from a computer system "that allows the Financial Institution to engage in sophisticated, high-speed, and high-volume trades on various stocks and commodities markets. . . . The Platform is capable of quickly obtaining and processing information regarding rapid developments in these markets. The speed and efficiency by which the Platform obtains and processes market data allows the Financial Institution to employ additional programs that use sophisticated mathematical formulas to place automated trades in the markets." Such trades "generate many millions of dollars of profits per year for the Financial Institution."

The following day, the Fourth of July, U.S. Assistant Attorney Joseph Facciponti laid out the government's case in a hearing to determine whether the wayward programmer could be freed on bail. The Justice Department was charging Aleynikov with what amounted to industrial espionage, a federal offense that could earn him twenty-five years in prison.

Goldman might have suffered massive damages if Aleynikov's scheme had succeeded, Facciponti said. "The bank itself stands to lose its entire investment in creating this software to begin with, which is millions upon millions of dollars."

Then, the thirty-four-year-old prosecutor dropped a bombshell.

"Because of the way this software interfaces with various markets and exchanges, the bank has raised the possibility that there is a danger that somebody who knew how to use this program could use it to manipulate markets in unfair ways," he told the court.

No one knew quite what that meant. But it was ominous. What kind of spymaster code was this? How dark and complex had the market become?

Despite the government's warnings, Aleynikov was released on a $750,000 bond.

Within days, the arrest was splattered in newspaper headlines across the country. Reporters quickly learned from Aleynikov's online work profile on the LinkedIn website that he was a programmer for Goldman Sachs.

The scandal cast a lurid light on high-speed trading. In America's heartland, mom-and-pop investors were stunned as they learned what had become of the stock market, the repository of their retirement dreams. It was hard to tell if they were reading *The Wall Street Journal,* Isaac Asimov, or Ian Fleming. Massive computers wielded by giant financial firms—or small firms they'd never heard of—were processing trades at warp speeds, popping in and out of stocks like bees in a hive. Some reports claimed that high-frequency trading accounted for as much as three-fourths of all volume on the U.S. stock market.

What was going on? Where had it all come from?

DAN Ivandjiiski was traveling in Poland when he received an e-mail containing a newswire story about the Aleynikov case. It was July 4, 2009, one day after the arrest. As he read through the story, Ivandjiiski, a pale, dark-haired blogger from Bulgaria, instantly knew something big had happened. A former trader himself, he'd been railing against high-speed trading for months on his new blog, called *Zero Hedge.* From his spare apartment on the Upper East Side of Manhattan, he'd been posting under the pseudonym Tyler Durden, the name of the psychopathic character in Chuck Palahniuk's novel *Fight Club.* Few outside his inner circle knew his true identity, but his savvy, numbers-centric analysis made it obvious to his blog's faithful readers that he'd been a Wall Street insider who couldn't take all the bullshit anymore.

Durden's primary target—some might even say morbid obsession—was Goldman Sachs. He'd become convinced that the powerful bank was manipulating markets for its own benefit. Now it seemed a federal prosecutor was confirming his suspicions.

By the summer of 2009, *Zero Hedge* had become a must-read for Wall Street insiders. The blog was breaking all the rules, calling all

of Wall Street a massive Ponzi scheme that was on the verge of collapsing, crashing the stock market and leaving the global economy
in ruins. The blog's observations combined the sentiment of a crack-
pot conspiracy theorist with hard-edged economic reporting, often
backed with complex analysis of statistics and charts.

With Aleynikov's arrest, *Zero Hedge* became an even bigger hit.
The story landed squarely in Ivandjiiski's wheelhouse. And he swung
for the bleachers.

From his hotel room in Warsaw, the blogger jumped on his laptop
and began typing feverishly. A few hours later he had a detailed post
live on his site speculating on what the Aleynikov arrest could mean.
"If the allegations are true," he wrote, "it looks like Goldman's hi-fi
quant trading desk was thoroughly penetrated by a 'spy.' . . . One can
only imagine the value of this 'code' not only to Goldman but to the
highest bidder."

Suddenly, *Zero Hedge* was getting swamped with hits, and the
mainstream press was soon hot on the trail. In a flash, secretive high-
speed computer trading was the subject of water-cooler gossip across
the country. By September, a *Forbes* magazine cover story called high-
frequency trading "the most wrenching, and controversial, transition
in the history of U.S. securities markets."

CRITICS of high-speed trading suddenly swelled in number. At the
front of the pack were Sal Arnuk and Joe Saluzzi, two former Instinet
traders who in 2002 had founded a brokerage called Themis Trading.
Themis was a throwback, a firm that bought and sold stocks for clients
using Street smarts, not AI-rigged high-speed algos.

Saluzzi and Arnuk had been on the attack against high-frequency
trading since 2008. On June 18, 2009, they published a white paper
called "High Frequency Trading: Red Flags and Drug Addiction."
Referring to a panel discussion he'd recently attended, Saluzzi wrote
that the high-speed traders participating in the symposium alongside
him "reminded me of the 'SOES Bandits' from the early '90s."

The paper zeroed in on the fact that high-frequency firms had virtually zero obligation to stick it out through thick or thin in the market. High-speed firms were canceling orders at a maddening pace. A staggering *90 percent* or more of all of the orders they pumped into the market were canceled. That was not real liquidity, they wrote, that was *phantom liquidity*, as insubstantial and fleeting as the wind.

"What happens if a major event causes turmoil in the market?" the paper asked. "Will these HFT's simply shut down their computers and walk away since their model has been corrupted? What happens to the 60% of the volume that they now control? Where will all that LIQUIDITY that they claim to provide go when the market doesn't suit them? A major vacuum will be formed in the market as multiple parties run for a much smaller than expected exit."

Experts within the high-frequency community roundly dismissed Arnuk and Saluzzi as cranks, reactionary Luddites who longed for the days of the ticker tape. They called them dangerous, liable to twist the minds of susceptible (and stupid) regulators, turning back the clock on the tech revolution on Wall Street and hurting America's ability to compete. Saluzzi and Arnuk were morons—and un-American to boot.

They felt otherwise, of course. Saluzzi and Arnuk were convinced that the market had been hijacked by computer traders while no one was looking—except the regulators, who inexplicably seemed to be helping them along. And they were hell-bent on making as much noise about it as possible.

The fight was on.

TED Kaufman knew all about fights—and long odds. In 1972, he'd worked on the long-shot senatorial campaign of a brash, twenty-nine-year-old Delaware politician named Joe Biden. Biden was going up against J. Caleb Boggs, a longtime, beloved figure in Delaware. No one thought Biden had a chance, not even Kaufman. On Labor Day, just a few months before the election, polls showed only 19 percent of voters were behind Biden. Somehow, the man who went on to become vice president in the Obama administration pulled it off, defeating Boggs by a nose. From then on, Kaufman believed anything was possible.

A trained engineer with an MBA from Wharton, Kaufman worked as Biden's chief of staff and close adviser for the next two decades. When Biden stepped aside to become vice president in January 2009, Kaufman took his seat in the Senate. Over the next year, the gangly, cerebral senator would become the most unlikely critic of high-frequency trading imaginable.

Kaufman's interest in computerized trading evolved out of his investigation into the SEC's move in July 2007 to abolish the "uptick" rule. The rule, which had been in place since 1938, mandated that short sellers—traders hoping to profit from a decline in the price of a stock—could only make a move after the price of the stock ticked up. That helped prevent short sellers from bear raids in which they piled onto a stock and relentlessly drove it down with short after short.

But in the late 1990s and early 2000s, an increasingly powerful group started lobbying for a repeal of the uptick rule: high-speed traders. The need to wait for an uptick in a stock before it could be shorted made it more difficult to jump in and out of stocks at lightning speeds. That, in turn, hurt their ability to provide liquidity to the market, hurting the little guy. Josh Levine, among others, pushed the SEC to repeal the uptick rule.

The SEC finally agreed, and on July 6, 2007, the uptick rule was no more. The move attracted little attention at the time. But by the fall of 2008, when the financial system was collapsing and shares of firms such as Lehman Brothers and Morgan Stanley were plunging, the SEC came under heavy fire. In March 2009, Kaufman introduced a bill, along with Johnny Isakson, a Republican senator from Georgia, calling on the SEC to reinstate the uptick rule within sixty days.

As Kaufman dug further into market structure, speaking with experts across the industry, he became increasingly alarmed by what he found. Rampant complexity. Secretive tactics. Hidden, unknowable risks.

To him, it all seemed reminiscent of the problems that had led to Wall Street's apocalyptic implosion in 2008, when highly complex mortgage trades led to the loss of hundreds of billions. The public's faith in Wall Street was near historic lows. What worried Kaufman most: a destabilizing event in the stock market triggered by computer trading. That could cause investors to turn their back on Wall Street all over again, hurt the ability of companies to raise funds, and severely damage the nation's economy.

Kaufman started firing off letters to the SEC and editorials to newspapers. "We seem to be learning more every day about certain order types, high-speed trading, colocation of servers at exchanges, dark pools, and other indications that we have a two-tiered market," he wrote in an open letter to the SEC on August 4, 2009.

The SEC had promised to take action. But it wasn't moving quickly enough for Kaufman. "We must act urgently because high-frequency trading poses a systemic risk," he told the Senate Banking Committee on November 5.

What kind of risk was Kaufman talking about? A rising concern was that a high-speed firm with poor risk controls could unleash a rogue algorithm into the market and trigger a destabilizing domino effect. A runaway algo could get stuck in a feedback loop, attempting to sell a massive amount of stock, and keep selling, relentlessly pushing the entire market lower. With trading systems able to act in microseconds across multiple venues, including dark pools, a destabilizing sell-off could occur in minutes or even seconds. One trading executive said he feared the "next Long-Term Capital meltdown will happen in a five-minute time period," referring to the 1998 implosion of a giant hedge fund that threatened to topple the global financial system.

In 2009, however, the majority of the electronic herd saw such concerns as the wild imaginings of conspiracy theorists. Critics such as Kaufman, Zero Hedge's Ivandjiiski, Arnuk, and Saluzzi were widely considered dangerous know-nothings raising false fears and spooking the public. High-speed traders believed they had created a flawless technological masterpiece—a market that was cheaper, more efficient, safer, and more transparent than ever before.

Kaufman wasn't buying the hype. He couldn't care less about what he saw as self-righteous justifications for what appeared to be little more than legalized profiteering. Kaufman wasn't worried about the powerful enemies he was making on Wall Street. Since he never intended to run for office again once his term ended in late 2010, he didn't have to worry about raising buckets of cash from deep-pocketed financiers for his next campaign. And despite his growing understanding that the forces he was challenging were far more powerful and complex than he'd ever realized, he refused to shut up and go away.

By early 2010, scrutiny of high-frequency trading had reached a fever pitch. Mary Schapiro, chairman of the SEC, realized she needed to act. And so she did what most Washington bureaucrats do in uncertain times: She commissioned a study. In January, the agency published a concept release on the structure of the stock market. After a decade of radical changes, the SEC was at last attempting to come to grips with a vast electronic trading machine that had risen up in the shadows of the market.

"The Commission is publishing this concept release to invite public comment on a wide range of market structure issues, including high-frequency trading, order routing, market data linkages, and undisplayed, or 'dark,' liquidity," the report stated. It highlighted several dramatic statistics that illustrated how times had changed. In 2004, the average trade size of a NYSE-listed stock was 724 shares. By 2009, the average size had dropped to 268—a result of high-speed algos slicing and dicing orders into easy-to-digest bits.

Speeds had ramped up dramatically. In 2005, it took ten to twenty seconds for an order to get filled on the NYSE floor, compared with just less than one second on average in 2009 (still far slower than the microsecond speeds on Nasdaq, BATS, Direct Edge, and Archipelago).

A flood of comment letters poured in from across the industry, sharply illustrating the rifts that had formed in the market. A number of fund management firms emerged as stark opponents of high-speed traders, whom they saw as little more than quick-draw bandits scalping their orders. The managers of Southeastern Asset Management, which ran the Longleaf Partners mutual funds and oversaw $30 billion in assets, attacked the shift toward automation.

"The market has become a servant to short-term professional traders, in particular high-frequency traders," they wrote. "As a result, the long-term investor—whether an individual, mutual fund, or hedge fund—incurs unnecessary execution and opportunity costs."

Perhaps the most curious—and thought-provoking—letter came from one R. T. Leuchtkafer. The name was a pseudonym: *Leuchtkafer* means "firefly" in German. No one knew the writer's identity. But the detail and sophistication of the comments, submitted on April 16, 2010, revealed Leuchtkafer as an insider who'd grown disillusioned with the state of play.

Right out of the gate, Leuchtkafer sounded the alarm. As Saluzzi and Arnuk repeatedly argued, the market was extremely unstable because high-frequency traders were likely to cut and run in a market shock, making the shock worse. "The last fifteen years . . . have seen the rise of new classes of very profitable, aggressive, and technologically savvy participants previously unknown in the U.S. markets," Leuchtkafer wrote. "When markets are in equilibrium these new participants increase available liquidity and tighten spreads. When markets face liquidity demands these new participants increase spreads and price volatility and savage investor confidence. These participants can be more destructive to the interests of long-term investors than most have imagined."

Leuchtkafer's greatest ire was directed against the electronic data feeds that exchanges provided to high-speed firms. The feeds contained so much information about what was going on inside the market—about the huge elephant or whale orders to buy and sell stocks by institutional firms such as mutual funds—that they gave their users a huge advantage. "A classic short-term strategy is to sniff out an elephant and trade ahead of it," Leuchtkafer wrote. "That is front-running if you are a fiduciary to the elephant but just good trading if you are not, or so we suppose."

He singled out Nasdaq's data feed—now called TotalView-ITCH— which, he said, specified whether hidden orders, which are typically used by large investors such as mutual funds, were buy or sell orders.

It was transparency turned on its head. In the 1990s, Levine had created the ITCH protocol to help light up the market—to allow traders to see behind the screen that the Nasdaq market makers had pulled over their activities. Now Nasdaq was selling the information to speed traders whose computers could crunch the data in milliseconds to determine whether big players were buying or selling. Using that information, they could jump ahead. If their computers, using TotalView-ITCH—or a similar data feed provided by the other exchanges such as BATS, Direct Edge, or NYSE Arca— detected a big elephant order to buy Microsoft, Leuchtkafer argued, the high-frequency firms would start buying up Microsoft, pushing up the price. Then they'd sell it back to the mutual fund—at a higher price, of course.

"The SEC must do an analysis and estimate whether and how much this data feed has cost investors over the years as HFT firms found hidden interest and ran ahead of it," Leuchtkafer wrote.

High-speed firms shrugged off the criticism. They seemed supremely self-confident, even arrogant, and had little doubt that they'd dramatically improved the market for everyone, especially small investors. If there were a few bad apples and some glitches along the way, that's life.

The critics didn't let up, however. In a February 2010 interview on Bloomberg TV, Saluzzi said he continued to worry that the market was vulnerable to a sudden, sharp sell-off because most high-frequency traders didn't have firm obligations to stay in the market.

"What happens is, everyone tries to sell at the same time and the bids and the buyers that you see in the market now will disappear," he told Bloomberg host Carol Massar. "The price vacuum will start, and we're going to plunge down. That's my big fear."

High-speed backers pointed to the stock market's resilience after the collapse of Lehman Brothers in the fall of 2008, when it seemed as if every other corner of Wall Street was shattering.

"We believe that the current national market system is performing extremely well," John McCarthy, general counsel for Getco, wrote in a letter to the SEC. "For instance, the performance during the 2008 financial crisis suggests that our equity markets are resilient and robust even during times of stress and dislocation."

McCarthy submitted the letter on April 27, 2010. One week later, the market crashed.

# CHAPTER TWENTY

# PANIC TICKS

Thomas Peterffy had seen it all. The Black Monday crash of October 19, 1987, the 1998 collapse of the giant hedge fund Long-Term Capital Management, the implosion of the dot-com bubble in 2000 and 2001, the credit crisis of 2008.

But this was different.

This was *fast*.

This was *high-speed trading*.

Peterffy was keeping track of the market from the seclusion of an oak-lined private study on his luxurious estate in Greenwich, Connecticut. Beside his desk hung a large painting by the French realist Gustave Courbet, a serene river in France reflecting a bright line of poplars in the distance.

All was not serene that day in the market, though. The founder of Timber Hill and Interactive Brokers could feel in his sixty-five-year-old bones that something was wrong. The market had been on its heels all day.

Now it was getting much worse.

It was the afternoon of May 6, 2010. In minutes, seconds, the chaos Peterffy was sensing on his screens would spiral outward, scrambling the most sophisticated trading systems ever created. Wall Street was about to crash into the shadows of fear and confusion.

As the market dipped lower shortly after 2:30 P.M., Peterffy turned up the volume on the giant flat-screen TV hanging on the wall opposite his desk, tuned to the financial news network CNBC. The befuddled anchors didn't seem to know anything, other than the obvious fact that traders were selling on fears of contagion from Greece's troubled economy.

Peterffy picked up the phone and called Timber Hill's trading desk, several miles away in downtown Greenwich.

"What the heck is happening?" he said.

"Don't know," the rattled trader replied.

"Well find out!" Peterffy shouted.

As the downturn picked up speed, Timber Hill's traders started seeing "panic ticks" pop up on their screens, automated warning signs indicating that their positions were violating key price gaps. The reaction to a panic tick was instantaneous: Cancel all bids and offers. Get out, *now*. Starting at 2:40, the panic ticks picked up speed dramatically. Timber Hill started dumping positions and pulling out as fast as possible.

Peterffy called the trading desk again to see if anyone knew what was happening. No one did.

PETER Brown had never seen the likes of it.

No one had.

The co–chief executive of Renaissance Technologies, the most sophisticated trading operation in the world, was sitting in his office, situated along a brightly lit hallway of a nondescript building that seemed more elementary school than state-of-the-art trading hub.

Despite all of his sophistication, Brown was at a loss concerning what was causing the market to tank. Fears about Greece had gripped the market for days. Riots on the streets of Athens had unnerved investors. But how could that explain what he was watching on his computer monitor?

Brown, a wiry man in his early fifties with masses of dark wavy hair, had, like Peterffy, seen his share of market panics — the Asian flu of the late 1990s, the dot-com implosion, the credit crisis of 2008. Along with Bob Mercer, his colleague for decades, dating back to their time developing AI language translation systems for IBM in the 1980s, he'd taken the reins at Renaissance in early 2009 from its founder, Jim Simons. It was one of the most plum jobs in all of finance.

Brown had never seen a market move so quickly. The speed of the decline was breathtaking.

He wasn't overly worried. Because of Renaissance's AI trading systems, alert to the mere whisper of trouble in its strategies, the plunge wasn't likely to impact the firm's $10 billion or so worth of holdings in its flagship hedge fund, Medallion. Brown knew that anytime the market showed signs of extremely unusual behavior, the computer algorithms Medallion used would react like sensitive fingers touching a hot stove: They'd jerk back. The programs juggled stocks so quickly, owning positions often for mere minutes or seconds, that they were able to dump most of their stocks in the blink of an eye and safely step out of the line of fire.

Brown was still a bit unnerved, though, by the blinding speed of the drop. He picked up his phone and called Simons.

"Jim," Brown said, "you should know, the market is down nine percent."

"It is?"

Simons wondered why. Brown didn't know.


ONE thousand, two hundred miles away from Renaissance's office, in a bland, cube-shaped building on the outskirts of Kansas City, Dave Cummings watched from his expansive second-floor corner office as the stock market unraveled like a ball of yarn.

The founder of Tradebot wasn't sure what to make of the steep market downdraft. The heavy volume was scrambling trading systems, leading to disparities in prices quoted on various exchanges. The decline in prices became so sharp that it made Cummings worry that it wasn't going to right itself. Like many others, he worried that a "fat finger" mistake by a trader—Wall Street slang for someone who pressed the wrong button or put too many zeros into a sell order—had triggered a downward cascade that was turning into a vicious feedback loop.

If there was an erroneous trade, that meant Tradebot's systems, which tracked all corners of the market for signals about future conditions, were operating on bad information. Keep trading and Tradebot might spread the turmoil elsewhere, like a contagious virus.

It could also risk the unthinkable: a loss for Tradebot.

He kept staring at his screens, drumming his fingers, biting his lip. Stocks were careening out of control. Cummings was nervous. Tradebot never, ever lost money in the course of a trading day. It was one of Cummings's mantras. He didn't want to risk it. Tradebot should get out, he decided. He gave the order. In seconds, Tradebot stopped trading.

A terrifying cloak of darkness was descending on the market. Even the most sophisticated traders in the world were lost, confused, running for cover.

SEVERAL miles away from Tradebot, a trader at the Kansas City fund company Waddell & Reed Financial was monitoring a massive order to sell seventy-five thousand S&P 500 E-mini futures contracts. Shortly after 2:30 P.M., the trader had given the order to dump E-mini contracts worth roughly $4 billion.

It was a huge move intended to protect the fund's positions from a downward spiraling market. The design of the algorithm used to execute the trade was fairly simple. It would sell at a pace that would consistently keep it at about 9 percent of the market's overall volume, with strategic thirty-second pauses to throw off the hunter-seekers. Whenever volume picked up, the algo would sell in order to take advantage of the activity.

The trouble was, volumes were surging exponentially.

Waddell's broker, Barclays Capital, executed the order in New York and it shot into the electronic matching engine for the Chicago Mercantile Exchange. As volumes spiked, more sell orders from the Waddell algo were triggered. In about ten minutes, it executed nearly half of its orders. Typically, this would have taken place over several hours.

On the other side of the sales were high-frequency funds. Immediately after buying the contracts from Waddell, they sold them to other high-frequency traders at a slightly lower price. A feedback loop erupted, a manic hot potato effect as algorithms popped in and out of the E-mini at lightning speeds, selling and buying and selling and buying. Shortly after 2:40, as Waddell kept selling, during a fourteen-second period high-frequency traders bought and sold an astonishing twenty-seven thousand E-mini contracts.

The market shot down like a rock.


PAUL Adcock was sitting on a conference call from his office on the eighteenth floor of the Hartford Plaza North building on the east bank of the Chicago River.

Adcock was in charge of NYSE Arca trading operations, the brains of the electronic trading arm of the New York Stock Exchange. An old hand at electronic trading, Adcock had been partners with Jerry Putnam all the way back to the early 1990s, even before Putnam founded Terra Nova and Archipelago. He'd come a long way and he'd seen it all.

On the afternoon of May 6, Arca's engines were being pushed to the limit, sucking in and pumping out terabytes of information per second.

It wasn't enough.

Adcock was manning the controls of Arca's central hub on South Wacker Drive in the Chicago Loop as trading leapt into warp speed. Orders were barreling into Arca's Universal Trading Platform, just upgraded a few months before, at speeds never before seen. Data detailing everything from stock prices to volume were pumping out of

Arca's computers to customers—hedge funds, mutual funds, prime brokers, high-speed traders—at more than ten times the normal rate.

Adcock was monitoring the situation on his computer screen as the conference call droned on. He was concerned, but he'd seen plenty of market turmoil over the past few years. Nothing seemed out of the ordinary.

Then the market snapped.

"I gotta jump," Adcock said, slamming down the phone and bolting out of his chair. He turned left outside his office door and darted into the expansive room, framed by wide windows overlooking the Chicago skyline, that housed the front-end of Arca's operation.

Volumes were going ballistic. Adcock was worried the intensity of it all would overwhelm Arca's clients' ability to handle the order flow, jamming their computers. He had to throttle back the speed to maintain control.

Everything seemed to be humming. Then Adcock noticed something strange. Nasdaq, the NYSE's biggest competitor, had cut Arca off. Normally exchanges routed orders to the venue that has the best price, a rule strictly enforced by regulators. At 2:37 P.M., Nasdaq had stopped sending orders to Arca.

Why? What was wrong?

Adcock didn't know.

ERIC Noll had been monitoring the stock market's bizarre behavior from his spacious office on the fiftieth floor of One Liberty Plaza, a towering steel skyscraper overlooking the vast reconstruction effort of Ground Zero.

Noll, a heavyset man with an unruly head of black hair and flaring Mephistophelean eyebrows, had only recently taken over the job as executive vice president of Nasdaq, replacing former Island lawyer Chris Concannon. He was in charge of one of the most sophisticated markets ever created—the very same system built by Josh Levine from the ground up in a small, cluttered room at 50 Broad.

Nasdaq's turbocharged trading engine was humming at top speed. Volumes were surging. Around 2 P.M., Noll left his office and walked one floor up to the Nasdaq Operations Center, known as the NOC, the state-of-the-art central hub of the exchange.

At 2:35, Noll began to notice a slowdown in a data feed from NYSE Arca—Adcock's operation in Chicago. Orders Nasdaq routed to Arca weren't getting executed rapidly. Normally, an order to buy or sell a stock would go off in a split second. But Noll saw that some orders, such as those for Apple, were taking two seconds or more to get executed. In the hyperspeed world of microsecond trading, that was unacceptable.

Something was wrong. Noll didn't know what, but he knew it couldn't continue. After consulting with his technicians, Noll decided to cut Arca off. Nasdaq stopped routing orders to the exchange— severing the link first established in December 1996 between Archipelago and Island as Putnam and Levine tested their systems in preparation for the Order-Handling Rules.

At 2:40, a wave of sell orders for Procter & Gamble, the consumer products giant, hit the floor of the NYSE. The market for P&G suddenly became unbalanced. There were far more sell orders than buy orders. A computer system to slow trading at the NYSE kicked into gear, routing orders to designated market makers on the floor.

That slowdown created another problem. Because traders couldn't sell on the NYSE, they routed their orders to other markets, such as Nasdaq. Waves of orders sloshed away from the NYSE to other corners of a rapidly fragmenting market. In a matter of moments, P&G shares collapsed, losing 35 percent of their value.

Across Wall Street, hundreds of trades started to occur at unheard-of price levels. Accenture, a global consulting company that normally traded for about $50 a share, swapped hands for *a penny a share* at 2:47.53. Boston Beer, the maker of Sam Adams brews, also hit a penny. Cigarette giant Philip Morris tumbled from $49 to $17.

Shares of funds that tracked the entire stock market traded for mere pennies. In total, roughly one trillion in assets vanished from the market like a conjurer's trick.

At the other end of the scale, Apple, which normally traded for about $250, sold for nearly *$100,000 a share.*

The explanation for this insanity went back to Nasdaq's integration of algo trading. Years before, high-speed market makers operating on Nasdaq were told that they always needed to stay in the market. But there was a loophole: They didn't need to post bids or offers close to the price of a stock. Instead, they could put up wildly wide quotes, such as an offer to buy for a penny or sell for $99,999. The trick allowed the firms to stay in the market without actually trading.

On May 6, after a number of high-frequency traders cut and ran, those quotes—called stub quotes—became the only live bids or offers left on many stocks and ETFs. Other investors putting in "market orders," a direction to sell at any price, hit those trades.

It was a broken market gone mad, out of control Bots trading back and forth at insane prices.

A massive, fine-tuned machine was seizing up.

In Stamford, Connecticut, traders in the vast UBS trading room were seeing alerts pop up on multiple data-feed systems. More than fifty-one thousand bits of trading data per second were ripping through the UBS network, ten times the average rate. Clients were calling, complaining about delays in executions.

UBS traders in U.S. stocks, working for an outfit that Will Sterling had built from scratch several years before, began noticing delays in quotes from several trading venues, including NYSE Arca.

To protect their orders, they started routing around those venues. The trouble was spreading.

MINUTES away from UBS's Stamford headquarters, Haim Bodek was scrambling to figure out what was happening to the positions of his high-speed options firm, Trading Machines. He'd expected from early in the day to see a big move in the market, something on the order of a 2 percent downswing. But what Bodek was seeing on his screens was off the charts.

Meanwhile, Bryan Wiener, a trader for Trading Machines who'd had experience in hectic markets working on the floor of the Chicago Merc, was trying to take advantage of the chaos. He was focusing on Apple, one of his favorite names.

A trader next to him named Eric was holding Apple positions that would benefit if market volatility went down (volatility goes down when the market rises). Wiener, however, thought volatility could go *up* (volatility rises when the market drops).

"Dude, I think you should flatten out," he told Eric. By *flattening out*, he meant Eric should purchase options that would benefit from a jump in volatility, offsetting the risk.

Eric refused. He thought the market was going to rebound, leading to a drop in "vol," as traders say.

Wiener was adamant. "If you don't flatten out, I'm going to punch you in the throat!"

Eric decided it would be wise to follow his advice.

Bodek, meanwhile, fretted that with all the chaos, multiple trades would be broken by the exchange. That could create havoc with his fine-tuned models.

It was too much.

"There's something going on," he shouted to the trading room. "Get out!"

THE Chicago Mercantile Exchange was straining under the pressure. Then, just before 2:43 Eastern time, a massive sell order for several thousand E-mini contracts hit the tape, eating right through the order book. At the exact same moment in New York, a massive wave of ETFs mirroring the S&P 500, the Nasdaq index, and the Dow industrials were sold. Research group Nanex would later theorize that the sell order came from the same firm capitalizing on a fourteen-millisecond delay in the time it took prices to move between Chicago and New York. It labeled the trade the Disruptor.

BACK in Chicago, the giant hedge fund Citadel was seeing system errors in its programs. As volumes surged, Citadel operators began noticing a slowdown in the data coming from NYSE Arca.

Citadel was one of the most prolific traders of NYSE and Nasdaq stocks in the world. It also executed many of the trade orders from retail brokers such as E*Trade and TD Ameritrade, an internalization business that ex–Island CEO Matt Andresen had helped build. Since internalizers matched buy and sell orders from clients "internally," rather than route them to an exchange, it was flow the exchanges rarely saw.

But at about 2:45, Citadel asked all clients to route their orders away from its computers due to a technical glitch. "We are currently experiencing Equity system issues," the firm said in an e-mail to its customers. "We are advising clients to please route away."

Suddenly, a wave of retail order exhaust flushed away from Citadel and into already overwhelmed exchanges such as Nasdaq and the NYSE.

AT 2:45.28 P.M., the pressure on the E-mini contract inside the Chicago Mercantile Exchange's matching engine became unbearable. A trigger snapped and the exchange's so-called Stop Logic Functionality halted trading in the contract for one, two, three, four, five seconds. Those few seconds gave the high-speed Bots the time they needed to catch their breath, as it were—it was far too brief a time period for most humans to even understand what had happened. The feedback loop was broken. The machines regrouped. Instead of selling, they started buying.

The market recovered—and then it surged.

BACK at Renaissance, Peter Brown was stunned as he watched the market whiplash. Just as quickly as it had crashed, it began rebounding.

Brown had called Renaissance founder Jim Simons to notify him that the market had plunged 9 percent. But he couldn't explain what had happened.

Then, shortly before 2:46 P.M., the rebound kicked in.

"Wait," Brown told Simons as the market ticked up suddenly. "It's down eight percent. Now it's down seven percent."

Exchange executives raced to contain the damage. At about two-forty-five, Duncan Niederauer took an elevator from his sixth-floor office to the floor of the NYSE. He met with Executive Vice President Joseph Mecane in the floor's Ramp Operations Area, where they could monitor the chaos.

A seasoned veteran of electronic trading, Niederauer was one of the primary architects of the shift toward high-speed markets, from his days at Goldman Sachs and his work with Archipelago to his assumption of the top perch at the Big Board. But like everyone else, he was at a loss to explain what had happened that afternoon. Mecane, for his part, had worked for years at UBS, alongside Will Sterling and Haim Bodek, and was an expert in electronic markets.

Phone banks were ringing like mad. A cacophonous roar reminiscent of bygone days at the Big Board filled the spacious trading floor.

With that roar as a deafening background, Niederauer and Mecane fielded calls from companies that listed on the exchange and were worried about the sharp, inexplicable drop their stocks had taken.

Soon after 3 P.M., exchange executives jumped on a conference call that lasted for several hours. SEC officials, including Commissioner Mary Schapiro, monitored the call. The main problem: figuring out a uniform level where they could declare that certain stock declines were "erroneous" trades. Such trades would be wiped off investors' books as a quirk of fate.

Nasdaq officials advocated a decline of 80 percent from the level where stocks traded at 2:40, when the mayhem started. They were worried about whether a more generous level would give investors the message that they could take risks and expect to get rescued in the wake of a big sell-off. NYSE executives, meanwhile, advocated a cut-off of 20 percent.

Eventually they reached a compromise: Trades in securities that had fallen 60 percent or more would be canceled.

At Nasdaq, 12,306 trades were canceled. No trades that were executed on the floor of the New York Stock Exchange were canceled, but 4,903 trades on NYSE Arca were canceled. Many stocks had snapped back, but the wild moves were unnerving. The recovery—the Dow finished down 347 points after tumbling nearly 1,000 points—helped calm nerves across Wall Street.

But the stomach-churning violence of the swing left deep scars—and deep fears that it could happen again at any moment.

# CHAPTER TWENTY-ONE

# VERY DANGEROUS

As the stock market plunged on May 6, Senator Ted Kaufman had been presiding as chair of the Senate during a debate over proposed regulations of the failed mortgage giants Fannie Mae and Freddie Mac. As they contemplated the latest financial disaster spawned by Wall Street, they began to be aware of another potential calamity. A wave of chatter rippled through the chamber as the senators, clicking on their handheld devices, stared in amazement at news reports of a major crash in the stock market.

Soon after the market closed, Virginia senator Mark Warner went looking for Kaufman. His chief of staff, Luke Albee, called Kaufman's aide-de-camp, Jeff Connaughton. "Senator Warner wants to talk with him about what just happened in the market," Albee said.

Connaughton replied that Kaufman was in the Senate chamber. Flustered by the market mayhem, Warner walked from his office to the chamber and asked to speak on the floor.

"I wish to comment on what happened in the market today," he said. "The stock market, at one point today, approached a loss of one thousand points, which, if it had held, would have been the largest single-day loss in modern history."

After describing a few theories that were bubbling in the media in the immediate aftermath of the crash, such as a single bad "fat finger" order, Warner motioned to Senator Kaufman. "I have heard, while sitting in that chair, my friend, the senator from Delaware, come to this floor time and again to talk about the challenges that have been created in the marketplace with the increased use of high-speed trading, flash trading, colocation, a whole series of technical terms but terms that we may have seen the first inkling today with what happens when these tools of technology do not work the way they are supposed to. . . . We saw a living breathing real-time example of the potential catastrophe that could take place."

Senator Warner sat down. Kaufman rose to speak.

"We basically went from a market that was a floor-based market to a market that was digitalized and decimalized," he said. "People came into the market and began to develop these high-speed computers. Human beings were no longer doing the trading, computers were. They developed these algorithms. It ran automatically. It grew and grew. There is no way to know what is going on."

He paused.

"No one knows what is happening in these exchanges when this trading is going on," he said. "We have a very dangerous situation."

Bob Greifeld was ready to go on the attack. It was May 7, 2010, the morning after the crash. The target: his archenemy, the NYSE. In an interview on CNBC, Greifeld lashed out at the Big Board. When the New York floor halted dozens of stocks at a time, trading became even more muddled, he alleged.

"It was really shocking what happened," Greifeld said. "They basically walked away from the stock. And so that lack of liquidity in the trading of their stock such as P&G or Accenture in that nervous period of time had a disproportionate effect in terms of what happened with the stock. When the fact is you have the primary market, the listing market, deciding not to support the stock, to stop trading, sent a signal through a very nervous market that there's something wrong."

Soon after Greifeld appeared, NYSE CEO Duncan Niederauer

sat for an interview on the buzzing floor of the NYSE. He tried to remain calm, but it was clear that Greifeld's comments had infuriated him.

"Let's stop the finger pointing," he said. "This is about trying to move the ball forward. Let's be clear about the facts about what happened. There's no walking away, there's no abandoning of our obligations."

Niederauer defended the performance of the NYSE floor, which had no canceled trades, and went on to attack fast-trading electronic systems such as Nasdaq. To those who'd followed Niederauer's career, the irony was rich. He'd been one of the chief architects of the push toward electronic trading. Now Niederauer was proclaiming the victory of the human floor trader and denouncing runaway electronic trading.

While extolling the NYSE's performance — there were no penny trades on the Big Board — he ignored the fact that NYSE Arca had seen as much chaotic, runaway trading as Nasdaq. What's more, it would be revealed weeks later that a technology breakdown on the NYSE had led to a massive delay in quote dissemination, scrambling some trading models and adding to the confusion.

Still, Niederauer recognized that something must be done. CNBC host Simon Hobbs pointed out that the NYSE had been unabashedly chasing high-frequency traders, hoping to get their precious flow.

"Do you think there's a conflict of interest with having to cozy up with this nuclear arms race that we have with technology?" Hobbs asked. "You're encouraging this nuclear arms race!"

Niederauer didn't bat an eye.

"Everybody has to compete on technology, and what we're all going to ask ourselves is how fast is too fast, when is enough enough," he said. He then conceded, "It's not sustainable."

It was a stunning admission from the head of the nation's largest exchange. Back in Washington, SEC chairman Mary Schapiro wasn't amused by the verbal fisticuffs. She sent a message out to the exchange chiefs: *Cool it.* The following Monday, she gathered all of the CEOs of the major exchanges together in a room in the SEC's Washington, D.C., headquarters—Niederauer, Greifeld, Joe Ratterman from BATS, Bill O'Brien from Direct Edge—and gave them their marching orders: Implement circuit breakers for individual stocks in order to head off another flash crash.

After years of pushing speed like an inner-city drug dealer, the SEC was shifting course. Marketwide circuit breakers, which would trigger a brief stop in trading if the market made a major move in a short period of time, were quickly implemented. They amounted to a reversal of the speed-freak frenzy that had hijacked the financial system in the past decade. It was time to slow things down.

Was it enough? No one knew.

In the weeks and months following the events the media dubbed the Flash Crash, the fierce debate over what had become of the U.S. stock market that had erupted after the arrest of Sergey Aleynikov grew even more heated. Angry words were exchanged in the halls of Capitol Hill, on financial television shows, and in the backrooms of giant trading firms in New York and Chicago.

Congress held panel discussions. The SEC grilled the previously unknown chieftains of the high-speed merchants—and their critics. Stephen Schuler of Getco, Dave Cummings of Tradebot, Thomas Peterffy of Timber Hill, as well as Themis's Sal Arnuk, spoke before an array of regulators who seemed more confused than anyone by what was going on in the depths of the market.

Privately, the high-speed firms were self-righteously indignant at the harsh light that had been cast on their business. Most believed they had improved the market by making it more liquid and cheaper for investors. They had little sympathy for the Everyday Joe who was baffled by what had become of the market, the bizarre *Attack of the*

*Clones* race for speed, the AI Bots, the massive data centers, the microsecond tap dance in and out of stocks—*their* stocks.

That's precisely what the speed traders missed, critics said. Mom-and-pop investors innocently believed the stocks they owned were *their stocks*—not fizzing electronic bits of information to be toyed with by whiz kids running supercomputers. They had already seen Wall Street destroy trillions during the credit crisis in the previous few years. Now the math geniuses were tampering with the holdings in their 401(k)s.

The Flash Crash sparked a crisis of faith in the market. Retail cash started flowing out of stock funds at an alarming rate after May 6, falling every single month for the rest of the year even as the stock market rebounded and vaulted higher. Many feared the specter of another crash. And who could guarantee a flash bounce would bail the market out the next time?

More bizarre action in the market added to those concerns. In August 2010, it emerged that a single Chicago high-frequency firm, Infinium Capital Management, had triggered a brief $1-per-gallon pop in oil prices due to a trading glitch that machine-gunned two to three thousand orders per second for an oil contract minutes before the market closed on February 3. Washington Post Company shares tumbled in the blink of an eye in June due to a computer-trading glitch, triggering new circuit breakers that had been installed to halt wild trades. In September, shares of Progress Energy, a North Carolina utility with eleven thousand employees, plunged almost 90 percent in a matter of seconds due to a glitch.

The complex, labyrinthine nature of the market vexed ordinary investors who hadn't been keeping tabs on the dramatic changes that had occurred in its electronic plumbing. Years ago, before the rise of electronic networks, most trading took place at the NYSE and Nasdaq. Now trading occurred in about seventy different venues, including giant hedge funds like Citadel or banks such as UBS. So-called private markets, including dark pools, accounted for nearly 40 percent of all U.S. stock trades up from just 15 percent in 2008, according to the market researcher Tabb Group. More and more, the markets were sliding into discrete pools of darkness.

It wasn't meant to be this way.

The architects of the trading technology revolution that took off in the 1990s — Josh Levine, Jerry Putnam, and others — believed they were bringing light to darkness, cracking the powers that be with competition, opening up the market to more transparency, making it cheaper to trade in the bargain.

But the computerization of trading had a perverse side effect. Secret formulas, like the code taken by Goldman programmer Sergey Aleynikov, became the currency of the realm of the new cyberkings of Wall Street. Trading had become a cloak-and-dagger game of hide-and-seek, of spymaster tricks, feints and dodges embedded in mysterious algos dueling in dark pools. Artificial intelligence programs, the cutting edge of computer science, became the new key to riches. The programs were so sophisticated that they could read breaking news and react, just like a human trader scanning the pages of *The Wall Street Journal*. Only the computers could do so in milliseconds. There was still a place for humans on Wall Street — keepers of the machines, the legions of computer programmers, physicists, and electrical engineers who kept the machines humming. The market had become a high-tech poker game of programmer versus programmer, algo versus algo.

And everyone wanted to know: *What should we do now?*

There were few good answers. The electronic genie was out of the bottle. The high-speed traders defended themselves, pointing to cheaper, faster markets, a more efficient system, the lack of corruption that had plagued the market run by Nasdaq dealers and floor specialists.

The Flash Crash had made a hash of those arguments, though.

The entire system was at risk, and there seemed little anyone could do about it.

Especially the SEC.

LIKE detectives swooping in on a crime scene, the market's top cops at the SEC swiftly swung into action to get a grip on what had happened. The crash was like a steaming highway pileup that could take weeks to untangle. In the days following the crash, few answers were forthcoming. Investors grew worried that, in fact, no one actually knew . . . *or could know.*

A crack team of investigators at the SEC and the Commodity Futures Trade Commission started poring over reams of data and quizzing players across the Street—high-frequency traders, exchange operators, hedge funds, banks, dark pools. The investigation was held under the aegis of the Joint CFTC-SEC Advisory Committee on Emerging Regulatory Issues, formed as part of a harmonization effort launched in 2009 in the wake of the financial crisis.

On May 18, just twelve days later, investigators released an extensive preliminary report on the crash. It was full of confusing charts and row after row of numbers. But behind the numbers was a shocking truth: The U.S. securities market broke apart into pieces—and was still broken.

"The decline and rebound of prices in major market indexes and individual securities on May 6 was unprecedented in its speed and scope," the report stated. A "mismatch in liquidity" was exacerbated by "the withdrawal of liquidity by electronic market makers."

The most disturbing aspect of the report was the admission that *anything* might have triggered the crash—even terrorism. Like everyone else, the SEC was in the dark.

"We have found no evidence that these events were triggered by 'fat finger' errors, computer hacking, or terrorist activity," the report said, "although we cannot completely rule out these possibilities."

# PART IV

TOTO, I'VE A FEELING
WE'RE NOT IN KANSAS
ANYMORE.

—DOROTHY,
*THE WIZARD OF OZ*

# FUTURE OF THE MACHINE

# CHAPTER TWENTY-TWO

# A RIGGED GAME

The Flash Crash was a clarion call about the dangerously fragile plumbing of the market. With trading spread out among more than fifty venues, a third of it taking place in the dark, all maintained by twitchy phantom liquidity providers and cheetah-fast scalpers turbocharged on AI, the market many once believed was the most sophisticated in the world had crumpled in minutes like a house of straw.

Yet in the months after the crash, little was done to fix the problem. Indeed, the spread of electronic trading picked up at a dramatic rate, and the high-frequency players were constantly on the hunt for novel methods to boost speeds. A number of firms had started to use nitrogen-cooling systems for their central processors in order to turbocharge their chips, an approach known as *overclocking*. A technology company called Hardcore Computer provided high-speed firms an overclocked workstation called Detonator. Another was called Reactor X. Tellingly, the technology had originally been invented for top-end video-game players.

While trading firms were deploying the most advanced technology available, the links connecting them to the market were ramping up just as quickly. In 2007, the NYSE had launched a $500 million initiative dubbed Project Alpha. The plan was to build a mammoth computer trading facility on the site of an old quarry in Mahwah, New

Jersey. The length of several football fields, the 400,000-square-foot building would allow computer-driven trading firms to put their computer servers right next to the NYSE's matching engine — the computers that brought buyers and sellers together in the frictionless ether of cyberspace. Twenty-inch-wide pipes pumped in water to cool the computers. Twenty surge protectors, each the size of a tank, protected the site against power outages.

In August 2010, just months after the Flash Crash, Project Alpha was ready for action. Evenly spaced around the large, nondescript building—nearly invisible to the traffic flowing around it on nearby roads and highways—were six buttonwood trees, planted in apparently un-ironic homage to the origin of the venerable stock exchange on Broad Street.

That exchange was all but dead. Mahwah was the new floor, a powerful confluence of capitalism and state-of-the-art computer technology. While tourists snapped photos of the exchange's marble façade on the corner of Wall and Broad, the real trading was taking place thirty miles away in Mahwah's vast air-conditioned floors of computer servers. Snap a picture there, and the feds might haul you off. Mahwah was classified as part of the critical infrastructure of the United States and therefore a potential terrorist target.

Demand for slots near the NYSE's matching engine had been red hot. All of the available colocation space available for the project's first phase, two 20,000-square-foot pods, had been sold out. Three more pods were set for rollout in the coming months, for a total of 100,000 square feet of turbocharged computer power. At a cost of up to $10,000 per pod per month, it was a highly lucrative business for the NYSE. How the setup fit in with the notion that electronic trading created a *level playing field* for all investors was another question.

Massive trading data centers were spreading around the globe. The Chicago Mercantile Exchange was building a 428,000-square-foot data center in Aurora, Illinois, thirty-five miles southwest of

Chicago. The NYSE was erecting another giant data center outside London. At an industrial site on the edge of Tseung Kwan O, on the outskirts of Kowloon, China, a data center was rising where traders could electronically swap stocks, currencies, and other contracts on the Hong Kong Exchange. Data centers were popping up in Mumbai, São Paulo, Melbourne, Singapore, and elsewhere.

The headlong push into electronic trading was going full blast. Computers were conducting more and more trades through complex AI-armed algorithms. In 2005, computer algorithms accounted for about one-quarter of all trading. By the end of the decade, they would account for two-thirds of all trading, if not more. Wall Street giants from J.P. Morgan Chase to Bank of America to Citigroup to Credit Suisse had teams of mathematicians and programmers who did nothing but design new algos all day, every day.

While Island had started it all, the level of the complexity was entirely new. The market had been altered beyond recognition by ultra-high-speed trading and the proliferation of AI Bots dueling it out on the expanding fronts of the Algo Wars. Spreads had narrowed dramatically, of course, but the new cyber–market makers were far more prevalent than the specialists who controlled trading on the floor of the NYSE had ever been. According to NYSE's own data, specialists were involved in only 28 percent of all transactions in 2000. By 2011, high-speed traders were present in as much as three-fourths of all trades, possibly more. The slices of the pie they were taking were smaller, but there were far more slices being snatched away than ever before.

And while spreads were narrower, the narrowing was something of an illusion. In the late 1990s, when spreads were typically about twelve-and-a-half cents wide, the amount of stock a market maker would buy or sell in a single trade tended to be in the thousands of shares. Now the amount was typically one hundred or two hundred shares. An investor who wanted to buy, say, thirty thousand shares (a relatively small order for an institution) could easily pay fifty cents or more above the initial offer. The reason? High-speed Bots were bidding up the price, sensing a whale in the ocean.

The upshot: Spreads simply weren't as pancake thin as they seemed. Over time, the impact on the 401(k)s of ordinary investors becomes monstrous. The lost nickels and dimes per share could amount to tens of thousands of dollars lost by the time investors retired.

Admittedly, the human traders and market makers the Bots had replaced had no one to blame but themselves. Nasdaq had been a nest of corruption, of scheming dealers colluding to enrich themselves at the expense of everyday investors. NYSE specialists had also been caught with their hands in the cookie jar. Good old-fashioned corruption and all-too-human greed had helped destroy a system that had lasted for centuries.

But were the Bots better?

WITH Project Alpha, high-frequency trading had officially taken over the Big Board. While the floor remained open for business, it was a shadow of its former self, a puppet show for TV. And there were other signs that the Bots were taking over at the NYSE. In early 2010, Getco had become a so-called designated market maker (DMM) — the new term the NYSE used for its floor specialists. Getco took more than 350 stocks from Barclays Capital, a British bank that had bought up floor spots from former specialists such as LaBranche, which had exited the business due to low profits. As a DMM, Getco gained a leg up on other investors, in exchange for obligations to maintain an orderly market.

Building on its edge, in November 2011 Getco said it planned to buy up Bank of America's NYSE floor business, giving it control of blue chips such as General Electric, McDonald's, Wal-Mart Stores, and Coca-Cola. The move made Getco the second largest DMM on the NYSE, just behind Barclays, trading 850 NYSE symbols, including stocks for 120 S&P 500 companies. Getco, a company that hadn't

existed more than a decade ago, would control one-third of the trading on the floor of the NYSE. The DMM push at Getco had been
spearheaded by former UBS executive Daniel Coleman, who in 2003
had hired Haim Bodek. Coleman in early 2012 would be named CEO
of Getco.

By then, only four DMMs existed—the other two were electronic-
trading giants Goldman Sachs and Knight Capital—compared with
the thirty-five specialist firms that had run the floor a decade earlier.
The shift was a complete reversal from the SEC's stated goal to increase competition in the market. Competition had been annihilated,
at least on the floor of the NYSE.

Getco had become a dominating force in the market. Its advantage came from a combination of space-age tech programming, the
most advanced telecom gear on earth, and a deep knowledge of
market plumbing. It used a bleeding-edge communications technology called Infiniband, which was estimated to be more than twice as
fast as most of its competitors. The firm was also said to use Nvidia
chips, graphics cards used in high-performance gaming systems, and a
new visual programming language called Kodu, used to create video
games on the Xbox.

With more than four hundred employees (as at Tradebot, they
were called "associates"), Getco had offices in Chicago, New York,
London, and Singapore and traded on more than fifty markets around
the world. Its chief trader in Chicago was Dave Babulak, Haim
Bodek's former colleague from Hull. Brian Nigito, the onetime Island
technologist, helped run the firm's New York office (Nigito would
leave the firm in 2011).

Getco was increasingly cozy with regulators in Washington.
Getco's general counsel was John McCarthy, who'd formerly served
as an associate director of the SEC's Office of Compliance Inspec-
tions and Examinations. In June 2010, Getco hired Elizabeth King, a
seventeen-year SEC veteran and an expert in options markets.

And now, with its move onto the NYSE's hallowed floor, Getco was taking its place as the new king of the hill in the stock market, the direct descendant of the traders who'd founded the exchange under a buttonwood tree in 1792.

The revolution started by Levine on January 16, 1996, with the launch of Island had come full circle.

WEEKS after the NYSE's Mahwah data center opened for trading, in early September, two old adversaries met again. The Financial Industry Regulatory Authority, formerly known as the National Association of Securities Dealers, or NASD, fined a New York trading firm $2.3 million and suspended several of its traders.

Its misdeed: Gunning fake orders into the market at high speeds in order to trick other traders into buying or selling stocks. The firm was called Trillium Brokerage Services. The case was the first hard evidence in the United States that firms were using rapid-fire algo trading strategies to game the market. But the trick used by Trillium was an old one — a trick a seasoned SOES trader might have used. According to FINRA, Trillium had jammed forty-six thousand phantom orders for stocks into the market in 2006 and 2007 in order to fake out other algo-driven traders.

The fake orders, which Trillium never intended to execute, according to FINRA, made it appear as if a big buyer or seller were in the market. That would cause other computer traders — such as firms using sensitive algos hunting for a whale — to jump in or get out, moving the price of the stock in a way that was advantageous for Trillium's traders. Trillium was blasting the orders into the market and canceling them before they had a chance to get filled. It was a classic bait and switch, conducted at high velocity. Regulators called the strategy "layering," an apt description of the layers of fake bids pumped into the order book.

It wasn't the first time Trillium had been caught playing a rigged game. In 2006, Trillium and its part-owner Schonfeld Group were fined nearly $500,000 by the NASD for entering phantom quotes during the start of trading on Nasdaq. As is typical with such cases, neither firm admitted or denied the charges—though they did pay the fine.

Trillium's history was well known to the regulators at FINRA who still remembered the SOES bandits of old. It was formerly known as Heartland Securities—formerly the trading arm of Datek Securities, formerly run by Shelly Maschler.

In charge of Trillium: Lee Maschler, Shelly Maschler's youngest son.

IN August 2010, a small team of construction workers plugged a one-inch-thick fiber-optic cable into a Nasdaq computer port at 1400 Federal Boulevard in Carteret, New Jersey. Trace the cable back 825 miles, over farmland in western New Jersey, through the granite and schist of the Allegheny Mountains in central Pennsylvania, across northern Ohio along the shores of Lake Erie and into Illinois, and you would come upon a nondescript data center in the South Loop of Chicago, steps away from the Chicago Mercantile Exchange and the futuristic trading engines of high-speed giant Getco.

More than two years in the making, at a cost of $300 million, the cable represented the cutting edge of superspeed computer trading. Rather than track the traditional route that most fiber-optic lines had used, along railroad right-of-ways, the cable was laid as the crow flies, a beeline cut through mountains and rivers with rock saws and dynamite. Its goal: to shave three milliseconds off an order's round-trip between that Carteret data center and Chicago—down from 16.3 milliseconds to 13.3 milliseconds.

That's one hundred million dollars per *thousandth* of a second.

Mississippi-based Spread Networks, the company that laid the cable, was pushing the high-speed arms race to a new level. It was betting that high-frequency traders would pay through the nose to be the first in line in the digital order books housed inside the data centers. And it was right. According to one estimate, a one-millisecond advantage could be worth more than $100 million.

Since there were only twenty slots on the cable, any firm that had a slot had a distinct edge over every competitor that didn't. Welcome to the new level playing field of high-frequency trading.

The phenomenon wasn't confined to the United States—it was going global. In October 2010, just months after Spread Networks plugged into Nasdaq, fiber-optic companies Hibernia Atlantic, based in Summit, New Jersey, and Huawai Marine Networks, of Tianjin, China, announced a plan to lay the first transatlantic fiber-optic cable built in a decade, a half-billion-dollar project that was projected to cut five milliseconds off trades between New York and London. Once complete, the three-thousand-mile cable would stretch from Halifax, Nova Scotia, across the North Atlantic to Somerset, England. As with the Spread Networks cable, the route would be shorter than other cable providers had used because it would cross shallow waters, where cable can be damaged by everything from fishing trawlers to sharks, which are attracted by the line's electricity. To protect the cable, two ships operated by Global Marine Systems, the *Sovereign* and the *Cable Innovator*, were burying it in a trench as much as six feet deep, dug into the seabed. The link was on schedule to go live in 2012.

Fiber-optic cables were encircling the earth, linking markets at high speeds as the Algo Wars expanded. And there were signs in early 2012 that even fiber-optic networks would soon be obsolete. A small group of elite high-speed traders in Chicago had started using microwaves to transmit trading signals at rates that dwarfed those boasted by fiber. First used to beam trades into the Chicago Mercantile Exchange, microwaves were now relaying trades between Chicago and New York through a series of microwave-station relays. The only problem: The signals could be disrupted by rainstorms or even geese. But the advantage was huge. According to industry estimates, microwaves could transmit a round-trip trade between Chicago and New York in ten milliseconds—a "whopping" three milliseconds faster than Spread Networks. The biggest firms were already using microwaves, insiders said, and more were coming onboard. Regulators, of course, had little if any clue about what was happening, and the high-frequency crowd was in no hurry to tell them.

It was hard to know if it even mattered whether regulators were paying attention. Because the Bots were going global, trading occurred in a supranational cyberspace that no regulator could control. The Tokyo Stock Exchange was the hub of Asia's fast-rising electronic trading matrix. In 2010, Tokyo launched its Arrowhead trading platform to cater to high-frequency traders, which made up roughly half of its volume. The SGX Singapore Exchange in the summer of 2011 launched its Reach platform, billed as the fastest matching engine in the world, with order speeds below ninety microseconds. Reach was based on the same architecture used by Nasdaq—the Island system.

Like the U.S. exchanges before them, SGX was aggressively courting high-speed traders. "To grow capital markets in Singapore . . . growing liquidity is first and foremost," SGX vice president Chew Sutat told *Singapore News* in May 2011. "HFT potentially could support growing liquidity."

Frustrated by the post–financial meltdown lack of volatility in the United States, high-speed traders were flocking to Asia. Firms such as Getco and Citadel were setting up operations in the Far East. A trans-Asian trading network known as the ASEAN Trading Link was rising, linking exchanges in Singapore, Kuala Lumpur, the Philippines, Thailand, Indonesia, and Vietnam.

In India, the National Stock Exchange, or NSE, first made thirty-five colocation racks available to traders' computers in the winter of 2009. International banks such as Goldman Sachs, Citigroup, and Morgan Stanley quickly signed up, leaving local Indian firms out in the cold. But more racks were opening up. With the high-speed players on board, the NSE rapidly lapped the much older and traditional Bombay Stock Exchange, accounting for nearly three-quarters of all stock trading in India by the end of the decade. Turkey's Istanbul Stock Exchange in late 2010 rolled out measures to cater to high-speed traders.

Algo trading was expanding in markets in Brazil, Australia, Israel, Canada, and Mexico.

Then, in 2011, BATS Global Markets took over the Chi-X Europe trading facility. Island, of course, lurked in the background. Dave Cummings had based the BATS system on Island, and Chi-X had been coded by former Island programmer (later Getco executive) Brian Nigito. BATS Chi-X Europe would handle more than 25 percent of all stock trading in Europe, making it the largest pan-European stock market.

Like a dominant species taking over an entire ecosystem, Island's pool was washing across the globe. From Nasdaq, INET—the Island system with all the high-speed bells and whistles tacked on—had spread to seventy exchanges in more than fifty countries around the world. And inevitably, as the Island system spread, it brought along its codependent species, the high-frequency traders.

Getco, of course, had established itself as king of the speed traders. In 2007, it had landed an investment of between $200 million and $300 million from private equity giant General Atlantic, a deal that valued the firm at roughly $1.5 billion. By 2011, that value was considerably higher. And the firm continued to bring on an army of quants to man its world-spanning trading machine. The following ad for Getco, for instance, appeared in January 2012:

CHICAGO, IL: Work with inter-disciplinary teams of traders & technologists & use trading models to trade profitably on major electronic exchanges; use statistical & mathematical approaches & develop new models to leverage trading capabilities. Must have Master's in Math, Statistics, Physical Science, Computer Science, or Engineering w/min GPA of 3.4/4.0. Must have proven graduate level coursework in 2 or more of the following: Stochastic Processes, Statistical Methods, Mathematical Finance, Applied Numerical Methods, Machine Learning.

Then, in the summer of 2011, a new contender for the high-frequency crown had emerged. Virtu Financial, the computer trading outfit that counted former Island attorney and Nasdaq executive Chris Concannon as a partner, merged with EWT, a California speed-trading operation that operated on exchanges around the world. (EWT was run by Rodney Faragalla, a former technologist at Island.) Industry insiders said the firm would handle as much trading as, if not more than, Getco.

The arms race behind the Algo Wars seemed endless. Speeds were hitting levels that defied rationality. A London technology company called Fixnetix claimed it had crafted the world's fastest trading microchip, a device that processed a trade in 740 nanoseconds. There was even chatter about measuring trades in *picoseconds — trillionths* of a second (a picosecond is to one second as one second is to 31,700 years).

The SEC, alarmed by the explosion of trading, and humbled by its inability to quickly explain the Flash Crash, rushed to come to grips with the market. To catch up with the machines, the agency planned to build a giant machine of its own. It called it the Consolidated Audit Trail, or CAT. The CAT, in theory, would be able to capture and analyze every single order placed into the stock market. This included not only the actual trades, but the mad frenzy of canceled orders clogging up the market's plumbing. The SEC hoped that its CAT would capture patterns in real time — much like an AI Bot — and discern whether they were manipulative. The cost of such a machine was unknown, but experts said it could run in the billions.

But few stopped to ask what the cost would be if nothing were done. Without the ability to peer into the market and learn who was doing what and why, the traffic police of the market were nothing better than Keystone Kops. Rogue traders could act with impunity in the full knowledge that there was little chance that they'd be caught. While the CAT smacked of some kind of Orwellian eye in the sky, it also seemed almost incredible that it hadn't been built already.

Because the terrifying truth was that the market by the late 2000s had descended into one vast pool of darkness.

Insiders knew this to be true. As the market continued to evolve into a speed-mad runaway train with no barriers beyond the laws of physics, some of the trailblazers of electronic trading started to question whether things had gone too far.

ON the morning of October 11, 2010, Thomas Peterffy stepped onto the dais of the ornate Opéra Salon on the ground floor of the Intercontinental Le Grand Hôtel in Paris. It was a gala event, the fiftieth annual meeting of the World Federation of Exchanges. Attendees included Bill Brodsky, chairman of the Chicago Board Options Exchange, the NYSE's Duncan Niederauer, Christine Lagarde, French minister for the economy and future head of the International Monetary Fund, Nasdaq CEO Bob Greifeld, and Atsushi Saito, CEO of the Tokyo Stock Exchange.

The speaker who would set off the most fireworks was Peterffy, the founder of Timber Hill, one of the early users of Island. He looked out over the podium at the upturned faces of his peers and grimaced.

Peterffy had become extremely disillusioned with the market he'd helped create. It wasn't just the deceptive tactics of firms like Trillium, it was the unregulated speed traders who were picking off his own firm's orders, with no firm obligation to stick in the market during tough times. The stock and options markets had been turned into a Wild West of dueling algos—and some firms, it seemed, had special advantages. Like Haim Bodek at Trading Machines, Peterffy was steamed that his orders were getting clipped time and time again. He wasn't going to take the abuse without fighting back.

He cleared his throat, adjusted his glasses, and launched into his speech.

"An exchange used to be a place, yes, a *physical* place, where people would come together to buy or sell, hoping to achieve the best price for themselves," he said. "The more the exchange was able to attract *all* of the buy and sell interests in a product, the more the prices on the exchange would reflect the true state of supply and demand."

It was the old mantra: *Liquidity breeds liquidity.* But something had changed.

"In the last twenty years came computers, electronic communications, electronic exchanges, dark pools, flash orders, multiple exchanges, alternative trading venues, direct access brokers, OTC derivatives, high-frequency traders . . . Reg NMS in the U.S.—and what we have today is *a complete mess.*"

He looked out at the crowd. Dead silence. Peterffy hadn't bothered to warm the audience up with a joke, a humorous anecdote. He cut straight to the point—and most of the people in the room didn't like what he was saying.

"It is not so much anymore that the public does not trust their brokers. They do not trust the markets, the exchanges, or the regulators either. And why should they, given our showing the past few years? To the public the financial markets may increasingly seem like a casino, except that the casino is more transparent and simpler to understand."

Visible tension spread through the room. Did Thomas Peterffy just call the market *a casino*? That was an attack they might have expected from the likes of Arnuk and Saluzzi or Senator Ted Kaufman—but from the founder of Timber Hill and Interactive Brokers, one of the godfathers of electronic trading?

Peterffy, of course, was fully aware that his words seemed to contradict his own history. Like Josh Levine, he had believed that computers would revolutionize markets. And they had. But something had gone wrong.

"I must confess to you that I was an ardent proponent of bringing technology to trading and brokerage. Unfortunately, I only saw the *good* sides. I saw how electronic trading and record-keeping could be used to force people to be more honest, to make the process more efficient, to lower transaction costs and to bring liquidity to the markets. I did *not* see the forces of fragmentation and the opportunity for people to use technology to keep to the letter but avoid the spirit of the rules—creating the current crisis."

He gazed out at his audience. Peterffy wasn't shocked to see the stern faces, the shaking heads and averted eyes. He was certain that he'd become their enemy—and he had little hope that they would listen. The computer-trading elite would never admit that the markets they'd created were deeply flawed. Still, he kept hammering away.

"It is vitally important that we bring an end to this crisis of trust before it spreads any further. That we bring back order, fair dealing, and trust in the marketplace. The financial markets of . . . the world's developed countries are at a turning point. Technology, market structure, and new products have evolved more quickly than our capacity to understand or control them. The result has been a series of crises over the past few years that have caused many investors to lose confidence or to think that the whole system is a rigged game."

After Peterffy finished speaking, there was silence. Then a scattered handclap. And then the room burst into loud applause.

Everyone realized: Peterffy had actually done it—he'd come out and said what so many were thinking, *what they all knew deep down*. The market was a complete mess. And the old guy was the only one with the balls to stand up there and call a spade a spade. It was a message Dan Mathisson at Credit Suisse would echo a few months later in his speech at the Fontainebleau Hotel in Miami Beach.

Soon after the speech, Peterffy was hobnobbing with the titans of the exchange world. He ran into Sandy Frucher, vice chairman of Nasdaq and longtime chief of the Philadelphia Stock Exchange.

"How are you, Sandy?" Peterffy said.

"I'm well," said Frucher, a gray-haired veteran of the exchange wars. "But I don't wake up in the morning thinking about which windmill to attack."

Peterffy understood exactly what Frucher was saying. In an ideal world, everyone would start behaving himself and stop focusing on the short-term buck, the quick hit. *We all know the truth. You know. I know. This is Wall Street. You're not changing a goddamn thing.*

In November 2010, one month after Peterffy's speech, the American Physical Society published a startling new study that made a radical prediction about the future plumbing of the global financial market. The paper was more proof that skeptics such as Peterffy had little hope of putting the brakes on the market's speed-demon evolution.

The paper, by MIT physicist Alex Wissner-Gross and Cameron Freer, an MIT mathematician, argued that it's in the financial interest of high-speed trading operations to build computer hubs at specific "optimal intermediate locations between trading centers" all around the world—between Shanghai and the Tokyo Stock Exchange, between the Tokyo Stock Exchange and Nasdaq, between Nasdaq and the London Stock Exchange. With these catbird-seat hubs, the firms would be able to trump their competitors in the race to capture opportunities in price discrepancies in stocks between the venues, say, Microsoft in New York and Microsoft in Tokyo, or West Texas crude in Chicago and light, sweet crude in Amsterdam. It was a race that went all the way back to Dave Cummings's insistence that Tradebot's computers be colocated with Island's at 50 Broad.

Wissner-Gross and Freer provided a map dotted with optimal hubs all along the earth's surface. Many of the hubs lay in the oceans, leading to the fanciful notion that particularly ambitious high-frequency trading outfits would plant themselves in the middle of the Atlantic or the Mediterranean or the South China Sea and get the jump on competitors using floating micro-islands populated by small communities of elite pattern-recognition programmers overseeing the hyperfast flow of data through their superservers.

Better yet: unmanned pods of densely packed microprocessors overseen by next-generation AI Bots processing billions of orders streaming out of other unmanned AI pods positioned optimally around the world, the silent beams of high-frequency orders shifting trillions across the earth's oceans at light speeds, all automated, beyond the scope of humans to remotely grasp the nature of the transactions.

The end game for Wissner-Gross and Freer had nothing to do with AI Bots and picosecond arbitrage. Rather, they saw this rapid expansion of powerful computer power around the planet as a step toward a sort of digital planetary transcendence that humanity could use to observe the world itself on a scale never before conceived. The floating islands would come equipped with sensors and the technical ability to crunch massive sums of data. Predicting long-term weather patterns, or even solving global warming, would then be much more feasible. "This is the first financially compelling reason to start to densely deploy computers all over the world's surface and make our physical planet smarter," said Wissner-Gross.

And yet few stopped to question the wisdom of linking every trading center in the world at blindingly high speeds. With optimized hubs connecting markets in a worldwide push-button money grid, and vast trading machines juggling every security known to man, the possibility of a next-generation crash, global in scale, was becoming all too real. Such an event had been dubbed the Splash Crash, chaotic pools of dark liquidity crashing like a tsunami across the world's trading system.

Now sprinkled into the toxic brew: experiments on entirely new breeds of artificial intelligence.

# CHAPTER TWENTY-THREE

# THE BIG DATA

E li Ladopoulos, aka Acid Phreak, stepped into Suite 1107 on the eleventh floor of 156 Fifth Avenue and shook the soot-black snow off his shoes. It was early spring of 2011. Snow still clung to the sidewalks of New York after one of the coldest Northeast winters on record. Inside the office, a row of high, dirt-smeared windows overlooking an endless cityscape in the Flatiron district of Manhattan let in a stream of grainy lemon-yellow sunlight.

The office of Kinetic Global Markets, a start-up New York hedge fund, looked like almost any high-tech trading hub. Narrow tables stacked with rows of computers, glowering twenty-somethings in jeans and sweaters and scruffy beards mesmerized by darting streams of data on their Acer flat-screens. Whiteboards sporting wild-looking flow charts and complex formulas hung on the walls.

The smell of cheap coffee wafted from a small kitchen by the office entrance as Ladopoulos walked in and pulled off his jacket. Flags for the native countries of various Kinetic's team members — Greece, Israel, Italy, Russia, the United States, and more — hung on a string that curved along the ceiling over the monitor-stacked tables.

Kinetic was trying to tap into what had come to be known among a cohort of AI aficionados as the Big Data. As computers spread across the world, more and more information was available about . . .

well, *everything*. Shipping trends in the Persian Gulf. The amount of wheat grown in Kazakhstan. Rainfall in British Columbia. Birth rates in Latin America. Oil shipments in the Strait of Hormuz. The list was endless. One fact was clear: The human mind could never process the Big Data. But a computer, perhaps? And, perhaps, a Big Data trading machine could troll the Web and other data systems and discover patterns, *untold patterns*. Those patterns, if all worked as planned, could provide signals that a machine could use to buy and sell stocks for a massive profit.

That trick, anyway, was what Kinetic and the trader formerly known as Acid Phreak—Ladopoulos—were attempting to pull off. It marked a new shift in the application of computers to the market. With the boom in high-frequency trading, computers had by 2011 easily defeated humans at the speed game. No human could trade hundreds of stocks in milliseconds.

But now programmers were attempting to build computers that could beat humans at the trading game itself, buying and selling stocks based on fundamentals such as sales trends and economic variables.

While the effort seemed almost quixotic, there were indications that it could be done. IBM, after all, had recently built an AI computer system called Watson that had defeated the world's elite *Jeopardy!* players.

The system Kinetic deployed resembled Watson in certain ways. Kinetic's task, however, was in reality far harder than cracking *Jeopardy!* Kinetic was trying to *hack the market* by mining endless terabytes of information stored on databases throughout the world. Its hacker in chief, Ladopoulos, was a charismatic, intense character with a shaved head, rimless glasses, a fondness for vintage tennis shoes, and a million stories.

Many of those stories went back to his previous incarnation in the early 1990s as an infamous hacker, back when being a hacker was actually cool, the closest a computer nerd could get to rock-star status. The hackers he ran with even had made-up names like rock stars: Phiber Optik, Corrupt, Outlaw, the Plague, Lord Micro.

Ladopoulos went by the name Acid Phreak. In the late 1980s, he'd founded a group of elite hackers in New York City called the Masters of Deception. The MOD's specialty was hacking phone systems, a skill set known as "phreaking" (hence Ladopoulos's sobriquet).

They were very good at what they did—too good. They hacked too many systems and eventually caught the eye of the feds. After getting caught for successfully hacking into AT&T's phone system, in July 1993 Ladopoulos and his partner in crime, Paul Stira (aka Scorpion), were sentenced to six months in prison and six months' home detention. The charge was conspiracy to commit computer crimes.

Ladopoulos seemed to have little trouble finding work after getting out of prison. His talents were in high demand from outfits that required protection from people just like him. At first, he worked on computer system security analysis for the military and intelligence agencies. Then he started researching the technology behind the stock market, and eventually, in 1996, he landed a job as director of global information security at Instinet.

In 1998, he came into contact with the legendary founder of D. E. Shaw, a giant New York hedge fund that used math and computers to mine hundreds of millions of dollars from the market year after year. David Shaw, who'd taught computer science at Columbia University before jumping into finance, helped convince Ladopoulos that the big money on Wall Street wasn't in security systems—it was in designing computer models to trade stocks.

It took years before Ladopoulos was able to build real-world models. To bone up on finance while working as a consultant for Instinet, he studied economics at the City University of New York. Then, in the early 2000s, he met David Leinweber, a finance professor at the University of California at Berkeley who'd been working on applying AI to trading for more than a decade.

Ladopoulos had been studying AI since the 1990s, but he wasn't convinced it could be used as an effective trading tool. Leinweber showed him that as computers grew more powerful, and more data was available on the Internet, AI would eventually become a reliable way to predict the future course of the market. For a time, they teamed up at a technology firm, called Monitor110, that searched the so-called Deep Web for information that hedge funds and bank prop (proprietary) traders could use to guide their trading decisions. Operating out of a sixth-floor loft just north of Wall Street, the operation scoured more than nine million sources of data, such as traditional news sites and blogs, for information on specific companies or on topics ranging from pharmaceutical trends to asbestos litigation. Ladopoulos worked for the research team that tested strategies. The results of the tests were used as a sales device — examples of how the system could work for potential users.

At Monitor, Ladopoulos met Roger Ehrenberg, the cerebral founder of the company and a venture capitalist who'd formerly run a $6 billion internal hedge fund for Deutsche Bank. Ehrenberg had been a longtime investor in Renaissance Technologies and was therefore well aware of the massive potential — and the massive hurdles — of using large-scale data and artificial intelligence to buy and sell stocks. It was possible, but only the best minds in the business — such as Bob Mercer and Peter Brown at Renaissance — seemed capable of pulling it off.

Despite its world-beating talent, Monitor was a failure. It was a needle-in-a-haystack business, and the firm found far too much hay and far too few needles. The information was overwhelming, impossible to spin into gold. The firm was wound down in 2008, and Ladopoulos's research team disbanded.

A few years later, the germ of the research team's work gave birth to Kinetic. Ladopoulos, Ehrenberg, and several others who'd worked on the strategies were convinced that the core idea they'd formed at Monitor still had massive potential.

Technology was improving at a dramatic pace. Cloud computing, the use of spare capacity on a distributed network of computers, was giving firms the ability to tap into glaciers of digital muscle power. Where Monitor had to buy and build its own server farm, a firm tapping the cloud could get the same processing and storage power at a fraction of the cost. Leaps in language processing and AI strategies also made the task of squeezing profits out of the Big Data seem more realistic.

The biggest step: shrinking the data set. The Information Super-highway was teeming with incalculable hoards of data that a smart trading system could exploit. The trouble was, as Monitor had found, there was far too much data. They needed focus—gold-standard sources of information that could collectively feed a model and present winning trading ideas. Rather than scan the entire Web, as impossible as boiling the ocean, they would scale down the project to a more realistic goal.

They went to work, building a database of websites and other machine-readable online sources, including government sites such as SEC.gov. To make sense of the information, Ladopoulos and several other programmers started to build an artificial intelligence program that could monitor the sites, hunt out recognizable patterns, and provide specific forecasts for stocks. The system might track respected blogs about Apple such as *Mac Rumors,* speeches by industry experts, shipping data out of China (where iPhones were built), employment sites measuring the number of workers with Apple experience looking for jobs (an uptick would indicate a round of layoffs, hence trouble and possibly an earnings miss). The system would scour SEC filings, data on Amazon.com or other retail sites that indicated sales performance, and Twitter feeds that mentioned Apple products.

Collectively, the AI program crunched the information like a magical data grinder and spit out a buy or sell recommendation with a certain probability, much like a Wall Street analyst—or IBM's Watson submitting a response on *Jeopardy!* That, at least, was the theory.

The goal: predict a company's performance *before* it became public. Effectively, they were building from scratch an AI financial analyst. Ideally, Kinetic would be able to detect a company's fortunes even *before the company's own executives and employees knew what was happening.* Sales trends, buzz on a product, a pricing war coming from a tough competitor—they were crystal balls into the future, if only you could find the right data and make sense of it.

So in 2008, full of Big Data dreams, Ladopoulos, Ehrenberg, and a small team of scientists, programmers, and mathematicians launched Kinetic. Their target was to create an AI-based trading system that could go live in 2011. The system would pick stocks only in the Russell 2000 index, a collection of relatively small stocks that weren't always actively tracked by Wall Street analysts. Since there was less competition in small stocks, they were low-hanging fruit.

But less competition also meant less information on the companies. That could be a good thing—the system wouldn't drown in oceans of data. But it was also a drawback. There weren't many people tweeting about Midas Inc. or blogging about Stanley Furniture, two companies in the Russell Index. Even scaled down, though, the amount of available information the machine would need to crunch in order to draw a realistic picture of the world for a specific company or sector was enormous.

It was a smaller pond, but it was still the Big Data.

ONE service Kinetic used was Selerity, a news-search system that deployed AI techniques to rapidly scan and interpret earnings releases for its clients. Selerity's algorithms would crunch through earnings numbers and hunt for red flags such as a big loss hidden in a footnote. Charged words such as *bankruptcy* or *default* or *merger* would trigger rapid alerts that Kinetic's trading machine could act on in milliseconds.

Sometimes this process struck gold. In January 2011, Selerity, using a trick deployed by too-clever-for-their-own-good active traders, plugged in an online address for Microsoft's earnings based on the address used in past releases. At 2:50 P.M. Eastern time, the release suddenly appeared—but Microsoft hadn't put the link to the page on its website yet, thinking it remained hidden. Microsoft was wrong. Selerity instantly downloaded the information. Its AI Bots went to work, sending the information to Selerity's clients, who were able to trade for instant profits.

Kinetic wasn't up and running by then, however. In fact, Kinetic was having an immense amount of trouble launching its strategies. It had initially planned to go live with its trading system in February 2011. But the system wasn't ready. AI programmers such as Ladopoulos kept tweaking the system, throwing more data at it in the hope that the machine would find the pot of gold at the end of the Big Data rainbow.

There was hot debate inside the firm about risk controls and which inputs to use in the AI system. The challenge was enormous—but the payoff seemed limitless. The Kinetic team kept working all hours. Work-free weekends became a luxury.

There was a firm commitment to the machine, a belief that the machine was *always* right. One telling conundrum concerned how to label Kinetic's strategies. It was difficult, because AI techniques by their nature could change over time. One month the strategy might cause the machine to pick cheap stocks. The next it might chase high-flyers.

"We have to be careful not to fool ourselves into thinking that the models we are creating should necessarily be treated like the name we are giving it," a Kinetic researcher wrote in an e-mail to the rest of the research team. "For example, if we assume that a model is truly a momentum model and try to manage it at the portfolio level as such, we may be hurt when the model stops behaving like a momentum model. That probably creates some challenges for how to manage our models at the portfolio level."

The machine crunched through a myriad of strategies. It would track the difference in trading volumes over the previous day, or the difference in price volatility—how much prices rose or fell—over a five-day period, or a ten-day period, or a twenty-one-day period, or a sixty-three-day period. It tracked the exchange rates between the dollar and the euro, the dollar and the Japanese yen, movements in Treasury bonds, the average range between high and low prices on the New York Stock Exchange. The signals could get dizzyingly arcane. One signal was the "maximum singular value of correlation matrix of all pairs over the previous 63 days."

It wasn't working. In its test runs, Kinetic's strategies, for reasons that baffled Ladopoulos, lost money (albeit fake money) far more often than they made money.

Kinetic was discovering that trading was far more complex than simply discovering signals in the market. Firms had to carefully measure their impact on specific stocks—whether their buy and sell orders were pushing prices around. This could be especially problematic for the small stocks Kinetic was trading, since few other firms were buying them on a regular basis. An order to buy a few thousand shares of Stanley Furniture could cause the stock to jump quickly (the reason: other AI Bots with order-detection systems on the lookout for whales). If Kinetic kept buying as the stock shot higher, the trade could easily end up a loser.

In other words, while Kinetic's signals might have been spot-on, its ability to execute the trades in the market was woeful. Ladopoulos had massively underestimated the ability of hunter-seeker Bots to detect his orders, trade ahead of him, and run up prices.

As the summer of 2011 wore on, Kinetic's dream of creating a foolproof AI trader proved increasingly elusive. The strategies weren't working. The data proved too difficult to manage. Some inside the firm started questioning whether Ladopoulos knew what he was doing. They thought he relied too much on machine learning, while not understanding fundamental quant strategies. Ladopoulos countered that it was not advisable to muddy the waters of the AI strategies with human influences.

Kinetic researchers also frequently debated a question: when to turn off the machine.

The answer: never. *The machine was perfect.*

"We are not going to stop trading," an internal Kinetic e-mail stated in the summer of 2011. "We need to be trading every day unless we encounter a severe drawdown, which is not possible given the risk management controls we currently have in place."

It was almost a religion, a faith in the power of the machine above all else. The machine knows all.

*Trust the machine.*

Another discussion concerned the difference between "rules-based" trading—the static, straightforward approach of the past that used trading models with fixed parameters—and the machine-learning approach—the dynamic, shifting, flexible method in which the computer learned on the fly how to trade.

Ideally, the latter approach gave the machine the ability to adapt to the market as conditions shifted. The machine encompassed *all possible strategies.* "We are not testing a hard-coded strategy over time, we are testing the ability of an algorithm to adapt to changing circumstances," one Kinetic e-mail stated.

But what if the machine somehow started tracking a bubble? The signals created by the bubble could cause the machine to start buying bubble stocks.

Don't worry.

*The machine knows.*

"Although consistent machine learning performance could correspond to some bubble, I think this type of problem would be less likely in a machine learning approach," the Kinetic e-mail said reassuringly. "It would be easy to unintentionally engineer a rule to correspond to some bubble. However, with our machine learning approaches we are frequently retraining based off our data, which is constantly being renewed. . . . In general, I think we have to be careful with applying evaluation techniques that are used with simple strategies to approaches that are capable of dynamically adapting strategies over time."

The problem was, the machine wasn't making money. So the Kinetic team, led by the onetime Acid Phreak, kept pushing the system, feeding it more and more data.

Unfortunately, the team's faith in the machine was misplaced. In August 2011, Ladopoulos and his research associates were fired by Kinetic's board of directors.

WHILE Kinetic had failed, the dream of creating a thinking trading machine lived on. And why not? Futurist Ray Kurzweil has predicted that as computer power and artificial intelligence expands to the point that it has the capacity to improve itself—computers effectively designing and creating more computers—the nature of humanity will become irrevocably altered, a fearsome event he calls the Singularity. Ultimately, Kurzweil says, we humans will bend the robots to our will, allowing us to transcend our biological limitations.

Less well known is that Kurzweil has tried to bend AI to a more prosaic goal: making money. In 1999, Kurzweil launched a hedge fund based on complex mathematical strategies called FatKat, short for Financial Accelerating Transactions from Kurzweil Adaptive Technologies. FatKat deployed algorithms to ceaselessly comb through the market for new trading opportunities. The algorithms competed against one another in a Darwinian death match—the algos that made the most money survived; the weak died off.

FatKat, in Kurzweil's eyes, represented the future of Wall Street. The inventor envisioned a future marketplace in which human beings had little input into day-to-day trading decisions. Rather, intelligent robots would be in control, swapping stocks with one another in a globally interconnected cybermatrix. In an ideal world, that would make the market less prone to the all-too-human frailties of fear and greed. Only the numbers, the cold hard facts, the ever-flowing streams of data, would matter.

There was little question the computer revolution that made the AI dream a reality was irrevocably altering financial markets. Information about companies, currencies, bonds, and every other tradable instrument was digitized, fast as light. So-called machine-readable news was a hot new commodity. Breaking news about corporate events such as earnings reports was coded so that superfast algorithms could pick through it and react. Media outlets such as Reuters and Dow Jones published machine-readable news that pattern-recognition computers scanned and reacted to in the blink of an eye. High-tech trading firms gobbled up the information and gunned orders into the market at a rate faster than the beating wings of a hummingbird.

· With masses of data streaming through thousands of miles of fiber-optic cables laced around the world, and more people plugged into the Web through social networks, entirely novel techniques for leveraging data for trading were cropping up. Twitter and Facebook, Google and YouTube became the new tools of intelligent trading machines looking to unearth the latest shift in retail sales or gauge the mood of entire populations.

While a few outliers such as Renaissance, Automated Trading Desk, and Getco deployed AI techniques known only to themselves, most firms over the years found AI to be severely limited as a trading weapon. It seemed to work only for very short-term horizons—a few hours, a minute, a second. Trying to project results beyond a few days seemed beyond the abilities of a machine.

But with new breakthroughs toward the end of the 2000s, AI was coming into its own on Wall Street. As data measured by the petabyte—one *quadrillion* bytes—blasted across the Internet every day (Google, for instance, processes more than two dozen petabytes *a day*), programmers with the right set of skills were attempting to marshal the latest breakthroughs in AI to find order in all the streaming chaos.

It was the Age of the Big Data, an era designed for and by AI aficionados such as Renaissance's Bob Mercer, whose mantra was "The best data is more data." Now access to data was exploding at rates impossible to fathom.

Kinetic showed that the Big Data was very hard to hack. But some other firms were having success. Case in point: a small start-up based in San Francisco called Cerebellum Capital. A pair of AI experts were behind the firm: David Andre, a scientist with a Ph.D. in AI studies from the University of California at Berkeley, and Eric "Astro" Teller, a director of Google's new projects division and grandson of hydrogen-bomb creator Edward Teller.

ANDRE and Teller had known each other since their days studying math and computer programming at Stanford University in the early 1990s. The two teamed up a decade later to run BodyMedia, a Pittsburgh-based company that marketed wearable computers that could help guide a client's diet. The system relied on AI techniques designed by Teller and Andre to crunch massive sums of data collected through the hundreds of thousands of users of the devices.

They started discussing other uses for AI technology. Repeatedly, finance came up. To an AI scientist, Wall Street was tantalizing—a vast system of digits and information scattered across multiple platforms. Andre and Teller theorized that just as their AI system crunched the waves of data spit out by their BodyMedia devices, a similar but more sophisticated system could find order in the seeming chaos of the financial markets.

It was a powerful and compelling idea, but the two had virtually no experience on Wall Street. One day after work, at a bar in the riverfront Station Square section of Pittsburgh, they discussed the pluses and minuses of making the jump into finance.

"It's a heartless, soulless world," Andre told Teller. "We wouldn't be helping the world like we are now. Right now we're changing people's lives."

Teller argued that they should view the project as an experiment, a way to conduct research on AI outside of a university setting or a large corporation.

"The success of the program will be proven by the results," Teller said. Plus, if successful, the research would fund itself.

That appealed to Andre, and they decided to make a go of it. They got an initial round of seed investing from several longtime acquaintances and started building their trading machine. With virtually no employees, they realized that they could exploit situations that much larger ventures might skip over because they weren't lucrative enough. Just as a great white shark might swim past a pool of tiny fish, large investors regularly skipped over small, slightly profitable trades. What's more, since Cerebellum would be discovering the strategies, the cost of doing business would be lower—no expensive traders demanding huge year-end bonuses.

Like the Kinetic team, they were in for a few rude shocks. Trading on Wall Street wasn't remotely as simple as it had first seemed. Large firms always had an advantage, since they were able to negotiate better terms with brokers and exchanges—lower fees, quicker data feeds, etc. It was also hard to raise money with virtually no track record. Big investors such as pension funds were a nonstarter—they would never put money into a start-up, especially one with just a few million in assets under management and pie-in-the-sky talk about mining the market for trading gold through AI.

Still, they forged ahead. In July 2009, they launched the Cerebellum Alpha Fund with just over $1 million in capital. Andre and Teller called their machine-learning program the Invention Machine. Using "genetic" algorithms, digital robots with programs that evolved through time, the Invention Machine ran simulations of various trades and tested them for positive or negative results. The algorithms, like mini-robot traders, would mutate and breed, much like Kurzweil's FatKat algos. The machine would kill off the traders that had done the worst and shift money to the traders that performed the best. This would lead to mutations in the strategies—entirely new algorithms. The Invention Machine ran this pattern hundreds of thousands of times a day, constantly combing through corners of the market while at the same time crawling through Internet sites for potential clues that could provide predictive signals. Generation after generation of computerized mini-BOT traders dying and breeding and mutating would lead, eventually, to profitable strategies. Or so they hoped.

Andre and Teller spent a great deal of time hunting for unique ways to grab information from the Internet. For instance, one way to gauge the bullishness of traders in a way that's not currently measured might be to ping the online restaurant reservation site Open Table, looking specifically at expensive haunts around Wall Street. Heavy bookings might signal that traders had grown optimistic about the market's prospects. While that signal alone would never be enough to trade on, when added to dozens or even hundreds of other signals, a clearer picture might emerge.

Deploying such techniques, Cerebellum's Invention Machine struck gold: Andre and Teller discovered an anomaly in the market that appeared to generate a nearly perfect, steady return of about 7 percent a year. By trading in and out of stocks and options—they won't disclose which ones—they could exploit a wrinkle in the market that no one else knew about. They quickly segregated the strategy into a new fund—they called it the Cerebellum ATM Fund—and launched it in December 2009. Investors piled in. By the summer of 2011, the ATM Fund had amassed $50 million in assets.

The experiment seemed to be working. AI *could* mine the market for strategies, discovering new trades and new possibilities. A fierce believer in the powers of the computer, Teller became convinced that the future of Wall Street lay in artificial intelligence. If people could trade, so could computers—but much better.

# CHAPTER TWENTY-FOUR

# ADVANCED CHESS

H aim Bodek rushed out the front door of his home, jumped in his all-black Mini Cooper, and sped to the train station in downtown Stamford, thrash metal pounding from the car's speakers. It was the morning of March 25, 2011, his last day on the payroll of Trading Machines. Bodek was scheduled to give a speech later that afternoon at Princeton University, at a conference called "Quant Trading: From the Flash Crash to Financial Reform."

As usual, he was running late. He hadn't written his speech yet, so he banged it out on his laptop on the train to Princeton.

It was hard. He wasn't sure what to say. He'd grown so cynical about the market that he'd become convinced that massive reform was required. But he didn't know if he should be the one to spearhead changing the rules of the game. He worried about his career, whether the new elite at the high-speed firms and exchanges who'd built the market's digital plumbing in the past decade would attack him and make it hard if not impossible for him to build another trading operation. He had a wife and three young children to support, and he was out of a job. The role of market-reform gadfly wasn't high on his list of priorities. But his creeping belief that the market had been hijacked kept bugging him, like a bee buzzing in his face. And it wouldn't go away.

In his talk, Bodek went halfway in calling for major changes. He spoke about the structural issues facing the options market, the evolution of algorithmic trading, and the negative impact stock market structure changes were having on the options industry. There was no mention of toxic order types or 0+ scalping strategies. He wasn't ready to take on the whole system—yet.

Matt Andresen also spoke at the conference. The year before, the onetime Island CEO had left his high-paying job at Citadel to launch his own computer-trading outfit in Chicago, Headlands Technologies. Andresen told his audience that top-shelf traders today need to know much more than quant strategies—they also need to have a deep understanding of market microstructure. They need to know the plumbing.

Another speaker was Andrei Kirilenko, who'd conducted in-depth research into the Flash Crash for the Commodity Futures Trading Commission. Kirilenko had discovered that high-speed gunners typically traded in the direction of the price movement of a stock for the first five seconds of a move, then flipped and traded in the opposite direction after ten seconds. On May 6, 2010, they followed the same strategy—but faster. The speedsters bought in the direction of price movements for the first two seconds, then reversed direction after four seconds. Later, a speaker on a career panel discussing jobs in quant trading said more universities needed to focus on high-frequency trading as a career.

Bodek couldn't believe it. Short-term flipping had nothing to do with real trading, he thought. The ability to take risk and make money on it, *that's* what mattered. The market had boiled down to a spy war of secret codes that exploited fraction-of-a-second glitches in the market's plumbing. As Thomas Peterffy had said, it was a complete mess.

Just a week before, former Goldman programmer Sergey Aleynikov had been sentenced in a New York courtroom to ninety-seven months in prison for stealing Goldman's trading code. (In February

2012, a federal appeals court overturned Aleynikov's conviction.) Earlier in the month, another algo trader, Samarth Agrawal, was sentenced to three years in prison for stealing high-frequency code from the French bank Société Générale.

Was this the future for the U.S. stock market, whose purpose was to give companies the ability to raise money and investors the chance to tap into the growth of the global economy?

The industry wouldn't have a chance, Bodek thought, if someone didn't stick his neck out and start taking on the madness.

Riding the train home that night, he decided it might as well be him.

MONTHS later, Bodek sat typing in a cramped room. It was just past 7 P.M. in the summer of 2011. He was testing a new trading platform on the SGX Singapore Exchange, which had just opened. And he liked what he was seeing.

Trading Machines, Bodek's firm, had been wound down months before. But Bodek wasn't going down without a fight. Operating from his home in Stamford, Connecticut, working out of a small office lined with computers, charts, and books, he was building new systems based on the hard lessons he'd learned in the brutal markets of 2009 and 2010.

Screeching Viking metal pounded from speakers as Bodek combed over the data showing the results of his latest tests.

He wasn't working alone. While most of Trading Machines' staff had left for new jobs, a few were sticking it out for the new strategy Bodek was building. There was Mark Shaw, a quant who'd worked alongside Bodek since his days at Hull Trading in Chicago in the 1990s, as well as Bryan Wiener, a trader who'd earned his chops on the floor of the Chicago Merc trading S&P options contracts.

Bodek felt like he was working against a stacked deck. Something had happened inside the plumbing of the stock market that had destroyed the strategies he'd learned during his years at Hull, Goldman

Sachs, and UBS. High-frequency traders had become so powerful, so ubiquitous, that it became virtually impossible to trade stocks without getting clipped time and time again.

Bodek knew his complaints sounded like excuses for failure. Critics would say he couldn't take the heat. But he was convinced there was more to it. Exchanges and high-frequency firms had been working hand in glove to design a system that gave an advantage to the speedsters. The speed traders had been working closely with the electronic pools for more than a decade, from Island to BRUT to Archipelago. They'd pushed for more speed, for more information, for new exotic order types. And the pools complied willingly.

It all added up.

In Bodek's eyes, there was nothing implicitly wrong with what had happened—at least at first. The relationship between high-speed firms and exchanges was in ways beneficial for all investors, he thought. The Bots pushed for better execution. That made the markets better for everyone.

But a problem developed. High-frequency trading became so competitive that on a *truly* level playing field *no one* could make money operating at high volumes. Starting in 2008, there had been a frantic rush into the high-frequency gold mine at a time when nearly every other investment strategy on Wall Street was imploding. That competition was making it very hard for the firms to make a profit without using methods that Bodek viewed as seedy at best.

It all came down to maker-taker, the trading incentive conceived more than a decade earlier by Josh Levine.

According to an academic study by a finance professor at the University of Illinois, by the late 2000s profits on rapid trading of Nasdaq stocks had turned *negative*, when accounting only for the spread between buy and sell prices. That meant the only way certain high-frequency firms—such as the scalper variety that profited on the difference between bids and offers—could make money was through maker-taker rebates, the fees they collected when other firms had to trade with them.

The trouble for the exchanges: *Everyone* wanted to pocket the rebates. Every reasonably sophisticated firm, including Trading Machines, was putting orders into the market designed to earn the rebate. That posed a conundrum for the exchanges, Bodek theorized, because *everyone couldn't get the rebate.*

Everyone couldn't win, because for every winner there had to be a loser. It was a zero-sum game—simple math.

And so, Bodek reasoned, a complex system was designed to *pick* winners and losers. It was done through speed and exotic order types. If you didn't know which orders to use, and when to use them, you lost nearly every time. Which is exactly what happened to Trading Machines. Worse, if you weren't getting the rebate, you were *paying the fee.* For a high-volume operator, the difference could mean a loss of tens of thousands of dollars a day.

To Bodek, it was fundamentally unfair—it was rigged. There were too many conflicts of interest, too many shared benefits between exchanges and the traders they catered to. Only the biggest, most sophisticated, connected firms in the world could win this race.

*Is that fair? Is that a level playing field?*

One apparent consequence of this hypercompetitive market was its fragility. Because high-speed traders were now competing for wafer-thin profits, they'd grown incredibly pain-averse. The slightest loss was unacceptable. Better to cut and run and trade another day. The result, of course, was the Flash Crash. It was an algorithmic tragedy of the commons, in which all players, acting in their self-interest, had spawned a systemically dangerous market that could threaten the global economy.

Bodek knew he'd made mistakes. He'd wasted months trying to hunt for a bug in the code of the Machine, when the problem was actually abusive order types.

Then he'd started using the order types himself to protect his firm from the abuses. But it felt dirty. He'd become one of the bad guys. One of the tipped-off insiders. Kill or be killed. He didn't like it, but it had become a matter of survival.

Bodek knew he wasn't alone. Thomas Peterffy, one of his idols, had been complaining loudly about high-frequency trading. He'd read the speech Peterffy had given at the World Federation of Exchanges. He also believed that Peterffy wasn't aware of how the toxic order types worked. If the founding father of electronic trading was in the dark, what chance did ordinary investors have?

It was not how the market should work. Investors should be rewarded for their intelligence, for being able to make accurate predictions and take risk—not for knowing the location of secret holes inside the plumbing (or, worse, *creating* the holes).

That was Bodek's biggest complaint: *The Plumbers had won.* And the SEC seemed content to help them along. A telling example emerged in June 2011, when the SEC approved a program created by BATS that would give certain traders with exclusive rights better prices than the general public. Market makers using BATS would be allowed to send two prices for an options contract to the market. One price—the worst price—would be displayed to the market. The better price would be dark. Only brokers that operated through the select market makers could get the better price. Only insiders could tap it. Indeed, under heavy criticism, BATS later backed down from the program. But it had tipped its hand, showing that it was more than ready to give certain clients a better deal than others.

Bodek became determined to reveal what he believed was a corrupt insiders' game that came at the expense of everyday investors. Was it outright collusion? He didn't have enough hard information to know for certain. Perhaps the exchanges that had rolled out the toxic order types were ignorant of the devastating side effects they could have. Perhaps, giving them every last benefit of the doubt, they believed they were doing investors a favor by rolling out orders that pulled in more high-frequency flow. The more Bot flow, perhaps they thought, the more liquidity. Tighter spreads, etc.

In his heart, Bodek didn't believe any of that. He believed the exchanges were locked in cutthroat competition, not only with one another but with the dark pools and the internalizers like Citadel and Knight. It was a dynamic that went all the way back to the late 1990s when Island, Archipelago, Instinet, and other electronic networks were engaged in a kill-or-be-killed Darwinian struggle. That struggle led to massive innovation and changes and, to be sure, benefits for nearly all investors.

But something else had changed along the way. The competition had become toxic, Bodek thought. The exchanges' backs were against the wall, and they'd made a deal with the devil at the expense of regular investors.

And would those investors care anyway? The toxic orders and all the other side effects of the system shaved only pennies off of every trade, after all. Who cares about pennies?

That, of course, was what they were counting on—*investors wouldn't care*. And if investors didn't care, lawmakers in Washington wouldn't care, and the regulators wouldn't care, either.

Bodek did care, however. The rigged market, he believed, had helped destroy Trading Machines and ruined all the dreams he'd put into it. But there was no way for him to know, with 100 percent certainty, the truth—without some serious help.

To that end, in the summer of 2011, he decided to explain it all to federal regulators. He hired a major law firm to help him use his understanding of toxic order types he'd gained from his exchange contacts while at Trading Machines, combined with the details of his understanding of high-frequency strategies he'd learned from the 0+ Scalping Strategy document, to lay out a road map. The road map detailed his argument that high-speed traders and exchanges had created an unfair market that was hurting nearly all investors.

■  ■  ■ .

BODEK wasn't the only one raising red flags about toxic orders that catered to a specific kind of trader. Justin Kane, a trader for Seattle money manager Rainier Investment, had been growing increasingly frustrated as he watched order after order from his firm get whacked. He decided to speak his mind at a market structure conference at the Downtown Marriott in New York City on December 6, 2011. He was on a panel alongside Direct Edge executive Bryan Harkins and Virtu's Chris Concannon, the former Island lawyer.

Kane for years had worked as a market maker in Jersey City, and he knew all the tricks the insiders played. Electronic traders, he told the audience, were using many of the same tricks the human market makers had used years ago. Worse, he said, exchanges were helping them get away with it.

Visibly agitated, Kane launched into an all-out attack against the high-speed market. His specific target: order types.

"Order types are being created to attract predatory traders," he said.

The market, Kane complained, had been twisted to cater to high-frequency traders, since it's in the economic interest of the exchanges to provide the traders an environment that is most conducive to making a profit. If the traders are making money on an exchange, they'll keep coming back.

But how can an exchange provide such *guaranteed economics*?

"An efficient market is one that brings together the buyer and the seller," Kane said, a statement Josh Levine would surely have condoned. "But this marketplace is set up to bring in the most intermediaries between the buyer and seller as possible."

They were doing this in part through order types—orders that Kane said were "harmful to our clients." He recounted a story in which he complained to one exchange that provided the toxic orders.

"We were told there was a stale feed," he said. But Kane wasn't buying it. "You can see the games that are going on."

Direct Edge's Harkins had played it cool during most of Kane's diatribe. But he finally returned fire.

"Anyone can look up our rule book and see how the orders work," he said. "Nobody is hiding anything."

Then he looked at Kane.

"Sounds like there may have been a bug in there," he said, implying that the problem lay in Kane's own trading system. It was the same response Bodek had heard when Trading Machines had run into problems more than two years earlier. Kane smirked. After the panel, an official with the SEC told Kane he'd like to talk.

Was the SEC listening? It was hard to tell. But there were signs that the SEC was sniffing around. In late February 2012, BATS reported in a regulatory filing related to its planned initial public offering that the SEC's enforcement division had requested information related to "the use of order types, and our communications with certain market participants."

Weeks later, on March 23, *The Wall Street Journal* reported in a page-one story that the SEC was "examining whether some sophisticated, rapid-fire trading firms have used their close links to computerized stock exchanges to gain an unfair advantage over other investors.

"Investigators are examining whether firms collude to limit competition or manipulate markets," the *Journal* said.

One of the exchanges in focus: BATS. Somewhat ironically, on the very same day the *Journal* article came out, BATS attempted to go public on its own exchange. It would have been the first company to list on the exchange — but the computer-trading gods weren't smiling on BATS that day. A computer glitch caused the listing to crash in seconds. Humiliated by the debacle, BATS decided to pull its listing.

In a follow-up article in early April, the *Journal* reported that Direct Edge was also coming under scrutiny. Specifically in focus:

"the use of routing and trading instructions, known as order types," the paper said. The article noted that one order type at Direct Edge, called Hide Not Slide, was "being scrutinized by the SEC."

BODEK, meanwhile, wasn't ready to give up on his dream of creating a world-beating trading machine. Working day and night from his home in Stamford, he started building a new system that involved predicting where stocks would go not in the next few seconds but rather in the next ten minutes—similar to the kind of strategy that had been perfected by the most successful hedge fund in the world, Renaissance Technologies.

Despite his downfall, Bodek remained defiant. To win the battle he saw coming, he was arming himself with a secret weapon: artificial intelligence. Specifically, machine learning, the same branch of AI used by Renaissance, Cerebellum, and others. While Bodek had for years used various forms of AI in trading, he'd never used machine learning, a much more dynamic variety of AI than what he'd used before. He'd attempted to apply it years ago in his first project at Hull. It had been a failure and he'd avoided it ever since. Now he was returning to his roots.

Bodek was convinced he had an edge—his intimate knowledge of the market's plumbing learned over more than a decade of trading in the trenches. His understanding of the inner plumbing of the market and the strategies he had helped design and implement through the years allowed him to peer into the depths of the market and see how it was shifting on a moment-by-moment basis. Indeed, as he well knew, in many ways he'd become a Plumber himself because he'd been forced to delve into the intricacies of the stock market's microstructure at Trading Machines. Using that edge, he believed he could design AI pattern-recognition systems aimed like snipers at the Bots.

Bodek was creating a man-machine integration that could in fact be the future of trading—a true *trading machine*. He'd be at the center of a vast digital web reaching into all of the pools, pulling the strings of his AI machines like a puppet master. Unlike the autopilot systems used by Renaissance or high-frequency giants such as Getco, Bodek would be part of the machine himself—and he'd be in control of it, keeping it in check, making sure it didn't run off the rails.

Whether or not Bodek would succeed, there was reason to believe the combination of human brains and boundless computer power could surpass the capabilities of the purely machine-driven systems. In 2005, an online chess-playing site called Playchess.com hosted a chess tournament in which human players using computers as an aid went head-to-head with chess supercomputers similar to the Deep Blue machine that in 1997 defeated world chess champion Garry Kasparov. By a wide margin, human players using laptop computers defeated the supercomputers. Kasparov himself dubbed the human-computer tag-team approach Advanced Chess.

The same human-computer partnership might triumph in the arena of the stock market. Bodek was determined to find out—and he soon had his chance.

In late 2011, Bodek started working with Chicago trading legend Blair Hull, founder of Hull Trading and Bodek's first employer on Wall Street. By the spring of 2012, Bodek started trading using his new system with money advanced by Hull himself.

He was returning to his roots alongside his mentor. He felt as if he'd come full circle.

While Bodek was quietly building his man-machine trading weapon, another small group of young mathematicians and programmers, working out of a bunker-like office in midtown Manhattan, was cobbling together a machine that could prove to be the next step in the evolution of computer trading: a digital Warren Buffett.

# CHAPTER TWENTY-FIVE

# STAR

Star was dying.

That's what Alex Fleiss thought. Every morning that Fleiss walked past the Neighborhood Playhouse School of the Theatre on East 54th Street and stepped into Rebellion Research's spartan midtown Manhattan office in the grim dawn winter hours of early 2009, he immediately checked to see what Star had done—what horrible thing Star had done.

*It was suicide.*

Fleiss, a twenty-six-year-old hedge fund whiz kid, would sit at his desk in the dark, windowless basement of Rebellion's office, stare in disbelief at his screen, and start to weep, face buried in his hands.

Star was dying. He knew it.

Star was an artificial intelligence program designed by Fleiss's longtime friend and partner at Rebellion, Spencer Greenberg, also twenty-six. Housed in a single Dell computer tower a few feet from Greenberg's desk, Star did one thing, and only one thing: pick stocks for Rebellion, the small hedge fund they'd founded in 2005.

Star picked stocks by scanning a dizzying array of statistics, from the price of commodities such as oil and corn to the performance of international currencies to the latest ticks of thousands of stocks around the world. More important, Star had *learned* its stock-picking strategies *on its own*. And as time went on, Star *kept learning*.

Star was akin to a digital Warren Buffett, a buy-and-hold computer program able to comb through nearly all tradable stocks in the world and determine which were the best and which the worst. It represented the next evolution in computer trading, pushing the process yet another step toward full automation. While Haim Bodek was experimenting with a man-machine "advanced chess" trading model, Rebellion was leaving the entire process up to the machine itself. It all came down to probabilities. Star would scan the market for patterns and look for correlations. If it noticed, for instance, that more than 50 percent of the time a rise in the euro coincided with a rise in oil-and-gas companies, it might start to buy oil-and-gas companies. Star continually recalibrated such signals even as it hunted for new ones.

In February 2009, however, the signals seemed to have gone haywire. Star was mad, just like HAL, the space-crazed AI in Arthur C. Clarke's *2001: A Space Odyssey*—or so thought Fleiss. The United States was trapped in an economic maelstrom, a calamitous banking crisis that threatened to collapse the world's financial system. Stocks were plummeting. It was the most deadly market since the Great Depression.

Star, however, didn't concur with the naysayers. Star was buying—hard. Financial stocks. Insurance stocks. Steel companies. The kinds of companies that would do well only if the economy steadied itself and rebounded.

At the same time, Star was dumping the defensive positions it had smartly started snapping up in 2007, when the economy had begun to fall off a cliff: the gold stocks, the cemetery companies, the discount stores and alcohol stocks, the stocks designed to hold up no matter what happened to the economy. Those stocks had helped Rebellion beat the market by a wide margin in 2007 and 2008.

But now that things were looking worse than ever, now that things were looking fucking catastrophic, Star was shifting gears. Star was getting bullish.

Fleiss couldn't believe it.

*Star's insane. Star's committing suicide—and blowing up all of our money in the process.*

EVER since he was a child, Fleiss had been watching the stock market alongside his mother, a hedge fund manager. During college, he'd worked with Laura Sloate, who, even though she'd been blind since the age of six, managed half-a-billion for a New York hedge fund. Fleiss had a strong background in stock fundamentals and economic forecasting. In another life, he would have made an ideal portfolio manager for a fund company like Fidelity or Vanguard.

His partner, Greenberg, was in many ways his polar opposite. A soft-spoken, slight figure with dark eyes and a perpetual three-day beard, Greenberg was a pure mathematician. He lived in a world of cold, hard numbers. He was the kind of person who brought a notebook with him on a date in case he got bored and wanted to work on a few equations. And few things could capture this pure crystalline world of math more perfectly than computers, Greenberg thought. Computers, it was clear to him, were improving exponentially, while humans were standing still. The math was simple: Computers are getting better; humans are not. Greenberg's money was on the computers, literally.

That's why Greenberg trusted Star, his own creation. Greenberg *had faith*. Those silly, emotional humans panicking and selling all of their stocks in early 2009 were flawed, prey to their irrational fears.

In Greenberg's eyes, Fleiss was a study in all of those flawed human emotions. Like a lab technician, Greenberg clinically enjoyed watching Fleiss for signs reflecting an illogical human response to day-to-day swings in the market.

Fleiss, for his part, didn't feel like he was being irrational. By his lights, Star was the crazy one. The math was wrong. The computer was nuts. The economy was plunging headlong into an all-out collapse.

Star, schooled on statistics that went back only to the late 1990s, was flying blind. It was Armageddon. This was the 1930s, Fleiss thought. Great depressions, grapes of wrath.

But Star seemed to think—*think!*—that everything was fine. For instance: On January 21, 2009, Star bought 3,903 shares of Kelly Services, a staffing company that had fallen sharply in the past year. Then, on February 2, it bought 1,103 *more* shares of Kelly.

Fleiss was furious. *Staffing company?* The economy was imploding—no one was going to be staffed.

*What the fuck!*

Fleiss told Greenberg it was a stupid move. Then, a few days later, Kelly plunged. So Star *bought more.*

"You do not buy a stock that just fell twenty percent!" Fleiss screamed at Greenberg. "That's what idiots do!"

"Don't worry about it," Greenberg said in his typical deadpan style. Investors were panicking, he explained to his friend—letting their emotions get in the way. It's the perfect time to buy. Star knew it. That's why he'd created Star: It was a perfectly rational, utterly unemotional investing machine.

Fleiss laughed derisively.

"Don't worry?" he said, his voice a hoarse screech as he flung out his arms. "Don't you realize that Star is saying the whole economy is going to rebound? Spencer, I'm *very worried.*"

"This is all crazy, Alex," Greenberg said calmly. "This will pass."

DESPITE Greenberg's confidence in Star, it was clear that Rebellion was in trouble. And money was tight.

Fleiss and Rebellion's two other founders, Jeremy Newton, a mathematician who'd started studying AI programming in the fifth grade, and Jonathan Sturges, a composer with a head for numbers, started eating frozen macaroni and cheese for lunch at a cost of $2.50 a meal. Greenberg, a vegan, lived on cheap salads and Chinese noodles. They stopped taking the subway to work and walked to the office through blizzards and pouring rain. While they all came from well-off families, none wanted to tap them for a handout. They wanted to make it on their own.

Day by day, it was looking as if they wouldn't. Because Star was dying.

As if things couldn't get any worse, late one night Newton was working alone in the office at his computer. He flinched as he heard a loud crashing noise in the basement downstairs, where Fleiss and Sturges worked. Furniture turning over. Computers smashing. Glass breaking. Someone—or something—banging on the wall, as if with a hammer.

He grabbed a baseball bat near his desk and started to inch down the stairs, terrified. It could be anything. Armed looters, a trapped giant toxic rat.

As he kneeled to peer into the room, Newton saw a large round hole in the wall beside Sturges's desk. A two-inch-thick cable was snaking through it—and kept coming. It had already destroyed Sturges's monitor and was crashing into furniture all about the room.

The phone company, it turned out, had made an error in how it fed a cable beneath the street. The cable had taken a wrong turn directly into Rebellion's office.

It seemed as if even the very wiring of the city was against them. The foursome started talking about moving in together to save on rent, or moving their headquarters to a cut-rate office in Connecticut. Fleiss began thinking about a new career—politics or teaching.

The market kept tanking, crashing hard into March. Star kept buying—and Star was dying.

Or was it?

SPENCER Greenberg was no stranger to the investing world. His father, Glenn Greenberg, ran Chieftain Capital Management, a New York fund manager that racked up annual returns of about 20 percent from 1984 to 2004, compared with 13 percent for the S&P 500.

Winning was also a family tradition. Greenberg's grandfather was Hank Greenberg, otherwise known as Hammerin' Hank, one of the greatest sluggers in the history of baseball. A first baseman for the Detroit Tigers in the 1930s and '40s, and a five-time all-star, Greenberg hit fifty-eight home runs in 1938, nearly beating Babe Ruth's sixty-one-homer record. Widely considered the greatest Jewish athlete in American history, Greenberg was also the first professional baseball player to embrace Jackie Robinson.

Growing up in New York City and attending the prestigious Trinity School on the Upper West Side, the younger Greenberg was slight and wispy, and he'd never been seriously drawn to competitive sports — or to Wall Street. Greenberg's early love had been computers. Rather than go out on Friday nights to parties and clubs with the hip, wealthy in-crowd at Trinity, Greenberg would spend his time writing video-game programs and dismantling laptops. Given to wearing a black trench coat and the same clothes for several days in a row, he was something of an outcast, reclusive and nerdy even among the high academic standards of Trinity. His best friend at school was Fleiss, whose nerdy ambitions could never match Greenberg's.

After graduating from high school, Greenberg attended Columbia University, where he studied engineering. Fleiss moved on to Amherst College, a small, elite institution in the rural Pioneer Valley region of Massachusetts. At Amherst, Fleiss learned about the overwhelming success of Renaissance Technologies, the Long Island hedge fund that had started using Island in the late 1990s. While Fleiss was good at math, his skills didn't come close to the abilities of a Jim Simons or a Peter Brown.

But he did know one person he thought could go toe-to-toe with them: Spencer Greenberg. Fleiss began an aggressive campaign to convince Greenberg to help him start a quantitative hedge fund. At first, Greenberg was skeptical that higher-order math could be used on the market. But as he learned more about Renaissance, he began to think there might be more to what Fleiss was saying. While at

Columbia, Greenberg started to consider various mathematical strategies that he could deploy in the market. The pair eventually teamed up with Newton and Sturges.

In 2005, using funds from Fleiss's stock market bets in college, which were based on an algorithm he'd designed, they set up shop in a six-hundred-square-foot office on 42nd Street in midtown Manhattan. Greenberg, just twenty-two, had been working on a data-mining project for a counterterrorism outfit that used AI to comb through public records and search for suspicious patterns indicating potential terrorist activity. After he had talked over his work with Newton, the two decided to see if similar techniques could be applied to the stock market.

One day in the summer of 2006, Fleiss was having lunch outdoors with his girlfriend at a restaurant on the Upper East Side. As they chatted in the sun after their meal, an elderly man dressed in a modest suit walked out of the restaurant and lit up a cigarette. Fleiss's girlfriend bummed a smoke off him, and they began to chat.

"So what do you do?" he asked Fleiss.

"I'm actually building a hedge fund that uses quantitative strategies to pick stocks," he said.

"Oh really?" The man laughed. "Where did you go to school?"

"Amherst."

"Good school. You know, I'm also in the quant biz."

Fleiss asked where he worked, but the man wouldn't answer. But Fleiss kept pushing. Finally, the man said he ran a fund called Renaissance Technologies.

Fleiss nearly fell out of his chair. He wanted to talk more, but a gleaming Bentley had just pulled to the curb and Jim Simons quickly disappeared into it.

As Rebellion built up its system, Fleiss began marketing the fund, mailing off descriptions of its strategy to deep-pocketed investors such as Donald Trump. Most of the time, he received form-letter rejections with stamped signatures. Others granted an interview. At a meeting with Highbridge Capital Management, a giant quant fund owned by J.P. Morgan, he and Greenberg were told they had zero chance of success. Far better to close up shop and join an established fund — like Highbridge.

"The only reason I took this meeting was to see if there's any talent worth poaching," the Highbridge manager told them.

In November 2006, Fleiss, Greenberg, and Sturges paid a visit to the office of a successful hedge fund manager in midtown Manhattan. They were escorted to the manager's cavernous office by a gorgeous secretary in a skintight skirt. Sitting down, they were handed large glasses full to the brim with water. Far away at the other end of the room, the fund manager sat in silence staring at nearly a dozen computer screens packed with flowing charts and data. One corner of the room was filled with roughly fifty umbrellas. The Rebellion team sat in silence, marketing briefs in one hand, full glasses of water in the other, and not a table to be seen.

Eventually, the manager looked up, blinking.

"Show me the numbers," he said in a gruff, booming voice. Greenberg stood, water sloshing out of his glass, made the long journey across the room, and handed over his marketing materials. They contained a description of several strategies, including one based on artificial intelligence, and their estimates for how well they'd perform. Since Rebellion hadn't started investing in the market, all of the data was based on screens they'd run on computers.

After scanning the data for a minute, the manager slammed a fist on his desk.

"This is horseshit!" he pronounced. "You can't do this!"

By early 2007, despite the naysayers, Star went live with $2 million in cash. The program would monitor dozens of factors that could impact a stock's performance, such as earnings growth, interest rates, or the economic health of its home country. The system would measure all of these factors, look for changes, and adjust its holdings on the fly. It used no leverage and didn't sell stocks short.

Right off the bat, Star plowed money into the residential real estate sector, which at the time was still in the midst of a record boom. Then, in April, it got spooked. The program dumped every single real estate holding, as well as its financial stocks. It also abandoned several Latin American stocks. Star was becoming extremely risk-averse.

In August, Rebellion moved uptown to a small office on 53rd Street. While its quarters remained small, with two floors and a small kitchen, it was a big improvement over the boxlike office on 42nd Street.

But investors remained scarce, and the fund pulled in only a few million in 2007. Still, its deft moves helped Star sidestep the shellacking the market took in late 2007, and it ended the year ahead by 17 percent, far better than the 5 percent gain clocked by the S&P 500.

Still intent on absorbing everything possible about how to apply machine learning to the stock market, Greenberg enrolled in New York University's elite mathematical-finance program. In early 2008, he was invited to a charity event at Jim Simons's palatial Upper East Side apartment overlooking Central Park. Simons seemed unimpressed that Greenberg had launched a hedge fund that deployed AI techniques.

"Just make sure you finish your Ph.D.," Simons told him. "You can start a hedge fund anytime."

After a brief run, the market started to turn ugly again in March 2008 with the collapse of the New York investment bank Bear Stearns. Star became more defensive, loading up on gold stocks such as Harmony Gold Mining and utility stocks such as GDF Suez, a French electricity generator. It had a large holding in crude oil stocks early in the year, but by June it had completely exited the position, just in time to miss a huge crash in oil prices that laid waste to energy stocks.

Instead, Star stocked up on health-care stocks such as Abbott Laboratories and dollar-store stocks such as Family Dollar. Heading into September, the entire portfolio was geared toward an economic disaster, holding only companies that were likely to survive in a depression. It was nothing less than an apocalypse portfolio. Then Lehman Brothers went bankrupt on September 15, and American International Group imploded, threatening to set off a chain reaction that would nearly crack the global financial system. Stock markets tanked. Hundreds of hedge funds shut down.

But not Rebellion. While its apocalypse portfolio lost ground—nearly every single stock in the world got clobbered in the weeks and months following the Lehman-AIG debacle—it still outperformed the broader market considerably. By the end of 2008, Rebellion was down 26 percent, beating the S&P 500's 39 percent plunge. (Since Rebellion didn't short stocks, it could protect itself against a downturn only by purchasing defensive stocks, and it didn't hold cash.)

In early 2009, the stock market continued to collapse. Many on Wall Street thought the financial system truly was on the verge of Armageddon—including Alex Fleiss. That's when Star started getting bullish. Star was scooping up banks and insurers—stocks that had been eviscerated by the collapse—in a way that showed no sign of stopping.

Fleiss panicked. He became convinced the AI had gone completely off the rails. Since the kind of economic and financial collapse of the late 2000s hadn't been seen in more than a generation, it was outside the data set that made up Star's worldview.

Every morning, Fleiss would come into the office and see the new bank Star wanted to buy, and he'd start to weep. He wept every day for weeks. He'd plowed millions of his own cash into Rebellion, convinced that Greenberg was the smartest person he'd ever met, a once-in-a-lifetime genius. And it was all going to melt down. Star was toast—and so was Rebellion.

But in March 2009, the market found its feet. And then it

rebounded—and few stocks rebounded more than the banks and insurance companies Star had gorged on. By the end of the year, Star had gained a whopping 41 percent, beating once again the S&P 500, up 23 percent in 2009.

In 2010, Star entered the year with a big bet on international stocks, which made up nearly 40 percent of its holdings. But as a credit crisis worsened, leading to a near collapse of Greece's economy, Star dumped its overseas positions rapid-fire and had whittled them down to less than 10 percent before the crisis had a major impact on the market.

All of its smart moves were paying off. Star got an impressive nod of approval in April 2010 when Jean-Marie Eveillard, a legendary French value investor, put a chunk of his own money into Rebellion. While Eveillard had little patience for most plain-vanilla quant funds, he'd been impressed by Star's performance. He loved its stock picks— some of which matched his own—as well as the fact that Rebellion used no leverage.

Star topped the S&P again in 2010, gaining 21 percent compared with the index's 13 percent gain. Well into 2011, Star had never once, in more than four years, fallen behind the S&P 500 in any rolling 365-day period. By then, Rebellion was getting noticed, and Greenberg was getting invitations to speak on TV and at financial industry events.

FROM behind a podium, Spencer Greenberg gazed out at the buzzing audience of several hundred well-heeled traders and wealthy investors and drew a deep breath. It was shortly after 2 P.M., February 16, 2011. Greenberg, who'd shaved off the ragged three-day beard he normally sported, nervously ruffled the eleven typewritten pages of his speech and scanned its opening lines.

*I'd like to tell you today a little bit about . . .*

His dead-serious face was innocent of all emotion. He looked up again at the audience as attendees took their seats around dozens of

round tables draped in white tablecloths, then glanced back at his
speech.

*. . . about the field of machine learning.*

Greenberg was about to address a roomful of elite Wall Street
moneymakers who, with the stroke of a pen, could help make his
dreams come true—dreams of hundreds of millions of dollars. Perhaps, if Star kept working, *billions*.

He'd never faced such an audience before. Greenberg was more
used to speaking before classrooms packed with computer programmers and mathematicians, fellow travelers out on the bleeding edge of
a new science that involved training machines to think and learn like
humans.

But Wall Street was clearly catching the AI bug. The computer
revolution, led by visionaries such as Josh Levine, had changed the
structure of the market in many ways, altering the very nature of how
stocks changed hands. Yet there had always been one domain that
had remained sacrosanct: the fund manager's brain. No one had ever
devised a strategy that could imitate how a long-term investor would
think and act, buying and selling stocks like Peter Lynch or Warren
Buffett—until Star came along.

Despite Star's success, Rebellion was struggling to gain investors.
It had just $13 million in capital, chump change in the hedge fund
business, where anyone with less than a billion was considered a start-
up. Artificial intelligence was widely considered too exotic, too unpredictable, too *weird*. Greenberg hoped to change that view—and he
had the results to back up his pitch. That's why he was there, preparing
to address a packed ballroom on the seventh floor of the New York
Marriott Marquis in Times Square.

The occasion was a gathering of mathematically inclined Wall
Street pros—and investors thinking about giving them money—
called "Battle of the Quants." Quants had been a rising force on Wall
Street for decades, and in the 2000s they'd come to dominate finance

through the use of sophisticated trading strategies and exotic derivatives. They'd also played a leading role in a catastrophic financial collapse that pushed the global economy to the brink. Many had lost huge sums, and investors had lost faith in their abilities.

But the quants were back and ready to fight, armed with new strategies, more powerful computers—and AI. There were few more knowledgeable about using AI to invest than Greenberg, which explains why he'd been picked to give the keynote speech to the audience that day. After a brief introduction, he took the podium.

"I'd like to tell you today a little bit about the field of machine learning," Greenberg said into the microphone as he began. "In particular, I'd like to discuss when this set of techniques is appropriate to use, and also touch on a few of the big ideas from the field."

Machine learning, he explained, is everywhere around us—it's used by Netflix to predict what kinds of movies we like based on past choices, by Apple's photography software to zero in on human faces, by e-mail firewalls to block spam.

And it is also a powerful method for investing, because a computer armed with a robust machine-learning algorithm can detect relationships in the stock market that people could never find. For instance, it can make the unlikely leap that when interest rates are falling, gold prices are on the rise, and utility stocks are gaining ground, European airplane makers are a good buy.

"Such an approach won't get a computer to learn to speak to the CEO, but it can get it to uncover fundamental principles of investing," Greenberg explained, speaking at a rapid clip. "The goal is to have our software learn, on its own, to become a *long-term-oriented* stock investor. We do not assume that we already know how to invest, and are not using machine learning just to optimize a few parameters in our model. Rather, we are leaving it up to our learning algorithm *to learn to invest.*"

This was an extraordinary statement.

And if this faith in the magic of AI trading algorithms caught on, it did not seem impossible to imagine that the future of the market would belong to programs such as Star. The plumbing of the market had been automated, turned into giant interlaced electric pools interacting at light speed through data centers around the globe. AI Bots manned the helm of a large part of the daily stock market action and were rapidly moving into commodities, currencies, bonds, and derivatives pools.

The machinery was in place. With intelligent computers such as Star coming on line and plugging into the system in the coming years, it seemed only a matter of time before the last human would simply turn out the lights and walk away.

It was a future, while distant, that Greenberg could easily envision. He began to wrap up his speech with a warning: AI could be a dangerous weapon in the hands of the ignorant.

"A terrifying example of this comes from a poorly planned military project that a computer scientist once told me about," he said. According to the scientist, Greenberg said, a group of military technicians were attempting to rig a learning algorithm to distinguish between photos of a forest without tanks and a forest full of tanks. After training the system, they found that it achieved remarkably good accuracy.

But when the researchers attempted to duplicate the experiment, it failed. They then realized, late in the game, that in the original simulation they had taken the photo of the forest without tanks on a cloudy day, while the photo of the forest with tanks had been taken on a sunny day. The AI was simply accomplishing the mundane task of noticing the difference between a sunny forest and a cloudy forest— it had nothing to do with tanks at all. The horrific results of such a flawed system being activated in the field could only be imagined.

Greenberg looked into the quiet audience, his face a cipher.

"Machine learning can be disastrous," he said, "in the hands of people who don't know what they are doing."

# ACHNOWLEDGMENTS

I thank first and foremost my wife, Eleanor, who knows more than anyone in the world the labor—the late nights, the weekends, the holidays (or lack of)—that went into writing *Dark Pools*. She helped me every step of the way. I also thank my agent, Shawn Coyne, who gave me encouragement throughout and was key in telling the story of Haim Bodek. I owe a great deal of gratitude to Bodek himself, who, in telling his own story to me, taught me about the electronic markets' insane complexities and hidden risks.

My Crown editors Rick Horgan and Julian Pavia offered excellent and detailed advice on nearly every single page of the book. Greg Klochkoff provided quick and helpful fact-checking work. RT Leuchtkafer—whoever he is!—provided me with invaluable data, research, and insights. The team at Rebellion Research was extraordinarily accommodating and I wish them well.

I first learned about the importance of Island from Jamie Selway, who gave me an enormous amount of his time and his thoughts. While Selway might not agree with the arguments voiced in this book, he is without question one of the most astute observers of the market today. Peter Stern, Chris Concannon, Matt Andresen, Mike Lazarev, and countless others helped me tell the incredible story of Datek and Island. And of course there's Josh Levine himself. I never met Levine, and I never spoke with him, but we exchanged dozens of e-mails over the past few years. He, more than anyone, gave me the vital information and perspective I needed to tell Island's story, which is also his story.

iii: **Dark Pools** The title of this book doesn't entirely refer to what is technically known in the financial industry as a "dark pool." Narrowly defined, *dark pool* refers to a trading venue that masks buy and sell orders from the public market. Rather, I argue in this book that the *entire United States stock market* has become one vast dark pool. Orders are hidden in every part of the market. And the complex algorithm AI-based trading systems that control the ebb and flow of the market are cloaked in secrecy. Investors—and our esteemed regulators—are entirely in the dark because *the market is dark*.

PROLOGUE: LIGHT POOL

1: **Loudspeakers boomed** I attended the 2011 Credit Suisse conference as a speaker.

9: **In other words, a vicious self-reinforcing feedback loop.** This is one of the most important points of *Dark Pools*. I expect that it will be dismissed by many in the industry. For an objective viewpoint, here is a brief snippet from an interview, on the blog *High Frequency Trading Review*, with Professor Dave Cliff, director of the UK's Large-Scale Complex Information Technology Research Initiative, and a longtime designer of artificial intelligence algorithms for Wall Street trading firms. He left the financial industry in the mid-2000s. The full interview can be found here: http://www.hftreview.com/pg/blog/mike/read/27568.

DAVE CLIFF: It's a big change that's happened in the last 10 or 15 years as everything has become computerized and as every computer can talk to any other computer. Suddenly, in principle, an error or a failure in one system, that would have been an isolated event, can have negative effects that ripple out in a chain reaction over a whole network.

HFTR: And then you have the whole "butterfly effect"?

CLIFF: Yes exactly. And one of the things that we have focused on in that project for the last five years is the extent on which the global financial markets are now essentially a single, planetary-wide, ultra-large scale complex IT system. And the extent to which there are failure modes like those I saw in FX back in 2005 might, in principle, ripple out over the entire system and cause big problems.

The 6th May Flash Crash was the first real sign that actually our concern was justified, that events could happen at an unprecedented scale, in terms of the magnitude of the drop and the speed at which it happened. The market is not supposed to crash while you go out and make a cup of tea.

HFTR: Yes, and then recover again while you drink it!

CLIFF: Exactly. So it definitely feels like we're not in Kansas anymore, Toto! The concern I have at the moment as a researcher and a scientist is to what extent are the dynamics and failure modes of these systems understood and to what extent are those bits we don't understand, risky or dangerous in the sense they might give rise to major market fluctuations or crashes that we really don't want to see?

## CHAPTER 1: TRADING MACHINES

13: **Haim Bodek, the founder of Trading Machines** Most of the material in part 1 comes from extensive interviews with Haim Bodek in the summer and fall of 2011, as well as with several former employees of Trading Machines.

## CHAPTER 3: ALGO WARS

40: **The Algo Wars had broken out** See, for instance, "Snipers, Sniffers, Guerillas: The Algo-Trading War," by Jennifer Ablan, Reuters, May 31, 2007; "Algo vs. Algo," by David Leinweber, *Institutional Investor's Alpha*, February 2007.

43: **"The maker-taker pricing model makes"** "Games People Play: Access More Liquidity with Gaming Technology," by Paul Daley, *Advanced Trading*, June 21, 2011.

CHAPTER 4: 0+

51: **No less than *USA Today*** "Are Computers a Culprit in Stocks' Volatility?" by Matt Krantz, *USA Today*, September 16, 2011.

62: **"Fears of algorithmic terrorism"** "Fixing the Fat-Fingered Faux Pas Epidemic," by John Bates, *TabbForum*, February 21, 2011.

62: **Neil Johnson, a University of Miami physicist** "A Great War of Algorithms Is Already Under Way," February 12, 2012, interview with University of Miami physicist Neil Johnson on the Portuguese website Janela na web (http://janelanaweb.com/trends/a-great-war-of-algorithms-is-already-under-way-scientist-neil-johnson/); "Financial Black Swans Driven by Ultrafast Machine Ecology," by Neil Johnson, Guannan Zhao, Eric Hunsader, Jing Meng, Amith Ravindar, Spencer Carran, and Brian Tivnan, working paper submitted to Cornell University Library, February 12, 2012 (http://aps.arxiv.org/ftp/arxiv/papers/1202/1202.1448.pdf).

63: **"HFT algos reduce the value"** "Enough Already!" by Eric Hunsader, *Nanex,* August 8, 2011 (http://www.nanex.net/Research/EMini2/2011.ebd.mnB.1.gif).

CHAPTER 5: BANDITS

67: **Joshua Levine darted up Wall Street** While I never met with or spoke with Josh Levine, I did exchange dozens of e-mails with him, in which he supplied me with ample information about the creation of Island. I also interviewed dozens of people who worked with him at Datek, Island, and other firms, including his original partner at the Joshua Group, McDonald Comrie, and Peter Stern, who helped Levine extensively in the creation of Island.

68: **Heading west toward Trinity Church** Shameless allusion to Michael Lewis's *Liar's Poker* here—the scene in which Lewis, around the same time, first arrives at Salomon Brothers and wanders around Wall Street.

71: **Maschler had recently left a nationwide brokerage** Several details about Maschler's early career were learned from conversations with people who worked with him in the 1970s and '80s. Some details about his career, as well as Jeff Citron's and Levine's, were taken from "Golden Boy? He's Dazzled Wall Street, but the Ghosts of His Company May

Haunt His Future," by David Barboza, *New York Times Magazine*, May 10, 1998.

81: **"Compared to this, the New York ticker tape."** "Terrors of the Tube— Computerized Traders vs. Market Makers," by Thomas G. Donlan, *Barron's*, November 7, 1988.

## CHAPTER 6: THE WATCHER

85: **One morning, Citron was sitting** The anecdote was provided by a member of the Datek Securities trading team.

86: **Take Jerry Rosen** I spoke with Rosen, now a real estate broker in Florida, about this incident.

90: **"a nation of day traders was born"** "Wall Street's Speed War," by Christopher Steiner, *Forbes*, September 27, 2010.

## CHAPTER 7: MONSTER KEY

106: **"We are slick, we are quick"** "Maschler Hits Heart of Wall Street," by Robert B. Cox, Loren Steffy, and Hui-yong Yu, *Bloomberg News*, January 26, 1995.

## CHAPTER 8: THE ISLAND

123: **in short order, his firm started trading on Island** "Hyper-Aggressive Day Trading Firm Wants to Take On Third Market Giants," by Heike Wipperfurth, *Investment Dealers Digest*, October 25, 1999.

## CHAPTER 9: THE GREEN MACHINE

134: **"Josh was incredibly open"** Interview with Furbush.

136: **In 1996, Datek Securities paid Citron and Levine** "Free Enterprise Comes to Wall Street," by Matthew Schifrin, *Forbes*, April 6, 1998.

## CHAPTER 10: ARCHIPELAGO

137: **Jerry Putnam picked up the phone** Much of the Archipelago story throughout the book is based on interviews with Putnam, Kevin O'Hara, Nelson Chai, Jamie Selway, and a number of other former Archipelago employees.

## CHAPTER 11: EVERYONE CARES

152: **There was also Datek Online** "Some Clouds Dim a Star of On-Line Trading," by David Barboza, *New York Times*, July 8, 1998.

CHAPTER 12: PALACE COUP

164: **Citron had to go** I learned the story of Citron's ouster from Ed Nicoll, Peter Stern, and John Grifonetti. I never spoke with Jeff Citron for this book and he declined to confirm any details.

CHAPTER 13: BAD PENNIES

171: **Goldman was spending billions** "Fear, Greed and Technology," by Neil Weinberg, *Forbes*, May 15, 2000.

174: **On July 3, 2000, Matt Andresen mounted a platform** Several of the anecdotes in these chapters are based on interviews and e-mail exchanges with Matt Andresen.

CHAPTER 14: DUMB MONEY

187: **Another high-frequency trader closely allied** "Dave Cummings, Tradebot CEO, Visits APM," by Joe Hall, *APM Quarterly* (http://web .ku.edu/~apm/Q2-2008.html).

CHAPTER 15: TRADE BOTS

193: **"We were getting overwhelmed"** Interview with O'Brien.

199: **"This is unfair, Matt"** Several details of Dave Cummings's career at Tradebot come from "Fast Lane: Firms Seek Edge Through Speed as Computer Trading Expands," by Aaron Lucchetti, *The Wall Street Journal*, December 15, 2006.

CHAPTER 16: CRAZY NUMBERS

209: **Smoke and ash poured through** "After the Attacks: A Test like None Before for the Computer Wizards," by Amy Harmon, *New York Times*, September 17, 2001.

211: **"The numbers got crazy"** Interview with Sterling.

212: **"We were seeing massive volume"** Interview with Hathaway.

213: **"We saw that they were trying to kill us"** Interview with Andresen.

220: **"It was like the New York Yankees"** Interview with Andresen.

223: **"We were lied to continuously"** Interview with O'Hara.

CHAPTER 17: "I DO NOT WANT TO BE A FAMOUS PERSON"

225: **To help with the switchover, Island** Island's name was officially changed to INET after the Instinet merger. For narrative simplicity, I largely continue to call it Island, since it was essentially the Island system.

225: **The final straw** SEC v. Sheldon Maschler, Jeffrey A. Citron, Michael McCarty, Erik Maschler, Heartland Securities, Aaron Elbogen, Moishe Zelcer, Raft Investments Inc., and JES Management Corp.

228: **"Talking to Josh was like staring into the sun"** Interview with Andresen.

## CHAPTER 18: THE BEAST

237: **Niederauer received e-mails** The e-mails are from documents in William J. Higgins v. The New York Stock Exchange, Supreme Court of the State of New York (http://www.nycourts.gov/comdiv/Law%20 Report%20Files/VOL8%20No.4/Ra-NYSE.pdf).

237: **Dick Grasso, watching the details of the merger** *King of the Club: Richard Grasso and the Survival of the New York Stock Exchange,* by Charles Gasparino (New York: HarperCollins Publishers, 2007).

237: **"The writing is on the wall for the floor"** "NYSE to Acquire Electronic Trader and Go Public—Archipelago Deal Signals Historic Shifts for Markets in Newly Competitive Era," by Aaron Lucchetti, Susanne Craig, and Dennis Berman, *The Wall Street Journal,* April 21, 2005.

## CHAPTER 19: THE PLATFORM

246: **It was nearing midnight as Sergey Aleynikov** Many of the details in this chapter come from testimony given in *U.S. v. Aleynikov,* U.S. District Court, Southern District of New York. I attended most of the trial.

249: **"This must be a mistake"** "Controversy over Alleged 'Confession' at Goldman Sachs Trading Software Trial," by Adam Klasfeld, Courthouse News Service, December 8, 2010.

252: **a *Forbes* magazine cover story** "The New Masters of Wall Street," by Liz Moyer and Emily Lambert, *Forbes,* September 21, 2009.

## CHAPTER 20: PANIC TICKS

260: **Thomas Peterffy had seen it all** I interviewed Thomas Peterffy several times for this book at his Greenwich estate, but unfortunately wasn't able to include much of his fascinating story due to space constraints.

262: **The founder of Tradebot wasn't sure** Along with a team of journalists, I reported extensively on the Flash Crash for *The Wall Street Journal.* See "Did Shutdowns Make Plunge Worse?" by Scott Patterson, *The Wall Street Journal,* May 7, 2010 (in which I reported that Tradebot and other HFT firms had pulled out of the market on May 6); and

"Computer Trading Is Eyed," by Tom Lauricella, Scott Patterson, and Carolyn Cui, *The Wall Street Journal*, May 8, 2010.

271: **At Nasdaq, 12,306 trades were canceled** Several details about the Flash Crash are derived from *Preliminary Findings Regarding the Market Events of May 6, 2010*, report of the Staffs of the CFTC and SEC to the Joint Advisory Committee on Emerging Regulatory Issues, May 18, 2010.

## CHAPTER 21: VERY DANGEROUS

272: **"I wish to comment on what happened** Congressional Record of the 111th Congress (2009–2010), Senate, May 6, 2010.

## CHAPTER 22: A RIGGED GAME

283: **At an industrial site on the edge of Tseung Kwan O** "High-Frequency Trading: Up Against a Bandsaw," by Jeremy Grant, *Financial Times*, September 2, 2010.

291: **There was even chatter about measuring trades** "The Rise of the Pico-second," by Michelle Price, *Financial News*, March 3, 2011.

## CHAPTER 23: THE BIG DATA

297: **The office of Kinetic Global Markets** Much of the Kinetic section of this chapter is based, as we journalists like to say, on "people familiar with the matter."

308: **Andre and Teller had known each other** This section is based on interviews with Andre and Teller.

## CHAPTER 24: ADVANCED CHESS

319: **Weeks later, on March 23** "SEC Probes Rapid Training," by Scott Patterson and Jean Eaglesham, *The Wall Street Journal*, March 23, 2011.

319: **In a follow-up article** "SEC Probes Ties to High-Speed Traders," by Scott Patterson, *The Wall Street Journal*, April 14, 2012.

## CHAPTER 25: STAR

322: **Star was dying** This chapter is based on multiple interviews with the four members of the Rebellion team in 2010 and 2011.

## ABOUT THE AUTHOR

**SCOTT PATTERSON** is a staff reporter at *The Wall Street Journal,* covering government regulation from the nation's capital. His coverage of the Flash Crash in 2010 won the Gerald Loeb Award. His first book was the *New York Times* bestseller *The Quants: How a New Breed of Math Whizzes Conquered Wall Street and Nearly Destroyed It.* He lives in Alexandria, Virginia.